Silver Saga

Mining the American West

Series Editors

Duane A. Smith
Robert A. Trennert
Liping Zhu

Silver Saga

The Story of Caribou, Colorado
Revised Edition

Duane A. Smith

Foreword by Robert G. Athearn

University Press of Colorado

MINING THE AMERICAN WEST SERIES

© 2003 by the University Press of Colorado

Published by University Press of Colorado
245 Century Circle, Suite 202
Louisville, Colorado 80027

 The University Press of Colorado is a proud member of
ASSOCIATION of UNIVERSITY PRESSES   the Association of University Presses.

The University Press of Colorado is a cooperative publishing enterprise supported, in part, by Adams State University, Colorado State University, Fort Lewis College, Metropolitan State University of Denver, University of Colorado, University of Northern Colorado, University of Wyoming, Utah State University, and Western Colorado University.

∞ This paper meets the requirements of the ANSI/NISO Z39.48-1992 (Permanence of Paper).

Library of Congress Cataloging-in-Publication Data

Smith, Duane A.
 Silver saga : the story of Caribou, Colorado / by Duane A. Smith ; foreword by Robert G. Athearn. — Rev. ed.
  p. cm. — (Mining the American West)
Includes bibliographical references (p.) and index.
 ISBN 0-87081-729-9 (alk. paper)
 1. Caribou (Colo.)—History. 2. Caribou (Colo.)—Biography. 3. Silver mines and mining—Colorado—Caribou—History. I. Title. II. Series.

F784.C37 S64 2003
978.8'63—dc21

                                                    2002155568

To Laralee

Contents

Acknowledgments

"America," William and Bruce Catton wrote in their *Two Roads to Sumter*, "is equally a tale of might-have-beens and used-to-be's, of ghost towns and shuttered mills, . . . and a thousand other evidences of blunted hopes and dreams gone sour." The success story we have featured; the famous and the infamous we know. But what of those average, unsung individuals whose lives and dreams passed unrecorded? Caribou is their story, and to them I owe a great debt of gratitude, particularly to the ones who wrote to the local newspapers about their camp and signed themselves simply "J.," "Miner," or "Western." This is intended to be a tribute to the pioneering souls who lived there, whose ambitions "gently trailed off into obscurity." I hope this is a fair measure of their lives.

Caribou, like a young man's first love, has captured a corner of my heart. Here I first came to wonder about what had transpired, to speculate about people who had gone to such a place to reside and work. My interest was whetted, my enthusiasm sparked, and I took off on a search that has led me to many other camps, but my excitement over this first one has never diminished.

My attempt to revive Caribou from the fast receding past was aided by many people, who generously gave of their time, energy, and memories to try to recapture a moment of history. Without the interviews of those few remaining Caribouites, much would have been unavoidably left out. All of them are gone now and with them an era.

Owen Sheffield earned a special thanks for his cooperation in providing the R. G. Dun letters and his willingness to share his knowledge of Dun and his company. And to Mrs. Seth Woodruff, my gratitude for opening this door to me. The Reverend Alfred Carlyon helped with the Cornish and Mrs. G. D. Dammers with translating the Dutch. Ken Periman graciously read some of the chapters and offered stylistic suggestions, and Carl Ubbelohde was most considerate with his time and expertise in assisting a young graduate student get his feet wet with research and writing.

To the staffs of the University of Colorado Western Historical Collections, Western History Department of the Denver Public Library, and the State Historical Society of Colorado, I am indebted for many favors over the past thirteen years. Special thanks must be given to Mrs. Alys Freeze, Mrs. Agnes W. Spring, and Miss Lucile Fry. The late Theodore Cobb was especially cooperative in allowing me to utilize the archives of the First National Bank of Denver. Sincere appreciation for assistance is given to the Fort Lewis College Foundation.

I would particularly like to acknowledge three individuals who were most instrumental in helping me with the Caribou project. Jerry Keenan kept the faith and got the manuscript over the final hurdle. The late A. A. (Gov) Paddock not only provided encouragement, knowledge, and interest, but also opened the archives of the *Boulder Camera*; his kindness and friendship are memories well treasured. To my wife, Gay, who loyally supported my interest in Caribou, there is little that I can say that has not already been expressed. Without her this would not have been possible.

I dedicate this volume to my daughter Laralee, who knows little about Caribou, but who has gladdened her daddy's life in so many ways.

Preface

To reiterate what I stated back in 1974, almost everyone remembers the first "love" of his or her life. My first love in mining was the camp of Caribou, Colorado, which, when I initially visited it in the early 1950s, had little remaining except a few aging, weathered buildings to tell what had once happened in this high mountain valley. The only thing a person could do was to imagine what might have occurred there during its heyday. It offered a lonely mystery that intrigued and captured me and, although I did not know it at the time, started me on a lifetime adventure with the fascinating history of western mining.

A decade later, in graduate school, I was asked what subject I might like to research and write about for my master's thesis. The choice proved easy, at least for me. It would be Caribou. My major professor, Robert Athearn, seemed not all that convinced, but he finally agreed. "Smitty," he said, "I'll let you do it because Caribou had a beginning and an ending." That makes research and writing easier, but Caribou's story, for me, did not end with that 1905 fire.

As Mark Twain wrote nearly a century before I fell in love with Caribou, "I was young then, marvelously young then, wonderfully young, younger ever again by several hundred years." With that enthusiasm of youth, I set out on a journey that has taken me to the far corners of the mining West. But I never forgot my first love. Studying it had taught me much and infected me with an enthusiasm for mining and mining communities. I was hooked on mining. I had contracted a case of mining fever. Even worse, it encompassed both gold and silver fevers and a touch of coal dust.

After I completed my thesis, I continued to follow Caribou's trail, finding more information as I journeyed along. Finally, this led to reworking the thesis and the 1974 publication of *Silver Saga*. That did not finish my fascination with Caribou. I remained on the lookout for anything that I might find about this intriguing community. Occasionally, just like mining, I dug up a new nugget or two. Sometimes, Caribou even worked its way into later writing. It became, unbeknown to readers, a type of personal trademark, along with the man who mined there briefly, Horace Tabor.

After the book went out of print, I always hoped to revive it, because the chronicles of the Caribous scattered about the mountains, deserts, and riversides are the heart and soul of the people who ventured optimistically and hopefully into the mining West. Caribou, and its contemporaries, had much to tell about times and people that had gone before and gave a lesson or two for today. Caribou also gained a claim to Colorado fame. It was Colorado's second important silver discovery. Only Georgetown preceded it, and Caribou ushered in the exhilarating silver seventies. Most of these mining communities, like Caribou, are gone now, but their stories are the bedrock of Western American mining history.

Three friends are primarily responsible for this continuation of the Caribou saga: Jerry Keenan, who never lost the faith and brought the original book into print; Tom Hendricks, who continues the Caribou story and ardently maintains his faith in mining; and Darrin Pratt, who resurrected my dream of reprinting *Silver Saga*.

—DUANE A. SMITH
November 2002

Foreword

The mining boom that visited Colorado after 1859 produced a myriad of "camps" strewn along the Rockies in what was then loosely known as the Pike's Peak region. Together they constituted a portion of what Duane Smith has called the "urban frontier," a sprawling collection of municipal seeds, most of which flourished briefly and then died on the barren granite slopes. In a sense they grew like weeds: rapidly, without careful cultivation or sense of direction, and with little hope of longevity. The camps were mere collections of buildings, and of people thrown together through the economic necessity of the moment; sites elected through chance where men hoped to "get and get out."

Perhaps a few residents thought of the future and entertained hopes of permanency for their town, but in the main even those who avowed such views secretly knew that theirs was an economy based upon extraction of metals and, as such, the future was at best risky. When the mines gave out, or metal prices sank, there was nothing upon which to fall back. During the 1880s Charles Francis Adams, Jr., president of the Union Pacific Railroad, whose subsidiary the Denver, South Park, and Pacific was floundering, made a bitter comment about Colorado mining. "The chief source of revenue of the road was in carrying men and material into Colorado to dig holes in the ground called mines, and until it was discovered that there was nothing in those mines the business was immense. That was the famous mining boom in Colorado . . . when everyone was crazy."

The term "camp" suggests a stopping place, a temporary abode, a place to be abandoned shortly. Despite the fact that residents of the incipient towns used the term "camp" and understood its implications, they could not bring themselves to abandon a heritage that bespoke of orderly rows of houses, and squares of rows, laid out in the traditional manner of a town. Nor were they willing to surrender what they regarded as "civilization" to a wilderness that suggested savagery by its lack of institutions. So, disregarding the question of tenure, residents of the camps proceeded on the questionable assumption that the name they had placed upon the map was there to stay, even though individuals might come and go on that fluid mineral frontier. The result was traditional municipal organization, with such variations as distance, climate, and the economy demanded. This largely male population did not want to live as prodigal sons, but rather in the manner of their fathers, and they sought to establish a well-ordered society boasting of refinements. To do this they had to overcome a reputation for civic wildness and disorder that seemed to accompany the birth of such camps.

One traveler who visited the West in the early 1880s remarked: "All the way from New York I have been told to wait 'til I got to Colorado before I ventured to speak of rough life, and Leadville itself was sometimes particularized to me as the Ultima Thule of civilization, the vanishing-point of refinement." Somewhat to his disappointment he found this particular mining town far from wild. On the contrary, he confessed that the place was "even flirting with refinements," and was peopled by a race "reverting to an old type," as he put it. To him Leadville was reminiscent of some English provincial town, and the manner of dress he observed along the streets reminded him of rural England.

After the "fifty-niner" boom had burst and a low point had been reached during the later 1860s, placer mining gave way to a more traditional and industrialized type of extraction characterized by a labor-management relationship, of heavy financial outlays, and usually of control by outside investors. Foreign-born workers were brought into many of the mining towns because of their expertise—the Cornish and the Welsh miners, for example—or because they were easily controlled, cheap labor. This social coloration, mixed with American traditions, gave the mineral cities a special flavor.

If one were to look for a good case study of such a mining camp, one that blossomed, lived for some thirty-five years, and faded away leaving behind a scene so unblemished by the marks of civilization that it might be called an environmentalist's dream, the ideal place to visit would be the site of Caribou, Colorado. High in the wind-swept Rockies, blanketed by subarctic growth, lies the grave of this once-proud, booming mining camp. Summer visitors see only a few stone foundations and an occasional scrap of warped and weathered lumber. Almost none of them have any idea as to the extent and vigor of a town that once grew on that little patch of mountainside and then died a quiet death along with dozens of sister communities in the region.

—ROBERT G. ATHEARN
UNIVERSITY OF COLORADO

Introduction: Silver Clarion

A front-page headline of the *Boulder Camera*, November 15, 1905, proclaimed to its readers, "CARIBOU WIPED OUT BY DESTRUCTIVE FIRE." To many who read the paper that evening the item meant nothing but the demise the previous day of a "once famous mining camp . . . but now mostly weather-beaten and decayed structures." Of more concern to the twentieth-century Boulderite was the crisis in Russia following the Russo-Japanese War and the 1905 internal revolution, and probably the fortunes of the University of Colorado football team. After the initial article, interest waned completely, as subjects more immediate than the passing of a relic of the frontier caught and held public attention.

A new generation had assumed leadership of the country, so recently a frontier. Theodore Roosevelt was president, a symbol himself of the twentieth century and the growing importance of the United States as a world power. The automobile and the airplane told of a world completely different from that of which Caribou had been a part. It was no wonder then that little time was spent mourning the loss of old times and places.

Caribou had flourished in another age, one more akin to the California gold rush and the Civil War than to the early twentieth century. At one time, the camp and its mines had been important to Boulder and Colorado, a time that had slipped away and its fortunes with it. Thirty-five years earlier Caribou had been founded; silver had been the cry then, and it was a magical one.

Silver or gold—it did not make much difference—the mania for precious minerals had gripped men for centuries. To acquire these gleaming metals they had bartered, stolen, killed, conquered, explored, and "sold their souls"; few were abundantly rewarded, most found only unfulfilled dreams. Caught up in the overwhelming lure of sudden wealth, men worked longer and harder hours in the mines than they would have back on the farm or in the family business. The minerals' value came not from nature—they have little intrinsic worth—but from the price that men placed on them. The cost in human lives and suffering to acquire such treasures has never been tabulated, but it would seem to surpass by far the total price of the minerals mined, purchased, or stolen.

Caribou was a part of the mining history of Colorado, which in turn was part of the Rocky Mountain mining frontier, and so it could be traced back to the days of the Spanish conquistadors who first excited Europeans to the mineral possibilities of the New World. The chance discovery of gold at Sutter's Mill in California in 1848 set off the chain of events that led twenty-one years later to prospectors heading for what became known as Caribou hill. The excitement generated by the 1849 gold rush to California impelled a generation to go in search of its own bonanzas. And they were found—in Nevada, and later in Montana, Idaho, and other Western territories. In 1859 the Pike's Peak country was the goal of eager prospectors and would-be miners. Out of it came a new territory, Colorado, and a mineral treasure house.

Silver was not the prize of the moment; it was gold that inflamed men's minds. Prospectors scurried around the mountains looking for it; then with pans, shovels, and picks they worked the streambeds to recover it. Free gold (placer mining) was what they were looking for. Crude settlements grew around their discoveries, with names such as

Gold Hill, Black Hawk, and Central City (or Central, as it was referred to in the nineteenth century). Meanwhile, in the valleys along
the mountains, other settlements arose to supply the mines in the
mountains; Boulder was an example. Placer mining quickly played
out and the miners found themselves confronted with the fact that
recovering the minerals from the hillsides was going to be tedious,
hard work, not at all like the easily obtained, quick wealth they had
imagined back home.

Colorado mining moved away from the feverish rush of excitement of 1859–1860 and settled into a familiar Western mining pattern:
stabilization and decline in older areas, continual search for valuable
ore in newer ones. Colorado's future rested on the success of these
searches, because prospects in the older districts were dimming. Long
transportation lines, complex refractory ores, lack of capital, and the
steadily increasing cost and problems of mining sobered the enthusiasm
that had once characterized the region. Hard rock or quartz mining
necessitated financial backing, different skills, and often complicated
milling processes, not simply ambition, willingness to work, and a pan.
Local resources proved inadequate and Colorado's golden dreams
seemed to be fading.

At this juncture, silver promised a bright new future. First at
Georgetown then at its near neighbor Silver Plume, silver mines were
discovered and opened. Rumors of silver had been circulating since
1859, but this was the first concrete news worthy of acting upon.
Georgetown was promptly dubbed Colorado's "Silver Queen" (the first
of many), but success did not come easily. Few men in the territory had
experience in silver mining, and fewer still had any practical knowledge
of smelting methods. The rest of the decade was one of experimenta-
tion, particularly in smelting, which was the key to success, silver rarely
being found in the native state. Trial and error produced numerous
processes, none of which could profitably handle both low- and high-
grade ore. Finally, the erection of Nathaniel Hill's Boston-Colorado
smelter in Black Hawk marked the beginning of a new scientific era
in Colorado's smelting and milling industry and the start of profitable
silver mining.

The 1870s proved to be the turning point in Colorado's mining
history. Cries of silver echoed from the mountaintops, as rich strikes
followed each other in rapid succession, culminating in the greatest
Colorado silver camp of them all—Leadville. Where gold had made
thousands of dollars, silver made millions. By the end of the decade
only Nevada's Comstock—the United States' first great silver district—

could match Colorado's production, and the latter was about to become the nation's number one mining state. The silver decade, it would be called, and it all started in a secluded, mountainous area of Boulder County in the northern part of the state.

Boulder County had been the site of one of the 1859 gold discoveries. What happened there paralleled the rest of Colorado. The county had been organized into six mining districts, each providing a means to file mining claims and a set of mining laws regulating operations. Of these six, the Grand Island District, encompassing a large section of the county's western part, had been prospected to some degree in 1859 and 1860, but the first recorded claim had not been filed until March 1861. Isolated from Boulder and Central City by the rugged terrain of the foothills and showing few apparent outcroppings of minerals, it suffered in contrast to the richer areas around it. Prospecting for gold continued haphazardly. The *Rocky Mountain News*, May 29, 1861, commented that a number of leads had been found, some of which were partially opened. Actually there was little to attract people to the Grand Island Mining District.

Where gold failed, silver triumphed. Caribou, located on the western edge of the district, finally brought prominence and settlement. Born of a silver excitement, it became Colorado's most northerly silver producing area and the rush to it in 1870 inaugurated the decade.

To the casual examiner, the saga of Caribou could be that of hundreds of other camps in the Rocky Mountain West. That nothing sensational, weird, or wild happened here is the joy of it. The Western historian, Hubert Howe Bancroft, wrote in the 1880s, "Twenty life times might be spent and twenty volumes written before the story of one mining-camp in all its ramifications could be told. The story of one mining-camp was the story of mankind; and to follow it after death was the story of the gods."[1] Though a bit flowery and pardonably exaggerated, Bancroft's words touched upon a fundamental truth.

Amid the few remaining gravestones in the Caribou cemetery is that of Mary Webster, on which is inscribed this familiar verse:

Remember friends as you pass by
As you are now so once was I.
As I am now so you must be
Prepare for death and follow me.

Mary, wife of Joseph Webster, born in Cornwall, England, died in Caribou, Colorado, 1879—a stark epitaph, a few lines—yet she lived;

and it is her story and that of those like her that needs to be told, not just those of her better-known contemporaries, who happened to become famous or infamous. The same is true for all the Caribous of the mining frontier.

Caribou was a pioneer settlement that assisted in bringing stability to a chaotic and trackless wilderness. Around the camp and the mines developed economic, social, political, and cultural institutions that eventually triumphed over the primitive environment. From Caribou's mines poured wealth to benefit the country, the state, and the nation, while its fame helped attract both needed settlers and money into the region. The camp's residents exhibited the attitudes, aspirations, successes, and disappointments of a generation of nineteenth-century Americans. Caribou's history is the narrative of its mines and people during the formative years of the American West.

Here, as in Mark Twain's Virginia City, "half of this little army swarmed the streets like bees and the other half swarmed among the drifts and tunnels. . . . Often we felt our chairs jar, and heard the faint boom of a blast down in the bowels of the earth under the office."[2] Now nothing remains. The wind and the changing seasons have come to reclaim their own; and the visitor is confronted with only the haunting knowledge that for three decades men once lived, worked, and died here. The cycle of Bancroft's "story of mankind" had been completed—and Caribou has a story to tell.

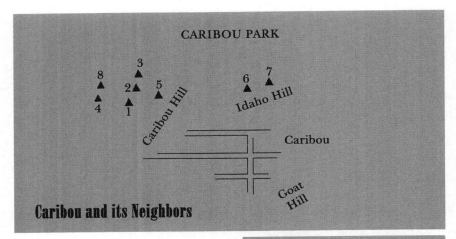

CARIBOU PARK

Caribou Hill

Idaho Hill

Caribou

Goat Hill

Caribou and its Neighbors

Major Mines

1. Caribou
2. Sherman
3. Poorman
4. Native Silver

5. No Name
6. Monitor
7. Idaho
8. Seven Thirty

Ward•
Cardinal
★ •
Central Black
City•• Hawk
•Georgetown
Silver Plume

•Boulder

•Denver

Silver Saga

Rush to Riches

An old-timer once said, "Silver runs in ledges, and gold is where you find it." Silver, indeed, was harder for the inexperienced prospector to find or to recognize, and it was not so common. The Caribou silver pocket was surrounded by gold-producing districts, but no other silver mines within twenty miles. A confusion of circumstances, which at this late date cannot be completely resolved, clouds the discovery.

Samuel Conger—hunter, prospector, and miner— figures prominently in all stories of the Caribou discovery. By his own admission he had come into the Grand Island District in the early 1860s and found an outcropping of blossom rock, the value of which he did not at that time recognize. Though some other men might have made a similar find, among those involved in 1869 there was a general agreement that Conger discovered the original

The Caribou Mine as an artist imagined it in 1870. Courtesy, Colorado Historical Society

float.[1] Beyond this point, however, the story rapidly becomes one of conjecture. Conger later stated he was in Ft. Sanders, Wyoming, in 1869, when he saw some Comstock ore that he instantly recognized as similar to that which he had seen years before in Colorado. He then returned to Boulder County, relocated the vein, and invited several of his friends from Gilpin County to join him. William Martin, George Lytle, Hugh McCammon, John Pickel, and Samuel and Harvey Mishler joined Conger in his venture. However, Conger's story has been challenged by some of these men who worked with him.

Martin and McCammon testified that Conger brought to Black Hawk some ore that Martin, who had worked in the mines at Virginia City, Nevada, recognized as silver. A grubstake arrangement was then worked out among the men; and Martin and Lytle, also an experienced miner, were sent on an expedition into the mountainous terrain to attempt to find the exact site. Working their way from Central City to the area Conger described, they found pieces of float and began to prospect toward the top of a large hill—soon to be called Caribou. Within a short time both men uncovered rich lodes: Martin, the Caribou; Lytle, the Poorman. The date was August 31, 1869.[2] Having discovered the lodes, they now faced the problem that had so discouraged mining previously in this region—the lack of roads or suitable means of transportation.

The reality of who and how is of little real importance for the significant thing was that ore of a very promising nature had been found. However, winter comes early to the high country and the partners found themselves pressed for time to prepare for its advent. The mines were worked and a crude trail blazed and cut through the timber to the wagon road from Central City and Black Hawk to Gold Hill. Except for one load taken out, the ore remained piled until spring again allowed easier access to the mills at Black Hawk. Meanwhile, a cabin, built on the site of the future camp, gave the men some semblance of comfort and a home. In December the partners filed a claim on the Carriboo [sic] Lode by right of discovery and location. Of some interest was the fact that the names listed did not include Samuel Conger. Sometime during the autumn or winter, Conger traded what interest he had in the mine for $500 and the others' shares in what they considered the less promising Poorman.[3] Conger, however, felt that the Poorman would eventually prove the richer of the two.

That winter the partners had the discovery all to themselves and vainly hoped to keep the news quiet. As spring approached, they shipped some of their accumulated ore, and rumors multiplied as the curious watched and wondered. Newspapers in both Central and Boulder quickly picked up the exciting news; the *Boulder County News*, June 1, discussed "belts of rich silver ores," and the *Central City Register*, June 22, gave careful instructions on how to reach the mines. The editor of the latter, either with tongue in cheek or through ignorance, stated, "All things considered the road is now good." It was not. A minor problem, though, for the rush was on.

Stories of the discovery spread out from Boulder County and Colorado like ripples after a stone strikes water. By fall even the august *New York Times* heralded on page one of the September 12 issue: "Wild Excitement Among the Adventurers of the Territory. The richest silver deposits on the Continent." The article that followed described the young camp and its mines and the continued rush to the new bonanza. Caribou had, indeed, come of age.

George Lytle, who had mined in British Columbia, gave the mine its name, Caribou, after either a mining district, a mine, or the animal indigenous to that area. Originally spelled with two o's, it was changed to "ou" because this was deemed to be the correct spelling of the North American reindeer and also to distinguish between this community and other camps to the north.

The site of the discovery was some eighteen miles north of Central City and twenty-two miles west of Boulder, the two nearest important settlements. The mines and future townsite were located within four miles of the Continental Divide. The altitude of the immediate area runs from approximately 10,000 feet at the site of the camp to 10,505 feet on the top of Caribou Hill. Bounded on the north by Caribou Park and Idaho Hill, on the south by Goat Hill, and directly west by Caribou Hill, Caribou sits at the head of a valley reaching downward toward Nederland, overlooking the foothills and plains. In 1869 it was heavily forested, unlike the present denuded meadow. A little creek, named Coon Trail, curves through the valley, bubbling briskly in the spring but almost dry the rest of the year. Several springs, now dry, furnished enough water for the immediate needs of the miners who first appeared there.

The Caribou District is part of the Front Range mineral belt; interestingly, the lead-silver veins uncovered were all located within a short radius of Caribou Hill, while a mile to the east gold predominated. An iron dike, much of it natural lodestone, runs nearby and is said by old-timers to attract violent electrical displays during storms.[4]

From Gilpin and Boulder counties the first men came, followed by others from throughout the territory and other Western mining districts. The equal of Georgetown—the new Comstock—some called it. Silver danced in many eyes as the prospectors staked their claims that summer. Two unidentified miners, who had been in Nevada's then prospering White Pine District, reportedly said that in its "palmiest" days the White Pine District did not exceed the Grand Island in richness of ores, and "the extent was not equal to it."[5] Each such statement increased the rush as men scrambled to find their bonanza. Not all believed so fervently in the prospects; in fact, some older districts clearly resented the publicity given to their new neighbor. Wrote a disgusted or jealous person from the nearby Ward District "There is room in there for several Cariboo [sic] cities, besides some splendid stock ranches."[6] Such feelings failed to stem the tide running in Caribou's favor in that summer of 1870.

By the end of June the original discoverers found themselves joined by sixty to seventy fellow prospectors. The scene changed rapidly. What once had been the site of a lonely cabin now assumed the air of a mining community. As an early visitor described it, "The camp contains two finished log houses, and three more going up. The larger number live in tents, brush and bark houses. Altogether they are as jolly, hopeful, busy, hospitable a set of men as we ever wish to see." The same visitor warned, however, that this was no place for greenhorns, for "prospecting in this district requires both hard and skillful work . . . old prospectors require at least a week to comprehend the country, before they are ready to strike a pick in the ground."[7] Such warnings went unheeded and the number of claims filed at the Boulder County Court House increased steadily during June, July, and August. Prospectors and miners searched and re-examined the entire district and many of the important mines were opened that summer, including the Comstock, Sherman, Spencer, and Idaho. The Idaho, especially, showed early promise, producing almost from its grassroots. With the shaft scarcely more than fifteen feet, the excited owners—including the city marshal of Black Hawk, Walter B. Jenness—raised $5,000 worth of ore. For each Caribou or Idaho numerous hopes went aglimmering as claim after claim produced little more than hard work and disappointment. However, each load of ore sent to a local smelter and each story or rumor of further discoveries lured more to come to try their luck or skill.

The lack of a decent road into the region continued troublesome; such public improvements were pushed aside in the excitement of the hour. Because no one else would, or felt inspired to do so, the owners of the Caribou Mine, who with their property opened and producing needed the road more than anyone, hired men to cut and grade a road. Not until the next year was the project completed. Snowdrifts hampered travel up the original trail, which went straight up the valley beside the creek, and the route was shifted along the south side of the ridge to get the benefit of as much winter sun as possible. The road, though steep, when completed compared "favorably with any in the mountains."[8]

With all the activity and excitement breaking around them, the partners—now called the Caribou Company—continued to develop their property. Despite a crippling inflow of water that had to be drained, work was pushed forward and high-grade ore sent to Hill's smelter in Black Hawk, with lower grades being stored for future shipment and milling. The owners had the experience, and a seemingly profitable mine, but lacked the money needed to develop it. However, the wealth of the Caribou had created speculative interest, especially after a rich ore shipment went to New Jersey. Prominent among those thus attracted were Abel Breed and Benjamin Cutter. These gentlemen visited the property; and in September the western half was sold to them for $50,000, and the eastern half bonded for $75,000 but retained by the Caribou Company. Thus Breed, who had the money necessary for development, became part owner of what an enthusiastic author now called one of the richest silver mines in America.[9]

Fifty-nine-year-old Abel Breed, from Cincinnati, was the outstanding figure in the early history of Caribou. Wealthy manufacturer of patent medicines and a partner in one of the country's largest undertaking firms, Breed had for some years invested in various mining properties, including numerous ones in Colorado. His interest in this property gave Caribou an example of what Eastern capital and promotion could do when properly applied. Associated with him was Cutter, an experienced mining man from California, who handled the actual operation of the mine.

Under Cutter's guidance, development of the western half of the mine was pushed ahead, and the Caribou Company continued to work the eastern part under a contract with Breed to pay him half of its net profit. Available records of the latter group show that for the period from October 1 to December 31, 1870, they sold eighty-eight tons of ore to Hill's Boston Colorado Smelting Works at Black Hawk for over $9,000,[10] helping convince Breed that he had made a wise investment. Another important step was taken when Cutter built two shaft-houses on the property to allow work to continue while winter winds and snow played havoc with mining.

Those who rushed to Caribou in the early summer of 1870 carried with them those supplies and equipment that might be needed immediately. The all-encompassing dream was to stake a rich claim as quickly as possible, but they found out here as elsewhere that mining was neither simple nor easy. Almost by chance a camp sprang up in the valley where the original discoverers had built their cabin the previous winter. Little effort was at first expended to promote comfort or permanence; time was the essential. Despite the discomforts and hardships of this pioneer stage, the *Caribou Post* within a year could rhapsodize over it:

> In a few weeks after the snows had disappeared there were
> from three to four hundred hardy prospectors on the ground,
> more than half of whom had their camps on the site of our
> town. They were as jolly and happy a set as we ever met. The
> scene after night-fall of the denizens of a populous mining
> camp gathered around the huge log fires,—made necessary by
> our high altitude, . . . ,—was one to be remembered as we may
> never see another like it in Colorado. From supper time till nine
> o'clock all was merriment and jollity, when "City Marshal" [Rob-
> ert] Haight would call "lights out" on his bazoo, and in a little
> while all were stretched on their couches of fragrant pine enjoy-
> ing the sweet sleep of healthful labor and, perchance, dreaming
> of silver bricks, or the girls they left behind them.[11]

The appointment of Haight as marshal reflected a desire by some individuals to preserve order, although the move was by no means dictated by a desperate situation. He probably served only unofficially. With no territorial or county officials on the scene, the settlers relied on the simplest expedient available. Whether the individualistic miners completely agreed with the nine o'clock curfew remains a moot point.

The rough edges smoothed surprisingly rapidly and rudiments of enduring settlement appeared. The need for a supply base near at hand was keenly felt, since a journey to Black Hawk and Central meant a long day's round-trip over roads that were, at best, dusty and rough. Not only supplies, but board and room and other refinements of a frontier society were craved by the men. By fall a change had taken place.

> Cariboo [sic] City has wonderfully improved in appearance during the past three weeks. Neat and substantial frames are supplanting the log and bark cabins of the first settlers; . . . the town site has been surveyed, cleared of timber and brushwood, and streets have been laid out and are being rapidly lined with new buildings. . . . The settlement has an appearance of permanence that it has not worn before. The citizens are confident of the future of the place, and believe with reason that they are in one of the best mining districts of the territory. . . . Billiard halls and other accompaniments for modern Civilization will soon be here, and school houses will soon be needed.[12]

Confidence and faith indeed were needed to venture to a new mining community, for a person gambled as much here on the future as he did on mining.

Not only mining and road construction, but also town building interested the members of the Caribou Company as they filed on 160 acres in the valley, hired a surveyor, and platted a townsite. Ambitiously, they laid out eighteen streets running approximately east and west, and four crossing them north and south. Of the former, only five received names—Pugh, Caribou, Idaho, Boulder, and Monitor—while the latter were simply designated first, second, third, and fourth.[13] Despite great expectation, most of the streets never developed beyond the planning stage, and the names—except for Idaho and Caribou—quickly passed from usage. At least a start had been made, however, and no longer could building be done haphazardly; it was required to conform to a camp plan. Caribou was gaining respectability.

With the plat filed, competition blossomed between Idaho and Caribou streets to see which would monopolize trade. Speculation on lots in the business district livened as prices increased; the lucky owner who guessed correctly stood to turn a sharp profit. Equally lucrative was the construction business as merchants and others moved into the area needing buildings and homes. Despite a shortage of lumber, work was pushed forward as rapidly as possible.

The new mines and camp attracted the curious, the miner, and the merchant—each one anxious to try his fortune. For a short period three stages a day were pressed into service from Central to meet the demands, and Denver's *Rocky Mountain News*, August 30, 1870, described the excitement as "great and increasing." It might have been, if one lived in Central or Caribou; not so if one were a Boulder merchant. Sadly and enviously, they watched as trade that should have been theirs went elsewhere for lack of a direct route to the camp, which, after all, was situated in their own county. Despite comments in Boulder papers to the contrary, by the end of the year Boulder's richest mining camp still was bound economically to neighboring Gilpin County and its major community, Central City.

For the merchant who could enter a new mining community first, vast potential awaited. The pioneer store at Caribou—Van & Tilney's—opened in July. Robert Tilney, after a rather short stay, sold out to his partner in October and moved to Boulder to later become the editor and publisher of the *Colorado Banner*. He left an interesting description of the problems faced during those early days:

> We pitched our tent, and with a partner opened up the first
> stock of goods, groceries and provisions ever taken so near the
> western line of Boulder County. The task of getting these goods
> there will never be forgotten. One half of our load was packed
> upon our backs up the steep hill (known as the ridge road), and
> although nearly worn out with fatigue, we managed to reach
> the place of rest safely. There were no fine buildings, no well
> laid-out and graded streets—nothing but a crooked wagon road,
> which led to the Caribou lode on the hill, then hidden from
> view by the heavy green timber. It was difficult to get through
> the camp with a wagon without hitting the hubs of our wheels
> against the stumps that dotted the main path every few feet.[14]

Within the same month a blacksmith shop and two boarding houses opened to answer other compelling needs of the miners.

By December the little village had grown considerably. Sheer numbers showed the increase decisively, for now there were four boarding houses, with another one being built. Press Pierce, one of the early

Caribou was young and hopes soared high when this photograph was taken in 1870 or 1871. Courtesy, Denver Public Library, Western History Department

pillars of the Caribou business community, had opened his meat market in the first frame building in the camp. Another general store, operated by Leo Donnelly, provided competition for Van. A combination bakery and brewery, two saloons, and a keno house offered recreational activities. The largest building in the community housed Sears & Werley's Billiard Hall & Saloon on the first floor, with offices on the second. To add further refinement it was lathed and plastered throughout. Completing the business establishments were two feed stables and a blacksmith shop. A total of about fifty frame buildings comprised the settlement. It had come a long way from the virgin pine forest of the previous year, or the site Tilney first reached in July. A compact camp looked out upon the world that winter with a confidence born of youth and prosperity that seemed endless.

The small-town professional class of post–Civil War America had not as yet reached Caribou, for it had neither doctors, lawyers, preachers, nor teachers. Nor had the fine hands of women significantly soothed this predominantly masculine world. In July a mere two women were reported in the district, and by September only twelve had moved into the area. Some of these probably left before winter settled in the Rockies. When women finally did appear in numbers, life at Caribou took on a decidedly different character and many of the cultural improvements then appeared.

Though lacking some of the entertainments and niceties of a more established settlement, the Caribouites cannot be said to have passed a dull summer and fall. There were mines to be opened and developed; a camp to be started; political matters to be discussed; and finally, when time permitted, recreational diversions to occupy the waking hours. Foremost in the minds of many, probably, was the establishment of their community, a trait common to Americans throughout frontier history. Not only would they benefit collectively, but stood to gain individually by increased property values, a better attraction for outside investment, and a more comfortable existence.

Just after the establishment of the camp, the residents petitioned to secure a postal route from Central to replace the private service that first responded to the need for mail delivery. A general meeting of the local Republicans decided to petition Washington, which after a slight delay granted the request. According to the petition, 400 voters resided at Caribou; this figure seems slightly exaggerated (perhaps in hopes of producing a quicker response). With the town surveyed and platted, the next step was to establish some rudimentary form of government. Anything more was not wanted, for the camp remained unincorporated and a large administration would mean high taxes—an idea that failed to gain widespread acceptance or support. As a result, in September a local election was held to select an assayer, justice of the peace, constable, and road commissioner for the district. Only 130 people voted, a far cry from the 400 mentioned in the petition to Washington.

Local contests were not the only area of political interest for Caribouites. While tied economically to Gilpin, the camp was politically a part of Boulder County. This dichotomy caused some painful problems which, it was hoped, would be overcome by an improved transportation connection between Caribou and Boulder. What better way to it than by railroad? Agitation had been carried on for some time to construct a railroad between Boulder and Denver, and Caribou was born right in the middle of a county-wide fight over a proposed railroad bond issue to do just that. The new camp took a hearty interest in the proceedings that promised them, if not a spur line, at least a wagon road up Boulder Canyon. Meetings were held throughout the county, including Caribou, by groups favoring both

Newness of construction and trees within the camp indicate this was Caribou in the early 1870s. Courtesy, Denver Public Library, Western History Department

sides. Few settings, however, were as picturesque as this new camp, which had no roof but the open sky, with a large bonfire for light and warmth on the chilly fall evenings, and a wagon for a rostrum. Caribou rolled up an impressive 92 to 33 vote in favor of the bonds, second only to Boulder's landslide 201 to 7. Despite the support of the rest of the mountain towns, the vote of the eastern half of the county returned overwhelmingly against the bonds and produced a rarity in politics, a tie vote—420 for, 420 against.[15] Here the matter temporarily rested.

When not involved in their own endeavors of making a living and working on a community or political project, the men could find numerous ways to spend their leisure time. One report from the camp described the efforts of the local actors to give performances of "The Merchant of Venice," "Merry Wives of Windsor," and other classics.[16] How serious these were may be doubted, for the reporter noted that numerous "Original off-hand essay and lectures" spiced the presentation, which for the sake of the "future peace and dignity of the camp" were not reported.

The saloons rivaled each other in their attempts to "relieve honest miners of troublesome surpluses" of money. Billiards, keno, faro, and numerous card games further helped pass a long evening. That the men had money to spend cannot be doubted, for the appearance of numerous merchants testifies to the fact. A hired miner's pay was about $3.25 per day, a good wage for Caribou and Colorado. The cost of living, according to newspaper accounts, was not much higher than in Boulder and Central, remarkable considering the isolation and newness of the community. For example, potatoes selling at 2¢ a pound in Boulder went for 3¢ in the camp.

As the fall turned into winter, the choice had to be made whether to retreat to the warmer and lower portions of the territory or remain in Caribou. Those choosing the latter had their first taste of a Caribou winter. On October 26, 1870, two feet of snow fell, and in December a correspondent offhandedly mentioned the heavy winds and occasional snows that had plagued the camp for the past two months.[17] Mining came to a halt, and many of the miners left to winter elsewhere until spring allowed some measure of comfort on Caribou Hill for those working there.

Sixteen months had passed since Martin and Lytle had discovered the Caribou and Poorman mines and a great deal had happened in the interim. As 1870 drew to a close, the face of the land had changed markedly; where once there had been a forest there now stood a mining camp and mines. Land that had previously known only the whistling of the wind and the quiet movement of wild animals resounded with the bustle of the mining frontier. The land had been opened and now awaited further development.

Caribou held out great promise, to which the ore wagons rumbling down the mountains toward the smelters at Black Hawk attested. It had been a busy, yet relatively quiet birth, a time of excitement, tinted with great expectation and, already, some disappointment. Much work had gone into the effort, along with unbounded enthusiasm and exploitativeness, so inherent in the frontier experience. Ahead loomed the pains of adolescence, a future date against which to measure the wealth of the district and the permanence of the camp. Few would have disagreed with this comment found in the *Rocky Mountain Directory and Colorado Gazetteer for 1871*:

> A careful examination of the mines, minerals and peculiar
> advantages and resources of the Grand Island district has con-
> vinced us that ere long Caribou will be a mining town of consid-
> erable importance, and the district one of unusual wealth.[18]

Queen of Caribou Hill

The fortunes of the town, and even the district, reflected those of its major mine, the Caribou. When the mine prospered so did the camp; when the mine played out the camp declined. No other mine poured forth its wealth in such abundance nor did so much to advertise and promote the region. No other could rival the "Queen."

Exploitative, speculative, and uncertain—mining is indeed all of these, and the Caribou clearly evidenced each characteristic during the decade of the seventies. As it had dominated the discovery period, so it continued to hold first rank. Little seemed to stand in the way of its becoming one of the most productive mines in the territory. During the winter months of 1870–1871, protected by its shaft house, this mine alone produced salable amounts of ore. The *Central City Register*, February

8, 1872, reported that since its discovery in 1869, $76,989 worth of ore had been shipped and at least another 500 tons of lower grade awaited only a more accessible mill. Divided by sale, the western half of the property, owned by Breed, forged ahead of that operated by the Caribou Company. Eastern money clearly could do more for Caribou than the small amounts available locally.

John Tice, a midwesterner on a tour of the Great Plains and Rocky Mountains, visited Caribou in the summer of 1871. As the Caribou Mine was the feature attraction, he soon found himself examining it, guided by William Martin, partner in and superintendent for the Caribou Company. After having been shown the surface workings and "liberally furnished with rich specimens," Tice descended the main shaft. Not particularly impressed, he left this description:

> The descent is by ladders, and the place was damp from drip-
> ping water of the side rock above, and gloomy, notwithstanding
> the star candles we held. It possessed no particular interest nor
> attraction, and we were glad when we returned to daylight.[1]

For Tice it might not possess any interest, but for the owners the mine held a great potential.

Progress was being made in expanding both the surface and underground works. The first serious mining problem appeared, however, when water from the melting snow started to seep into and fill the main shaft. Cutter met the challenge by installing an engine to pump out the shaft, but the dilemma remained. The deeper the shafts sank, the greater the potential water volume from underground sources.

Water hampered operations; but even more immediately troublesome were the time and money needed to transport ore to the smelters in Black Hawk. This situation allowed only the best grade of ore to be worked, leaving the majority unprofitable, thereby retarding the development of the mine. The answer, of course, was to build a mill nearer the mine. Breed, concerned with his profits, took the step. He picked a site only a few miles from his property (present-day Nederland), a location well chosen, with water and wood available and near the main thoroughfare between Central City and Gold Hill.

Breed was fortunate, since he could base his planning on the trials and failures Georgetown and Clear Creek County had experienced in the past six years. Silver mining had been greatly retarded in that region because of little success in separating the valuable minerals at a reasonable cost to both the miner and millman. By the start of the seventies, a process based on amalgamation was being used on the majority of the ores, and Breed selected it for his operations. The pan amalgamation method was used extensively in the West for the extraction of silver, having first come into prominence in Nevada.

Cutter was made supervisor of the construction. Work starting in early May 1871, proceeded rapidly, and within two months the granite foundations were nearly completed. Hampered by a lack of lumber, Cutter sought to insure a steady supply by erecting a sawmill, and pushed on with the construction. August, the planned completion date, passed with work continuing on the superstructure. Not until December did the mill start, and then costly stoppages for repairs prevented continuous use. Although reported to be in full, successful operation the next month and meeting the "expectation of the proprietors,"[2] numerous trying delays continued. Defective castings from the East proved particularly vexatious to the owners until they secured a large number of replacements from Gilpin County foundries. By the end of 1872 the mill finally operated for three consecutive months without stopping for repairs.

When completed and placed in working condition, the mill was one of the finest in the territory. The Boulder and Caribou papers, with understandable pride, lauded the achievement. The building measured 100 feet by 165 feet, with five terraces arranged so that ore brought from the mine and placed on the upper level gradually moved down through the remaining levels until it appeared as bullion at the end of the run. The process was based upon roasting and amalgamation. Explained simply, it operated as follows: after the ore was crushed, dried, and then reduced to powder under a battery of stamps, it was roasted for eight hours to desulphurize, expel base metals, and chlorodize the pulp remaining (salt was added to induce this). This pulp was then mixed with mercury in amalgamating pans, where the silver, now in a silver chloride combination, combined with the mercury while the remaining pulp was run off. The last procedure was to heat the mercury-silver, separating the two and leaving silver to be poured into bars. The mill, when running at capacity, could handle twenty tons of ore per day at a reported cost of slightly over five dollars per ton in 1871, although later reports place it in the fourteen-dollar range.[3]

The mill enhanced the value of the mine and the future of the whole district by providing nearby facilities. Breed had done well; his choice of a site showed good judgment and the method was one that had already proven successful. His mill, once the early problems were ironed out, was one of the best-equipped and -operated in Colorado. For the rest of the decade it remained the best in Boulder County, and until the great silver mills of the Leadville era, it ranked among the finest in the state. With fine disregard for conservation and all those who relied on Boulder Creek for a water supply, the waste was allowed to seep into the stream.

With the mill completed, Breed could realize the entire wealth of the Caribou. To consolidate his holdings, he completed his purchase of the eastern half of the mine from the Caribou Company for a reported $75,000 in the autumn of 1871.[4] Now in control of the total property, he vigorously pushed operations forward. By the end of the year eleven shafts had been sunk—the main one 329 feet. The pay vein pursued was rich and kept the miners and ore sorters busy. The editor of the *Caribou Post* likened the aboveground scene to that of an old-time New England farmhouse with a blazing fire in the fireplace of the ore-sorting room and the men gathered around working. Breed was carrying on legitimate mining on a scale not practiced before at Caribou.

Water, however, continued to hinder operations, most of it seeping in from the annual runoff. By pumping, mining could continue everywhere except the very bottom of the shaft. As the vein dipped, however, Breed had no choice but to find a better way to drain the water. He planned to dig a tunnel from the north side of the hill to intersect the main shaft, thereby easing the pumping distance and cost. Once again he turned the project over to his lieutenant, Cutter. Work commenced in 1871 but progress was slow. Finally, three years later, the tunnel intersected the shaft at the 290-foot level after drilling 752 feet. The Breed or Caribou Tunnel, as it became known, did help to drain the mine, but by the time they joined, the shaft had long since passed that depth. Water now was pumped out from the level of the tunnel rather than the surface. While this was some improvement, it still left the basic problem unresolved.[5]

Rumors of a possible sale of the Caribou Mine were bandied about for most of 1872. Almost from the time Breed came upon the scene, speculation had been rampant to this effect. Back in December 1870, ore was sent to England to help convince "John" of the riches of the district, but particularly of this one mine. The following May the Caribou was rumored bonded to an English company for $500,000; in July a mysterious Mr. Goldring from England visited the camp and sent Caribou ore to London; and finally in November the mine was reported sold. Nothing came of these rumors, but the *Boulder County*

News, January 5, 1872, openly declared that Breed had rejected a one-million-dollar offer from England. Other proposals reportedly were made from England, with the price continually increasing until it reached one and one-half million. Breed or the English buyers, or both, failed to be satisfied and the speculation continued.[6]

The rumors and activities of Breed at Caribou caused the questioning of his intentions. Had he purchased the mine as a speculative venture to sell, once it started to produce large quantities of ore; or had he intended to maintain ownership? While the answer cannot definitely be ascertained, the former alternative would seem to have been his intention. Neither Breed nor Cutter was a novice in the mining game. Their mining activities had been quite legitimate, and under their guidance the whole operation had been placed on a developmental—later a profitable—basis. An indication of Breed's plans appeared in two letters he sent to William Martin. In the first, undated but presumably sent in 1871 or 1872, he wrote that he had a man to examine the mine for the English partners; and on April 10, 1872, he noted that the prospect of a sale was very favorable and warned Martin not to mention it to anyone.[7] To be sure, the expense into 1872 had been great in building a mill and opening the mine and tunnel, but the ore produced some return and the amount in sight promised even more. This was a good time to sell for, as Breed knew, those in mining gambled and no one could say when the ore vein might pinch out. With new equipment, a mill, and ore reserves, the Caribou presented a very attractive, tempting offer.

By the spring of 1873 the mine was producing very well indeed. The Georgetown *Mining Review* reported in March a daily average of twenty-five tons, worth $160 to $200 each, being mined. Meanwhile, Breed's interest had turned from England, across the channel to The Netherlands. Here, too, money was available to invest in American mines. In mid-March a party from that country, as a local Boulder paper commented, with "unspellable and unpronounceable names" visited and examined the Caribou.[8] Apparently satisfied with what they saw, the Mining Company Nederland purchased the mine for three million dollars.

The sale price caused comment in the local press. The *Boulder County News*, at first slightly hesitant, came to the conclusion that the mine was not overpriced, and it seemed that both the company and the county stood to gain. The *Central City Register* regarded the purchase as a sound business transaction from the first. The *Mining Review* alone opposed the sale and with prophetic foresight stated:

The *Review* has but little to say in any way congratulatory, concerning the business, except that unexpected wisdom was shown by the purchasers (if we are correctly informed) by partial payment for the property, in stock. The mine is now to be put to a fearful test, and whatever may be the immediate advantages to the district in which it is located, of the influx of capital, there is, at least, an even chance that the end will not be as rose-colored as the beginning.

If, however, the expectations of its new owners are not fully realized, the time will come when those members of the Colorado Press who have unqualifiedly applauded this sale, will reflect with bitterness the records of the past in their own districts, where once sanguine capitalists were too fond of investing, but now can not be induced to; and the honest miners of Boulder County, who have pushed their district up to its present prominent position, will have a warm and forcible curse, for one who shall come among them for speculative purposes, and taking advantages of flood tide, leave the little fish to struggle for life through the long and discouraging ebb.[9]

On April 30 the company took possession of the property, which included the mine, mill, and right-of-way in the Caribou Tunnel. Breed, however, retained ownership of the tunnel, although with growing indifference, for correspondence shows that by 1878 he did only the minimum work possible to retain it. In 1878 it was "jumped" and he was compelled to go to court to force the squatters out. Despite Breed's seeming lack of interest, the tunnel remained essential to the draining of the Caribou. Eben Smith, then superintendent of the Caribou, was particularly anxious, as he wrote, to oust "the damned scoundrels . . . at once."[10] Breed also owned other property at Caribou that he retained, apparently in hopes of selling at a later date.

The Mining Company Nederland was officially organized in April 1873 by, among others, Dr. Pieter Philip van Bosse, former minister of finance and colonies; Jacob de Bruyn Kops, member of Parliament and former professor of political economy; and Hugh Hope Loudon, member of The Hague Town Council. The company received the Royal Assent on April 18, with registered capital of seven million guilders divided into shares of 1,000 guilders each. Its sole property and hope for profit was the Caribou Mine.

Power was retained by the Dutch, for at least five of the seven commissioners and the director were required to live in The Netherlands. The American stockholders had the right to elect one commissioner. To represent the company in the United States, a general manager would be sent to Caribou. Yearly meetings were scheduled in The Hague, where the progress for the year would be analyzed and the news received of dividends, supposedly 7 percent for holders of preferred shares. Five percent of the profits would be set aside for the commissioners and a like amount as a bonus for employees. With all powers, duties, and responsibilities carefully delimited, the Mining Company Nederland was ready to start operation.[11]

From the very beginning this venture proved a possibility, not a probability, for the Caribou had never produced ore enough to warrant the purchase price. Not all the three million had been paid in cash, as the *Mining Review* hinted. Breed's agent, Moses Anker, a mining promoter and speculator, received a commission of 3,500 shares of stock, the balance in cash to Breed and his associates. Even with this, the company ventured its entire capital and had no money to work the mine. As represented to them, however, they needed none. When the Dutch had visited the mine, they beheld an estimated 34,000 tons of ore ready to be mined on the various levels.[12] This, plus the known history of the mine, was enough to convince them that it was a bargain that should be seized.

Upon assuming control they made a disheartening discovery: the enormous ore reserves of the previous March had disappeared. Breed, feeling sure of his sale, had apparently gutted all available ore in a frenzy of mining before the final transfer—a serious charge to levy, but contemporary sources accused him of it, and bullion shipment records show an increased activity.[13] Breed finally exposed his true interest in mining. Later Breed invested in Aspen mines and received this scathing comment from the local *Rocky Mountain Sun*, July 21, 1883: "[he showed] some of the meanest characteristics of the human race." With the profits of the sale and last minute mining in his pocket, he leaves the story, his legacy an improved mine and new mill. But the former needed a good deal of dead work before it would again be profitable for its owners. The exploitation of the mine ended its first phase.

Despite the shock this revelation must have been to the company, it started forth resolutely with what remained. To supervise the operation it employed Peter H. Van Diest, late chief of the Mining Department of The Netherlands, East Indian Colonies, and sent him to Caribou as resident director. Van Diest was well qualified and never lost faith in the mine, writing as late as 1876 that, when opened thoroughly, it would undoubtedly pay large dividends.[14] Under his guidance, work was pushed forward; but the Caribou remained in no condition to pay the quick returns envisioned by the stockholders in The Netherlands. To further complicate the matter, Mark A. Shaffenburg, U.S. marshal of Colorado Territory, who temporarily preceded Van Diest as managing director, had purchased new mining machinery reportedly worth $100,000—to add another burden to the company. By the end of the year, though, three shifts worked around the clock; and at last paying quantities of ore appeared to be in sight.

Trouble was not long in coming, however. The company seemed burdened with an excessive number of officers in Colorado. The initial problem arose between Van Diest and chief stockholder Moses Anker, over the ore reserves and how to develop them. Reports from Van Diest were more conservative, but Anker sent glowing letters of prospective yields. Anker—whom the Central City *Daily Register* called "the irrepressible"—had been promoting Colorado silver mines since at least 1870, when he was in Baltimore trying to interest local money to move west.[15] The stockholders desired to read of yields; and pressure, in turn, was placed on Van Diest to produce profit rather than expensive, though needed, exploration and development. In disgust, Van Diest resigned to be replaced by Anker. Anker, not himself a mining man, placed experienced men under him. Despite optimistic forecasts, the expenses continued and ore amounts did not match expectations. Again it was hoped that a change of management would do wonders for the company, and H. J. De Bruyn Prince succeeded Anker. Grumbling was now heard from many sources, including the foreman of the mine, Richard Harvey, who felt he was not receiving a fair wage. Fortunately, some of his letters have been preserved and shed light on the situation at Caribou. He reported differences between the men in charge of the mill and the mine. He hinted at, but did not clearly describe, activities that were for the benefit of interested parties in America and not the Mining Company Nederland. And finally, some months after he resigned as foreman, he wrote to a friend:

> But I will here state that the reason I left the Caribou Mines was, that two parties of the Stockholders in that property—the Dutch and Americans—got at loggerheads about working the property. The Dutch would not furnish any working capital to put the Mine in good working shape, but persisted in working it on its own merits, or with the false economy of taking out the ore whenever they could find it.[16]

Caribou mines in the mid-1870s—Caribou, Sherman, and Poorman. Courtesy, Duane A. Smith

Clearly, the company and the mine were now in trouble. Confused management, too little capital, and conflicts were steadily taking their toll.

While the troubles of the company and its mine took the major share of the attention of the interested onlookers, the *Mining Review*, like a fire bell in the night, warned of another problem. In its July and August 1874 issues it observed that the prominent mines of the district were being rapidly absorbed by large corporations, which were, from a financial standpoint, capable of sustaining a long fight. Fight? Yes, because the No Name vein cut and apparently faulted the Caribou, and the Sherman and Poorman lodes were found to have merged in the Caribou Tunnel. "Undoubtedly, with greater development, there will be the necessity . . . of a greater number of the legal fraternity. It is sincerely to be hoped however that the curse will not linger there as it has in other sections of the mountains." No one heeded this still, small voice.

The years 1874–1875 witnessed the culmination of the exploitative policy that followed Van Diest's resignation. Despite optimistic stories in local papers about production and development, the situation continued to deteriorate. Harvey had written on March 22, 1875,

"They put off the pay again from the 15th until the 25th. We questioned and asked them why it was that they could not pay the men at the regular day, seeing they were taking out so much bullion."[17] He continued by stating they received the following answer: "They were paying off old outstanding debts, and saving money to pay off Anker who was over in Europe all the time plaguing the Company for money." Only time would tell if the company could meet its obligations, and time was running dangerously short. Van Bosse, president of the company, wrote as early as September 1874, "There exists some tension between the Dutch and the American counterparts, the last being not very happy with the modification and also under suspicion of mischievous intentions."[18] Unfortunately, he was not more specific as to what tensions; both parties apparently had grounds for uneasiness over the developments.

The situation in Colorado reflected displeasure in The Netherlands. A Dutch journal charged that The Hague gentlemen had been "badly sold." It further accused the Americans of placing the mine in its present condition by useless expenses and poor mining practices. In conclusion, it was assumed the "tricky Americans had calculated" to buy the mine back for a song and then resume profitable production.[19] How much truth supported these charges cannot be known. However, Harvey's comments, Anker's activities, and the history of the mine lend credence to the accusations.

On Friday evening, December 3, 1875, the mine was suddenly closed by the miners. One week later, 150 miners' liens on the property were filed against the company in the Boulder County Court for wages and money due from contracts and for materials from October to December. Other creditors, realizing the situation, also filed suits to attach the property for debts owed them. The District Court, with no other recourse, finally ordered the property, machinery, and buildings to be sold to satisfy the creditors. Among those hoping to get their money before it was too late were some familiar figures, including Moses Anker and Mark A. Shaffenburg. Anker, in fact, was awarded $139,000 by a Boulder jury in 1877, but found to his dismay the award did not mean he would be able to collect from an organization no longer in existence. The other major attachment was by Jerome B. Chaffee for $47,933.[20]

Charges and countercharges flew as to who should be blamed. Despite accusations of fraud and corruption against him by a dismissed company bookkeeper, De Bruyn Prince continued as resident agent. A shakeup was in order among some of the lesser positions, and

Abel Breed serving himself from a tea/coffee set made from Caribou Mine's silver. Courtesy, Garry Bryant

Van Diest returned now as superintendent of the mine. The Caribou reopened under his guidance, but the situation remained tense. Even Van Diest, though popular, could not salvage the wreck. The company, devoid of funds, provided no assistance and no foreseeable improvement. By spring the situation had become so critical that the miners took over control of the mine and worked to secure their back pay. Van Diest acted as the mining manager for the men in dealing with creditors and getting the ore milled, the mill at Nederland being in the hands of the sheriff. A visitor to Caribou during these tense days left the following description:

> No person employed not about the mine, or not known to be friendly to the party now in possession is allowed around the mine, and extreme vigilance is exercised to prevent the agent of the Nederland company, Mr. Prince . . . [from] gaining admittance to the works, or getting information in regard thereto. On the outside of the building, over the mine, an ominous sign is displayed, bearing the inscription "Positively no admittance except to employees," on one end of which is a rude drawing of a skull and crossbones, and on the other a gallows whereon is suspended the figure of a man, supposed to represent the fate of the person bold enough to disobey the injunction.[21]

The miners were at least making some money, but the situation was too unstable, and the future depended on what the company planned or could do as a remedy.[22]

The Mining Company Nederland made some efforts to revive itself. The Amsterdam *Handelsbad*, February 13, 1876, reported an attempt was underway to have the stockholders contribute money to satisfy the claims of the creditors.[23] All this proved to be too little and too late, for by the middle of March the company went into bankruptcy. A rumored last minute attempt to salvage something by selling the property to an English firm came to nothing. The company's mine, mill, and other Colorado assets awaited only the auction block.

The Mining Company Nederland lost its Caribou property. In three years a mine that had exhibited a great deal of promise had become almost worthless, thus raising the question: why?

A Dutch journal, as previously discussed, accused the Americans of misrepresentation in the original sale and a plan calculated to force the company into bankruptcy. Concerning the former charge, there was a good deal of truth relating to Breed's activity. The other claim, however, does not seem to be as valid. In 1884 the *Rocky Moun-*

Caribou Hill looks peaceful on this summer day. The large wood stacks beside the Caribou and Poorman mines will cause trouble one day. Courtesy, Duane A. Smith

tain News labeled Moses Anker as a notorious promoter of mining stock swindles and accused him of manipulating the sale. The American press charged that the collapse resulted from inefficient management, un-principled manipulation of stock, downright fraud, absolute theft, and dissension among the stockholders.[24] Shaffenburg, who originally put the company in debt for machinery and later harassed it by lawsuits, was removed in 1875 as a U.S. marshal, convicted of mismanagement of official business, and sentenced to Leavenworth Penitentiary. No direct evidence, however, connects him with mis-appropriation of mining funds. There is no doubt that internal fighting over stock and mining methods hurt the company. Harvey's letters confirm this, but to charge the Americans with deliberately ruining a company based in The Netherlands with Dutch control of the mine seems to be an extreme accusation.

The original cost of the property, and Breed's ambitious mining before the sale, set the company back and it never fully recovered. Nor did the purchase of expensive machinery provide the needed impetus. The relative inexperience of the Dutch further aggravated the situation. Short of working capital, they resorted to exploitative mining for quick profit rather than exploration and development. Richard Harvey's letters clearly point out the fallacy of this practice. Eventually, the ore reserves ran out and the company had no capital for the dead work that was now required.[25] In desperation they turned any way to try to find another ore pocket, but with no success. Burdened with a three-million-dollar debt and inexperienced and high-salaried officials, plagued by distance between the headquarters in The Hague and Caribou, and a disappointed dream of a mining bonanza, the Mining Company Nederland failed to develop what potential it had. It would have taken a fortunate series of circumstances to save the company; these did not appear.

In the end, with the Caribou Mine in a depleted condition, unable to meet even the most fundamental of obligations and displaying on the books only expenses, no profits, the company folded. Once again European capital went to the American West, only to disappear with small return to the investor. The future of the Caribou was left in the hands of the "tricky" Americans, while the Dutch had learned an expensive lesson in American mining.

The history of the Caribou Mine plagued Dutch investment for years. In 1879 the influential *Engineering and Mining Journal* reported that a group of Dutch investors was considering purchasing mines in the San Juan region of Colorado. If the sale went through, it would be the first American mining property disposed in Holland, commented the Journal, since "the unfortunate Caribou sale."[26]

Eastern Investors
Try Their Luck

While the discovery and opening of the Caribou mines was being carried forward intensely, much of the rest of the United States was going through a period of turmoil. Industrialism had made solid strides toward dominating American life since the war. Then came the panic of 1873 and depression, checking for a while the country's growth. Reconstruction, meanwhile, plowed its sordid way through the South, and in the White House sat the Civil War hero, U. S. Grant, benightedly watching over his nation while scandals rocked his second term. Passing almost unnoticed in 1873 was the signing of a bill that abolished the coinage of silver dollars and placed the nation on the gold standard, on which it had been in practice, if not principle, for years. The West, which would be affected most by the abolishments, was being rapidly settled, and at the moment had its attention focused on the Indian-White struggle, as it moved remorselessly toward a climax and a triumph for the invaders.

Such events were noticed only in passing at Caribou. Even the panic and depression failed to impede the growth of the camp, for as long as the mines kept producing, Caribou remained insulated behind a silver wall. Eventually, to be sure, the Caribouites would take heated notice of the "Crime of 1873," as the coinage act became known. Not now, however, for the price of silver remained high, the mines produced, and capital flowed in—the prospects seemed unlimited. In the spring of 1871 the future appeared particularly radiant:

> All the shafts sunk last fall were filled with drifting snow of winter; some were yet even full of snow, and undisturbed. At others the miners were engaged in cleaning out the snow, and in others this had been done and the work of mining was progressing. Within a circle of one-half mile from town there are no less than seventy lodes; fifty-six pay well, and all would pay if there were means for reducing the ores.[1]

That fifty-six could be paying well seems impossible, for never in the history of the district would that many be profitable. Listening to the hopes of the owners, the author of the statement, John Tice, came to an overly inflated conclusion. Optimism, like the wind, permeated the atmosphere, inviting all to whiff and succumb.

Such optimism was not localized; it wafted as far as New York and across the seas to Europe. In the hands of agents and speculators Caribou mines were being offered to prospective mining magnates. From Cincinnati came Leonard S. Root to spend several weeks examining the *Grand Island Mining District* and then going back to New York and London to put property on the market. With activity such as this, Caribou advertised itself and lured capital. Many mines besides the Caribou had been located in 1870–1871, but none, as previously mentioned, would prove so wealthy or significant. At some time almost all the major rivals became involved with the Caribou Mine through common ownership or legal dispute. This led, as the *Mining Review* warned, to repeated trouble.

In the spring of 1871, however, all this was still in the future. Little, if anything, clouded the eyes of the miners as they went forth to open their mines. The tempestuous atmosphere of youth and boom times overrode all other considerations. Certainly a mill was needed, but on both Caribou and Idaho hills, evidences of rich silver veins had been uncovered.

Running parallel to the Caribou but north and lower on the hill was the Sherman Mine. From the start regarded as one of the best in the district, it still had an undistinguished early career. The owners, apparently lacking capital, leased it in 1872. Unlike so many mines in this circumstance, the Sherman was developed carefully and profitably. Having an even quieter early history was the No Name, which diagonally intersected both the Caribou and Sherman veins. Not until 1873 did it rate notice by the newspapers; production that year and the next prompted the *Boulder County News*, October 9, 1874, to overenthusiastically call it the "king of the whole county."[2] Local ownership, however, never was able to place mining on the level with Breed and the Caribou.

Enough ore had been produced and enough promise shown, though, to tempt Eastern investors. In the late spring of 1874, Levi M. Bates, a New York merchant, became interested in the two mines and eventually purchased them for a reported $80,000. Bates appointed Martin A. Smith, a resident of Fremont Center, New York, and apparently a mining promoter and lobbyist, as his resident agent and turned to what he hoped would be a profitable investment.

The history of Bates's venture curiously parallels that of Breed. New machinery was installed, surface buildings constructed, and exploration pushed ahead. Bates, too, became convinced of the need for a mill for his property and built one in 1874–1875. He picked a site about three miles from Caribou on North Boulder Creek. The mill, when completed in July 1875, was an impressive structure. From the sketchy reports that appeared, it can be deduced that the process involved crushing and roasting, followed by the introduction of chlorine and some special silver precipitant. Able to handle only fifteen tons per day, the mill cost Bates $25,000 in addition to the money he had already invested.[3] Ore from the mines had been stored until the opening, but the reduction process proved unsatisfactory for unspecified reasons and the first of several remodelings was undertaken. The *Mining Review* in August 1875 remarked that the "so called 'chlorine process' has not turned up trumps yet in this property."

Overcoming these initial setbacks, the mill, employing twenty-five to thirty men, operated at or near capacity for the first half of 1876. It ground to a halt later that year due to difficulties at the mines, apparently never resuming production. The little village of Batesville, or North Boulder, grew up by the mill. It housed the workers but had no stores or business houses. Relying on the mill for its existence, the settlement did not survive its benefactor.

Operations in both mines were on a large scale in 1874 and 1875. Smith was not only the resident agent but also invested his own money and launched an intriguing career in Caribou mining. Bates, either tiring of his mining speculation or seeing an opportunity to make a quick profit, sold his property to William Fullerton and Robert Graham Dun on October 30, 1875. Smith retained his interest and apparently purchased part of Bates's stock, for he is listed as a partner with the other two. The mines and mill changed hands in the transaction, but control remained in New York, where all three men had homes.

Although having sold the mines, Bates was far from being finished with Caribou matters. In a series of letters to the Central City law firm of Teller and Teller, who represented him in Colorado, Bates, during the following two years, discussed his troubles. He found himself involved in several lawsuits concerning old debts, and he could not seem to get the situation clear in his mind.[4] He felt he was being unfairly involved and, as he wrote on April 25, 1876, he wanted Henry Teller to be "fully ready for those scamps." His problems, however, were minor when compared to what happened to Fullerton and Dun.

The prominent member of this partnership and the best-known Easterner to purchase mining property at Caribou was Robert Graham Dun, owner (1859 to his death in 1900) of the internationally famous agency then known as R. G. Dun & Co., now the much larger and extensive Dun & Bradstreet, Inc. The growth and development of Caribou depended on the investments of outside capitalists and none individually contributed as much over so long a period as this man.

Dun was forty-nine years old at the time of the transaction. Joining in 1851 the agency that was to bear his name, he rose within four years from employee to partner and, in 1859, to sole owner. Dun had practically no experience with the mining industry when he grew interested in the Caribou area, but by the 1870s he was wealthy and eager to invest some of his money in speculative stock. What contact Dun had had with mining was through his older brother James. James Angus Dun had mined in California and Nevada and in the late 1860s became assistant manager for the Dun & Co. office in San Francisco. Here he came to know William Ralston, Nevada Comstock mine owner and San Francisco banker, and through him his younger brother met Ralston. R. G. Dun took a trip to California and later corresponded with Ralston. What influence this contact may have had on Dun may only be speculated; conceivably the two discussed the prospect of silver mining.

A major influence on Dun was his friend William Fullerton. Fullerton, a lawyer by profession, became nationally famous when he served as counsel for the plaintiff in the sensational and scandalous *Tilton vs. Beecher* case in which the widely known and respected Rev. Henry Ward Beecher was charged with alienation of affection by Theodore Tilton. While well versed in law, Fullerton's knowledge of mining probably was less than his partner's. Several years later in 1877 he confessed, "I know nothing about mining and have to depend entirely upon the judgments of others." As early as 1872 these two men were considering purchasing a Utah silver mine, but Fullerton found himself unable to raise the funds and nothing came of the plan.[5]

Dun's start was fairly modest. In a letter written November 15, 1875, he noted that he and Fullerton had jointly bought 1,250 shares of the Sherman and one-half of the No Name Mine, with Fullerton becoming president and cashier of the company.[6] Smith's role in the partnership remains rather mysterious. Appointed general manager, he returned to Caribou; Dun's correspondence quickly indicates, however, that he was no longer a partner. Dun, in fact, suspected him of being involved in dishonest dealings.[7] The legal status of the No Name and Sherman during these years is unclear—both the local newspapers and Dun's correspondence refer to a Sherman–No Name Company and separate organizations for each mine.

Dun and Fullerton planned to go to Colorado to inspect their purchase but were unable to do so because of other pressing business problems. Dun, meanwhile, sent his brother Jim to Boulder to look after his interests and to be his "eyes and ears." Distrusting the "very flattering accounts of new and rich developments in the mine" that Harmon Minckler wrote and telegraphed, Dun hoped to learn the truth. Minckler, whose rather checkered Caribou career was just starting, held an unspecified position. Dun confided to Jim, "Of course you will get as much into the confidence of every one about the place—but at the same time hold to your suspicions of every Mothers son of them." In the same letter he mentioned his suspicion that the new owners of the Caribou were up to something. These new Caribou owners, Jerome Chaffee and David Moffat, also controlled the First National Bank of Denver (which held Fullerton's note for $13,000 on the property), and Dun felt they might be trying secretly to get an attachment and "gobble" his mine and mill. He did not really trust Minckler in this matter either: "Of course I hardly think Minckler would lend himself to such an outrage but you know how a matter of

Robert G. Dun found that investing in mines can be an expensive adventure. Courtesy, Ross County Historical Society, Chillicothe, Ohio

a few thousands to Moffat would be a small matter to accomplish such an object and to Minckler it might prove a tempting bait."[8]

During 1876 the partnership and friendship became increasingly strained, as Fullerton proved slow in supplying his part of the money needed to continue operations and reduce the note signed in the original transaction. This situation was reflected in the operation of the property. Mining came to a halt, which, as previously mentioned, shut down the mill. The No Name was leased while the internal struggle continued within the partnership, and the Sherman was worked only spasmodically the rest of the decade. Already tired of the venture, the partners tried to sell; but the prospective buyers, after seeing the property, refused to make the purchase.[9] Dun's misfortunes at Caribou had just begun.

Hard-pressed for money to support his Eastern ventures, Dun sincerely wanted to sell his Colorado property. Not only had expectations been unmet, but the company, as Dun wrote a Denver creditor, "is temporarily embarrassed for means—principally by reason of Smith's extravagance and mismanagement."[10] Despite his desire and need, he did not wish to sell the property under false pretenses, and became angry when a report was sent to a prospective buyer from Caribou telling of a new $1,000 per ton strike in the No Name. Dun, who had not received such a dispatch, called it a bogus attempt to induce a quick sale and would have nothing to do with it.[11] Far too few mining men at Caribou upheld such high business ethics when selling property or stock.

The year 1877 did not improve the worsening relationship between the two men nor relieve Dun's worries over his investment. Fullerton continued to drag his feet, and Dun found more and more of the responsibility being shifted to him. Money was needed in Colorado to make payments on the outstanding debts, and only by a hurried effort was he able to prevent the public sale of the Sherman to satisfy a lien against it in January. The lien on the property had been assessed against the Sherman Mining Company in March of the previous year by the Caribou business firm of Scott Bros. for default of payment for materials. After a trial the court ordered the sale of the mine, but Dun's last-minute efforts prevented this. This proved to be only the first of eight suits brought against either the Sherman or the No Name in 1877 and 1878, which helps to explain why the two were not in operation and why Dun lost interest in his mining venture. In each case the court awarded damages to the plaintiff against the companies, the largest amount being $14,522 in a suit brought by the First National Bank of Denver.[12] Dun, who was in New York, found himself at a distinct disadvantage in trying to achieve a clear picture of what was happening and to untangle the legal complications enveloping his property. Writing to his brother-in-law, William James, on March 6, 1877, he complained, "The d——d old mine has harassed me almost to death aside from embarrassing pecuniarily. I only wish I were out of the operation and had back one quarter of what I have in it."

To make matters worse, Dun and Fullerton did not entirely control the property and the former apparently had little idea at first who the silent partners were. On January 26 he wrote:

> Until very recently I never knew who represented the other interest. It now turns out it is all in the hands or at least under the control of the Fullertons—that being the case they should have furnished at least double the funds advanced by me, but instead I have put in more than half of all furnished.[13]

Dun shed no further light on who the "other interest" might be, but another suit brought by Scott Bros. on July 30, 1878, perhaps gives an indication. Named as defendants were Steven Fullerton, brother of William; Harmon Minckler; Martin A. Smith; Levi Bates; and James Dun, although the last two disclaimed any interest during the trial, and action against them was dropped. James became involved only as the representative of his brother. That Minckler had a share in the company was indicated in a letter from the New York law firm of Davies and Work, sent to Teller and Teller concerning their mutual client Levi Bates. Writing on December 27, 1875, Henry Work stated, "I think I am not far wrong in saying that they [M. A. Smith and Minckler] represent themselves as well as other parties in the purchase."

Dun was becoming rather leery of Fullerton's activities and even hinted that he considered his partner had not been very "candid or square" about the operation. The two men now did not even visit one another, writing only when the circumstances warranted. To complicate the situation further, the No Name was involved in a lawsuit with the owners of the Caribou Mine concerning overlapping claim rights. Dun, to try to break part of the impasse involving the property, purchased the Sherman outright in early 1877. Rather than working it and risking more money, he hoped for a sale to recoup his losses.[14] His partnership in the No Name continued and it was this mine that gave him so much trouble. Meanwhile Dun launched his own investigation into what he thought were, at best, shady operations involving members of the company. Martin A. Smith now reappeared on friendly terms with Dun, although he was at the moment going through involuntary bankruptcy in a New York City court. Smith informed Dun that he had shipped 69,000 ounces of silver to Fullerton, while Fullerton's statement to Dun showed only $40,000 in receipts. Silver, in 1877, averaged $1.19 per fine ounce in New York. Smith, according to Dun, "came clean"; but Harmon Minckler would not confess anything.[15] Minckler's whole connection with Caribou remains perplexing. He served as general manager and superintendent of the Sherman and No Name at various times but his previous career is unknown. Even the spelling of his name is varied—Mincler, Minchler, and Minckler—the last being the most commonly used, his first name appearing both as Herman and Harmon.

Dun wanted to go through the accounts with Fullerton but never indicated in his letters whether he had such a meeting with him, nor did he ever mention concrete proof of misdeeds. His suspicions remained strong, however, down to the end of the partnership. Not only had Smith leveled the charges about the silver shipments, but he also told Dun that he believed he had found a buyer for the mines. Dun was again destined for disappointment, for no sale was arranged.

The tribulations Dun had suffered the previous two years were repeated in 1878. Throughout this period, although receiving profit from his firm, he found himself hard-pressed for money to support his numerous undertakings, of which the mines were only one. The No Name, its vein intersecting the Caribou Mine and yielding no profits, caused a great deal of his worry and legal trouble. To make matters worse, it was mortgaged and Fullerton continued unable or reluctant to bear his share of the responsibility. Finally, in September 1879, Dun settled the issue, gaining complete control by purchasing the title to the property. He now had, he estimated, $100,000 invested at Caribou.[16]

In the four years since he had begun purchasing Caribou mining property, R. G. Dun had learned a great deal about the intricacies of absentee ownership. Probably the most aggravating issue he faced, outside of his controversy with Fullerton, was the reliance he had to place in someone else at the scene to forward information to him. He complained that even his brother Jim sent unclear and often confusing reports. Nor did conflicting stories from other sources help clear the clouded picture. Excerpts from a letter written to Harmon Minckler, November 19, 1879, illustrate clearly Dun's predicament, involving not only lack of information but misinterpretation of instructions as well.

> I am afraid you are going into much greater expense with the Spencer Mine [Dun had a bond on the property] than I contemplated. I only wanted a very small shaft house put up and I did not expect to buy an engine. . . . You are not keeping up your promise to write frequently. I would like to hear from you almost daily and learn just what you are doing in the mine and out of it. . . . I don't want to trouble you to write long letters, but just have you jot down items that you think will interest me.

Dun's business practices also left something to be desired; it appears that he did not know for several years the complete structure of ownership. Perhaps his friendship with Fullerton explains this lapse, but it does not condone it. Gradually Dun found himself dragged further into mining than he originally intended in order to protect his increasing investment. The end, however, was not in view, despite Dun's fervent wish to put the property in first-rate condition to sell it.

The issues faced by Dun and his partners recurred in the transactions of other Eastern investors who purchased property at Caribou. The Native Silver Mine, located on Caribou Hill, first came into prominence in 1874 when owned by New Yorkers. The owners, referred to only as Aden Alexander and Hale by local papers, worked their mine into promising shape and sold it to the New Jersey Mining Company.

This company, comprised of Eastern capitalists headed by ex-governor Andrew Gregg Curtin of Pennsylvania, had extensive plans for its property. Despite the name, it had been organized under laws of the State of New York and had capital of $1,000,000.[17] Curtin was the most prominent member. Known as the "soldier's friend" during the war, he had been governor from 1861 to 1867 and minister to Russia from 1869 to 1872. Following the now well-established pattern, the directors decided they needed a mill, not several miles away, but near the mine at Caribou. For the rest of 1875 and the next year as well, mining continued; but time was marked until construction on the mill was completed.

The cry had long been sounded for reduction works at Caribou. Neither the Nederland Mill nor Bates's ill-fated undertaking on North Boulder Creek filled the need. The arguments in favor of construction were based on the necessity to treat the lower-grade ore profitably, for the cost of freighting and the limited selling price prevented mass shipment any distance. With a larger profit margin offered by a mill on the site, more mines could be opened, thus stimulating the entire district. It was as simple as that, but in the eyes of the Caribouites it was a godsend.

An earlier attempt in 1871, based upon smelting, proved abortive. Henry Kearsing constructed a small reverberatory furnace near the town. Unfortunately, very few of the local ores could be reduced by smelting and none in reverberatories, without enormous loss of silver. From the start this small operation was a failure and it lasted hardly a year.[18] Kearsing, like many others in neighboring Clear Creek County, built a mill without accurately sampling the ores and found to his dismay that his process proved unsuitable. The contrast with Breed's operation was all too clear.

The site chosen for the new mill was about a quarter of a mile south of the main part of town. Work started in June 1876 with "a large force of graders [keeping] a cloud of dirt in the air." It proved to be a most rewarding summer for the local people, as they watched their long-cherished dream come true. In late December milling operations began at a final construction cost of $65,000, for a mill with a daily capacity of ten tons. The process was similar to Breed's—crushing and roasting—with important differences in the final stages. After roasting, the ore was dissolved, then passed through a series of wooden vats that finally left the silver precipitated on copper plates. Called the chloride leading process (similar to a Clear Creek County process), it was hoped that it would be both an efficient and economical way to treat local ores. To supply the mill with water, a ditch was dug around Caribou Hill from Caribou Park, slightly over a mile away.[19]

David Brunton, the mining engineer who had been brought in to construct and oversee the operation, lasted only one winter before he had had his fill of Caribou. One winter was enough, he wrote, the mill being covered with snow for four months with nothing visible but the ventilator and the smoke stack. To get from the general offices to the mill, he had to tunnel through the snow. He willingly accepted another offer elsewhere in the spring.

The New Jersey Mill, meanwhile, was launched with a flourish, prompting the *Central City Register*, May 5, 1877, to call it one of the best and most successful silver reducing mills in the country. It would be nice to say that it continued along such a propitious course, but it would not be true. Within a fortnight, scarcity of ore forced it to shut down. Operations for the rest of the year were sporadic and the high optimism began to wane. After overhauling and improvements, it resumed work in the summer of 1878, only to face a continual ore shortage, despite the fact that it was processing ore from several mines, including the No Name and Native Silver. By the end of the year the Nederland Mill purchased the tailings of its rival, which had closed and showed little prospects of reopening.[20] Occasionally, some person or company attempted to revive it during the remainder of the century but nothing of a permanent nature evolved.

Gone aglimmering was the dream of a local mill and the multitude of benefits to be derived therefrom. The reasons advanced were almost as numerous as those who stopped to analyze it. Unfortunately for the New Jersey Company, it chose the worst time in the 1870s to open a mill. None of the bigger mines, except the Caribou, was operating steadily, and their own Native Silver proved unable to furnish enough ore. Lack of mining experience among the Eastern owners created difficulties, as shown by their overexpectations and their determination to build a mill without sound investigation. This burning desire for a mill was endemic to the West. Several managerial changes at the mill hinted at trouble, but whether they were due to inept personnel or just an attempt to find someone who could operate it successfully cannot be determined. This and other examples caused the *Engineering and Mining Journal*, July 13, 1878, to editorialize about the insane and foolish idea most Eastern mine purchasers had that they must erect an expensive mill. It had, the *Journal* concluded, proven to be one of the most fatal blunders committed by owners and operators.

Local newspapers hinted at dishonest activities but offered no proof, a dodge too often used by Westerners, to explain a multitude of sins. Unfortunately for the New Jersey people, instead of being the savior, the mill depleted company resources. First came the initial outlay, then replacements, plus operational expenses, all of which went for naught when the mill failed and badly needed capital vanished. A more thorough examination of the ore, the mineral reserves, and the process itself should have been carried out before the initial outlay; it was too late now except to hurl accusations concerning who was at fault. Nor should the venture have been undertaken until careful consideration had been given to Caribou's isolated condition and what this meant in added cost for materials needed for construction and operation.

The company should not have to take the entire blame for the miscalculation, however, because the idea that produced it seems to have been prevalent among others at the time. Times were changing, although this is easier to see with hindsight than foresight. Outside of the Caribou operation, none of the mines, nor even a combination of several, proved rich enough to support a mill. As the shafts sank deeper, the marginal operators found themselves with their backs to the wall, faced by increasing expenses and declining profits. Many quit mining altogether or turned to limited mining by the mid-1870s. The answer of incorporation and joint operation would be tried later. In the 1870s individualism still predominated. Perhaps if the mill had opened in 1871 instead of 1877, it might have been a profitable enterprise. Nevertheless, a fond illusion was shattered by the experience of the Native Silver Company and no more mills would be built. The district's ore from now on would be sent to Nederland or elsewhere to be smelted.

The downfall of the mill seriously hurt the company. To make matters worse, their mining operations ran into a series of difficulties in 1877. As the main shaft went lower, water became a problem, and then in the spring the boiler blew up and the mine was closed temporarily. Work did not resume until the next year, when the mine was leased to Joseph Irwin, a well-known and experienced miner. Irwin continued to mine the property into the 1880s and became the resident agent for the company.[21] Once again an Eastern firm resorted to leasing to prevent its property from standing idle and to provide at least some income.

Eastern money did not always come to grief, nor did the investors always find themselves dragged further into a mining morass. Although operated on a much smaller scale than the previously discussed mines, the Seven Thirty proved a lucrative investment. Located west of the Caribou, it had been a promising lode but did not realize these prospects in its early days. William Martin, of original discovery fame, leased the mine in 1874 and some progress was made, although water was a problem. Not until 1878, when Gilbert Lehmer of Cincinnati took a lease on the mine, did its fortunes take a turn for the better. Lehmer, by careful management and developmental mining methods, brought the Seven Thirty's production to rank among the best on the hill.[22] With ore reserves uncovered and experience in mining, Lehmer took the next step and purchased the mine in late 1879 or early 1880. Unlike other Eastern owners, he chose from the very first to live in Caribou and supervise operations, and he chose to lease and carefully mine before purchasing. Lehmer, from his base at Caribou, broadened his operation to include Aspen mines in the 1880s.

One of the larger mines that did not come under Eastern control was the Poorman. Second only to the Caribou in point of discovery, it was rated the equal of the "Queen" by some, including Samuel Conger, who, as already noted, traded his interest in the Caribou to gain control of the Poorman. The mine, located parallel to and immediately north of the Caribou, proved to be a coquette during the 1870s, always promising but rarely fulfilling. Although a rich pocket of ore was discovered early, Conger leased the property in 1870 and sold out three years later. The claim was divided in half and Neil D. McKenzie, who played a prominent role in the history of the mine and mining at Caribou, became the owner of the west half.[23] During the rest of the 1870s the mine was worked almost continually, McKenzie operating his half personally with lessees generally mining the other. By 1879 it had once again become united under one management, with McKenzie a principal owner. Though the mine failed to equal its early promise, McKenzie managed to expand the workings and maintain at least some outflow of ore.

There were other mines at Caribou, some little better than glorified prospect holes, others of some worth to the owners. On nearby Idaho Hill the Idaho Mine was the best of a small group. The mines there never produced the quantity of ore of those on Caribou Hill. The only mine within the city limits, the Potosi, produced well early in the decade, then reports of it disappeared from the papers. Other mines worthy of noting in passing were the Belcher, the Grand View, and the Spencer, all on Caribou Hill. In 1876 Van Diest, in his *Grand Island Mining District*, listed another sixty besides those already discussed. Many hopes no doubt were dashed when these prospective bonanzas failed to pan out.

Mining conditions at Caribou fluctuated from prosperity to semi-stagnation during the 1870s. Reports show that the years 1871 through 1875 were good ones for the Caribou mines—the apex of mining in the district for the decade. In the spring of 1872 a change in approach toward mining—with a shift from a passion for new discoveries to production of ore—served to stabilize the situation. The appearance of shaft houses and other buildings alleviated the hardships of winter. Water was, as always, the most vexing single problem, even with the introduction of pumps and the construction of tunnels, of which the Caribou tunnel was only one. In 1876 the camp and mining production slumped noticeably, with comments such as

The New Jersey Mill had become a relic of wasted investment by the late 1890s. Courtesy, Duane A. Smith

"having a dull season" and "the appearance of a dead town" being used to describe conditions.[24] Within two years the district rebounded, although not to previous heights.

The recession of 1876 resulted from several factors: the collapse of the Nederland Company and subsequent litigation over the remains, which crippled the major producer; dismay and continued expense to Eastern owners, who curtailed their activities and cut off the needed flow of capital to other mines; and the continued drain of money into mills that failed to resolve the dilemma of ore reduction and placed a heavy burden on the investors.

The compulsion for a mill died hard during the decade, resulting in several expensive "funerals." Breed succeeded, while Kearsing, Bates, and the New Jersey Company failed, showing the advantages of having a major producing mine, financial reserves, good judgment of conditions, and employment of competent men. Each of these proved important to the success or failure of a milling operation. The mere selection of a site on important traffic arteries, near water power and wood, and within economical hauling distance of the mine, got Breed off to a fine start. He selected the then-popular roasting and amalgamation process, which proved correct for the ore

At its peak, the Caribou, or Nederland, Mill was one of the finest in Colorado. Courtesy, Denver Public Library, Western History Collection

available, while the rest disastrously experimented. In the end his advantage proved too much for the others in a camp that never really proved that it could support more than one mill, even in its peak days.

The first phase of mining, small operation on a shoestring budget, ended in the late seventies. It now took a greater quantity and/or a better grade of ore to continue profitably. The transition from individual to corporate operation, though painful, was a necessary expedient if the district hoped to survive.

Two definite and important trends emerged: consolidation and Eastern ownership. The former was noted in the years from 1875 and the latter from 1870. The consolidation of two or more mines or lodes by one company or owner benefited the district with better and more efficient operation, but it also caused serious injury when a company stopped work, closing a large segment of the hill. Eastern ownership and capital both helped and hurt the district. The capital brought into Caribou was advantageous to the mines and town. Consider, for example, the No Name, which was principally developed with outside assistance, as opposed to the locally owned Poorman. While men like Curtin and Dun helped, they also hindered. Their absentee ownership and inexperience in mining and milling methods led to costly mistakes and failures; nor did the desire for a quick profit encourage constructive development. While they gained the needed experience, the whole camp suffered. The best-operated mines on the hill were those leased and run by local men or owned by individuals who lived in the area and took an active interest in their property. Unfortunately, their mines also proved to be smaller and could not carry the district alone. If a mine were to continue to be a steady producer, it had to be operated under a program that was neither speculative nor ravishingly exploitative. This lesson was hard to learn.

"It Takes a Mine to Work a Mine"

During the spring and early summer of 1876 the local people anxiously awaited the outcome of the contest over the remains of the Caribou Mine. To no lower depths would Caribou fortunes dip in the decade than during this time of uncertainty. Finally, the day came for the sheriff's sale; the property was bid for and purchased for about $70,000 by Jerome Chaffee, who headed a syndicate of several men. One who witnessed the sale and signed himself "a miner" wrote that the failure of the company stood out boldly as a "monument of folly" to the employment of inefficient and incapable men to run and manage such works. To his mind this "kid-gloved gentry" did more loafing around hotels, driving fast horses, drinking fine whiskey, while drawing large salaries, than trying to promote the owners' interests.[1] Thus did an

American take a parting shot at the now-defunct Mining Company Nederland.

Chaffee's connection with the lawsuits that led to the sale resulted in questions about his real intentions from the very start. Insinuations of deliberate "mine butchery," of attempts to demoralize the Dutch stockholders, and even that he had been involved originally in the three million dollar sale were made. To his defense came the *Central City Register* and *Denver Mirror*. The former stated that he had other mining properties worth more than the Caribou Mine, and his only idea was to protect himself and the First National Bank of Denver from heavy loss. The latter accused the Democrats of perverting the truth to injure a political opponent. It flatly denied that Chaffee had anything to do with the property until claims had been brought against the company.[2] Despite such denials Chaffee was never able to clear himself completely from the taint of these charges.

For the first time since 1870 the Caribou Mine was again locally owned. Chaffee was well-known throughout Colorado as a mining man and a politician, having served as territorial delegate to Congress in 1871–1875; he would later be a senator from 1877–1879. The Democratic *Rocky Mountain News* referred to him as "the Caribou man in the senate." He was joined in this mining venture by David Moffat, a partner in the First National Bank of Denver, who would gain fame and suffer bankruptcy while driving the Moffat Tunnel through the mountains west of Denver. Both had been interested in Caribou for some years; the *Caribou Post*, July 22 and August 5, 1871, reported that they had visited the camp. Moffat had some connection with the visit of the Englishman Goldring, for the two of them came to Caribou together. The New York *Engineering and Mining Journal*, November 21, 1871, stated that Moffat was offering the Caribou Mine for sale. This came to naught, however. These two men had experience in Colorado mining, and, equally as important, had financial connections that promised a more thorough development of the mine than had been possible earlier.

The Caribou had never been completely inactive; a small force of independent miners worked it until Chaffee formally took possession. Immediately, an ambitious program of development was launched, starting with the appointment of the well-known mining man Eben Smith as superintendent. Smith, whose full first name was Ebenezer, had been engaged in milling and mining in California before coming to Colorado in 1860. Chaffee and he became partners in Gilpin County mining and milling and both helped organize the

Colorado senator and mine promoter Jerome Chaffee knew when to get rid of a mine at the right time. Courtesy, Colorado Historical Society

First National Bank of Denver in 1865. Considerable dead work had to be done to put the mine in profitable working condition again, and particular attention had to be focused on the water problem. Smith wrote a revealing letter to Moffat concerning developments at the mine and plans for the future:

> I am putting some wood as it must be done now or not at all and we would be compelled to stop in midwinter we have used during the first month about 40 cords of wood and aside from this all or nearly all of the supplies are ordered. All of our mine work will hereafter be done by contract of course we will have to employ engineers bucket dumpers one timberman and black smith by day. We have the East shaft now nearly ready to con- tract and when that is done we only have to clean out one winze thus we hope all of our roustabout work will cease.

He concluded that the rock at the bottom of the main shaft looked promising, but "the vein is not yet settled" and the rock as a whole is low grade.[3]

Eighteen seventy-seven was a year of innovation: steam drills were installed; hired miners for the main operation were combined with les- sees for the smaller areas; and finally a brief joint working agreement was negotiated with the Native Silver to lessen expenses. Although the consolidation failed to last, it indicated what the future might hold. Overall this was a profitable year for the owners, and for the first time in months heavily laden wagons left the mine daily to wend their way down to the mill at Nederland.

The mill had also been purchased by Chaffee and was put back into operation in 1877, after being closed for about twenty months. The Mining Company Nederland had run it successfully during its tenure, but the failure of that company closed it. The major complaint against this enterprise had been the dumping of impurities into Boulder Creek, which, according to reports, changed its color from "crystal to a dark and muddy looking stream." The citizens of Boulder did not appreci- ate this spoilage. Apparently in the summer of 1873 some correction was made, for the complaints ceased. Smith now supervised the mill as well as the mine and reduced expenses by operating with a smaller force that produced good results.

While work was being pushed forward at the mine, Chaffee was busy clearing the final encumbrances from the property. The surplus of money from the sale of ore during the working of the property in the winter of 1875–1876 had been deposited in the First National

David Moffat, partner of Chaffee, played a shrewd game at Caribou. Courtesy, Colorado Historical Society

Bank of Denver by the Boulder District Court. Anyone who had claim against the company was required to apply to the court for reimbursement. To clear this sum and all claims against the property, Chaffee filed suit against the company, the bank, and the creditors in Boulder in February 1877, only to have the case transferred to Arapahoe District Court.[4] At the same time, Chaffee found himself sued by William Fullerton for damages when Caribou miners accidentally broke into the No Name. Fullerton suspected that the Caribou was working the No Name vein, but he was groping in the dark, because he did not know the situation in the former. He hoped that both companies would allow experts to examine the mines in order to reach a verdict acceptable to each.[5] Legal proceedings were suspended, however, in hopes of reaching a peaceful settlement; and the conflict between these two mines was delayed for a short time. Free finally to operate as he pleased, Chaffee held out the best chance Caribou had had in several years.

The prosperous condition of the mine in 1878 reflected the mining practices of Smith and Chaffee, especially the former, who earned praise from the local newspapers. Chaffee's mining rival, R. G. Dun, had other ideas. As early as March, he wrote his brother that he had no doubt the Caribou was taking ore from the No Name, and he wanted him to learn all he could about its operation.[6] Dun, though, was involved in clearing up the problem with Fullerton and other matters in New York and did not for the moment follow up his accusations. Dun previously had dealings with both Moffat and Chaffee, relating to the No Name and claims against it, through their connection with the First National Bank.

By the next year the mine had become a steady producer. The *Boulder News and Courier*, April 4, described it, with a certain amount of local pride, "undoubtedly the best developed, finest equipped and richest mine in the state." Nor was this a complete overstatement; Smith and Chaffee had done a fine job opening and improving it. The main shaft was now over 740 feet in depth, with a two-compartment or double-way bucket operating in it. The mine had a total of seven shafts and thirteen levels, all connected by winzes with well-timbered walls. A Knowles double-action pump was located within the mine to drain it with the aid of the Caribou Tunnel. The surface structures were equally impressive. The hoisting house enclosed the main shaft and one other and contained a blacksmith and tool shop, air compressor, sorting floor, tramway cars, the office, and other equipment. Over two of the other shafts there were also buildings and machinery.[7]

Having put their mine in top condition, Chaffee and Moffat, like Breed before them, decided that the future held more for them from selling than from continued mining. The price, however, had come down from the $3,000,000 paid by the Dutch; the mine now sold for $900,000 and the mill for $100,000.[8] A good profit, nevertheless, considering the original investment by Chaffee and Moffat. Unlike Breed, however, they did not strip the mine and leave nothing but a shell. The new owner, the Caribou Consolidated Mining Company, was a New York–based firm and some of its organizers had operated the Native Silver Mine with indifferent success. The president of the Caribou Consolidated, Andrew Curtin, owned considerable stock in the Native Silver Company and John T. Graham was treasurer of both. Curtin, however, would soon be replaced as president by Brayton Ives, New York stock broker and banker, who had just finished a term as president of the New York Stock Exchange. The headquarters of the new company were located at 33 Broad Street on the same block as Ives's own business house. With a capitalization of $1,000,000, the company planned to carry forward the development started by the previous owners. Eben Smith was retained as superintendent and work went on as usual.

The company declared three dividends during the summer, but it had hardly begun operations when a damaging setback was suffered on September 14. On that date a fire swept over Caribou Hill, burning the shaft house and destroying valuable machinery. Insurance amounting to $10,000 did not start to cover the loss. Smith immediately began rebuilding the destroyed shaft house, replacing the machinery, and constructing a temporary boiler to keep the main pump going to prevent the flooding of the mine.[9] By November the work had been completed but the Caribou Consolidated had suffered a severe blow; its stock dropped from $6.50 before the fire to a low of $4.25 a share. The future prospects had been dimmed considerably.

The other mines were somewhat more fortunate than the Caribou when the fire raged over the hill. The Native Silver and Seven Thirty marshaled their miners and checked the holocaust on the west side of the hill, but it circled around them and caught the Caribou Mine. The *Boulder News and Courier*, September 19, credited Harmon Minckler and his crew from the No Name with saving that property and the Poorman and Sherman shaft houses. Minckler had the "foresight and judgment," according to the account, to fill his tanks with water and thoroughly wet down the buildings before the fire hit, but even he apparently had a very hot and dangerous fight before the

Eben Smith, capable mining man, revitalized the Caribou, but Dun had some un-answered questions about him. Courtesy, Colorado Historical Society

flames surged elsewhere. Many of the smaller shaft houses in its path were consumed. For another reason the struggle was important; had the fire jumped the ridge here it would have swept into the main business district of the town, probably wiping out the whole community.

Trouble now appeared for the Caribou Consolidated from another direction: Dun took the company to court to recover damages for ore taken from the No Name property. This proved to be just the first of a series of lawsuits that engulfed not only the Caribou but the majority of the major mines on the hill. The mining claims at Caribou, like those in many other Western mining districts, had been hastily drawn and filed in the county courthouse. Vague or vanished claim markers meant conflict if an owner thought his property or vein was being worked by another party. Such was the case here, and the Caribou Consolidated Mining Company found itself right in the middle of costly litigation.

Dun sought a temporary injunction against the Caribou Consolidated to restrain it from working part of what he claimed to be the No Name lode. He also ordered his brother Jim to sink a shaft on the mine to reach Caribou workings. His purpose was to prove his claim. In September the shaft broke into the Caribou workings, and Dun found himself faced with a countersuit by the company, which charged that it had been ousted from its property. It also asked for damages.[10]

Colorado newspapers took up the dispute, which was being waged from Caribou to New York City. James Dun, angered by charges of blackmail and other accusations, took it upon himself to present the Dun side of the story in January. He refuted categorically the charge of blackmail and restated his brother's contention about ore stealing. He hinted at misdeeds by Chaffee when he wrote, "Messrs. Chaffee and Company have not been so pure in their transactions that they can afford to throw charges of this kind." The *Rocky Mountain News*, reflecting an anti-Dun attitude, waxed indignant over the omnibus charges of the *Denver Republican*, which accused Chaffee of "running the camp, bulldozing legitimate mining, lowering wages, stealing ore and operating for stock-jobbing purposes solely." Not so, said the News, for Chaffee had built up the camp and put the mine "at the head of paying lodes in Colorado." The old charges against Chaffee were renewed, but the News countered by accusing the No Name Company of running into debt, jumping the country, and for all intents and purposes being dead. It summed up its case by claiming that the Caribou Company had the "firm support of the respectable element of the town," and that "legitimate mining" could not afford "four, five or six dollars per day for fighting men as the No Name company are compelled to do."[11]

The Caribou owners faced not only Dun's claims but even more spectacular ones, which involved Gilbert Lehmer and his Seven Thirty Mine. Miners from the latter, in February 1880, broke into the Caribou No. 6 shaft from their own underground diggings. Believing that Seven Thirty ore was being stolen, they built a fire of "noxious and offensive substances," whose fumes permeated the Caribou workings, stopping work. To further intimidate the miners, Lehmer proclaimed that he had placed a supply of giant powder in his shaft to "blow them to hell," unless they got out. Finally, Lehmer settled the issue with action by leading a group of his men in demolishing the No. 6 shaft house, which he claimed was built on Seven Thirty property. No one as yet had been "blown to hell," but the Caribou Company met the challenge by promptly securing an injunction to keep Lehmer from working his mine. Action shifted to the Boulder District Court where the injunction was dissolved. This did not end the issue. Lehmer and his men were arrested for creating a riot, and a "crowd" of witnesses and prisoners was transported to Boulder for the hearing, at a high expense to the taxpayer, complained a Boulder paper. The fight between the two dragged on through the courts for some time, finally reaching the state supreme court before it was "dismissed for want of prosecution."[12]

Both sides took up their pens in defense of their positions, Eben Smith writing to the *Engineering and Mining Journal*, while Gilbert Lehmer answered in the *Mining Record* (New York). Lehmer, in the April 17, 1880, issue, was particularly vehement in stating his views. After calling the charges against him "trumped up," he particularly challenged Smith's account and stated that, as far as he knew, no mob violence had interrupted mining. The issue soon died, as events moved swiftly to resolve the impasse on Caribou Hill.

Ubiquitous Harmon Minckler, now resident manager of Dun's Sherman, Spencer, and No Name mines, gave an exclusive interview concerning these events at Caribou to the *Boulder News and Courier* on May 21, 1880. Heartily sick of the so-called war between the rival factions, he felt the time had come to stop the "miserable contention and cursedly expensive litigation" and allow legitimate work to proceed. Of more significance, he spoke openly of a proposed consolidation of the two mine groups—Dun and Caribou Consolidated—which he claimed now needed only to be ratifed by the stockholders to make it official. This would end the "war" and in his estimation was all "that stands in the way of magnificent reports from Caribou."

Minckler's statements confirmed a rumor that had been circulating for some time in Caribou and Boulder. What easier method existed to end the dispute if a fair agreement could be reached? Dun had contemplated such a plan for several years. In 1878 he had toyed with the idea of suing the Caribou owners for $100,000 or possibly $150,000, to bring them "to their knees" the probable result being consolidation.[13] The suit against the Caribou was not pressed at this time, but the intriguing merger idea loomed larger in the ensuing years.

The company, by the winter of 1879–1880, could not hope to remain solvent long under the type of situation unfolding before it. Eben Smith said as much in a telegram to the New York owners, warning them of unusual expenses and disrupted shipments of ore. The price and transactions of Caribou Consolidated stock on the market mirrored the situation. The high for the week of January 26 had been $6 in a moderately active market. By late February the price had sagged to $3⅞ and by March 31 to $3 with only scattered sales.[14]

Confronted with the lawsuits on one side and the losses from the fire on the other, the Caribou officers approached Dun and his attorney, Chester A. Arthur—the future president of the United States—with the possibility of consolidating the two mining properties. As early as the fall of 1879, feelers had gone out, and Dun had talked with Graham and later Brayton Ives. Dun, apparently believing he controlled the situation, would not consider any value placed on the Caribou higher than one-tenth or, at the outside, one-fifth of "the whole." Dun felt the company put on a bold front but "are very sick at heart and want to settle on the best terms they can," and were in a "hell hole with their stock." The negotiations took a new twist, however, after the start of the year. The court temporarily denied Dun's injunction against working the Caribou, requiring only that an account be kept of all ore mined. At the same time, $25,000 in bullion was shipped to New York by the Caribou Consolidated. Dun was certain that this ore came from the No Name and wondered why Jim was not getting similar production out of his property.[15]

In New York Dun found himself severely handicapped in trying to understand the complicated matters in Colorado. The lawsuits particularly confused him, but the stockholders of the Caribou Consolidated were in no better condition. Although groping in the semidarkness of absentee ownership, both moved toward the common goal of consolidation.

Behind the scenes the two groups were working; Dun met with what he termed the Caribou people—Chaffee, Moffat, Ives, and Graham—which indicated that the former two must have retained some control or stock in the company. The first indication of a modified position appeared when Dun wrote Jim that he was now willing to allow the Caribou a quarter of the whole. On January 29, 1880, Dun, writing to his brother, discussed a meeting of the previous night at which time he had promised to use his influence on Jim not to place items of an antagonistic nature in the papers and to restrain from commencing any other suits at the present. Dun, at this same meeting, proposed a three-man committee to arrive at the relative value of all properties involved in the suggested merger—Caribou and mill, Native Silver, No Name, Sherman, and Spencer. The Caribou people countered, suggesting that a third of the consolidation go to Dun, but this he would not entertain. Negotiations dragged on in this vein for several months.[16]

The Steady Fall of Caribou Stock, 1879–1880

Date	Price per Share
Aug. 9, 1879	$6–6$\frac{1}{2}$
Sept. 6	5$\frac{1}{8}$–5$\frac{7}{8}$
(fire on Caribou Hill)	
Sept. 20	4$\frac{3}{4}$–5$\frac{7}{8}$
Oct. 4	4$\frac{7}{8}$–5
Nov. 22	4$\frac{1}{2}$–5$\frac{3}{4}$
Dec. 27	4$\frac{7}{8}$–5$\frac{1}{4}$
Jan. 24, 1880	5–5$\frac{1}{4}$
Feb. 14	4$\frac{1}{2}$
March 20	3$\frac{1}{4}$–3$\frac{1}{2}$
April 17	2$\frac{3}{8}$–3
May 15	2$\frac{1}{4}$
(consolidation)	
June 19	2$\frac{5}{8}$
July 3	2$\frac{1}{2}$–2$\frac{5}{8}$
Aug. 7	2$\frac{1}{4}$

The amount of stock sold steadily declined with the price. Quotations from the *Engineering and Mining Journal*.

Wracked by outside troubles, the Caribou Consolidated now was running into internal ones as well. The crux of the matter can be gathered from a meeting Dun had with Moffat in February. Dun commented that Moffat had the reputation of being very sharp, but he felt he would be a good man to have on his side for the reasons illustrated in the following quotation:

> The programme now is that he [Moffat] will set to work to smash up the Caribou stock and buy the control of it and then he will negotiate terms as an individual with me, and I am now of the opinion this will be my best show to get my money out of the mines. He thinks we might capitalize the whole at $20,000,000 in low priced shares (not over $5) and thus get out. . . . Moffat can now control some 40,0000 shares of the stock of Caribou with which he thinks he can break down the stock into a dollar or less per share. And if he does not succeed in this he says he can easily have a debt credit against the Caribou and have the property attached, or else order Eben Smith to shut down the mine.[17]

Dun noted that this was Moffat's own game and he would have nothing to do with this matter; regardless of his attitude, he stood to gain by the outcome. Moffat never succeeded in driving the price of Caribou stock as low as $1, but by mid-April it had sunk to $2½. Several factors probably brought about this condition, including Dun's finally securing the temporary injunction to restrain the Caribou people from working his lode, and new court cases involving the two factions.[18]

In New York, meanwhile, Dun was becoming less sure of his position. He suspected Minckler might in some way be tied up in a plot with the Caribou people to gain control of the entire hill. Dun had mixed feelings about this man. He employed him to operate his mines, particularly the Sherman, and on occasion gave him small gifts of money; yet he never completely trusted Minckler, for several times in 1879 he warned Jim about him and later called him a scoundrel. Still no agreement was reached, as Dun turned down an offer of a third in the consolidation. Toward the end of April, Dun had a long talk with Eben Smith—who had come east—and Graham, in which a plan to end the expensive fight was finally agreed to by both sides. Dun was to put only the Spencer and No Name into the merged company, retaining sole ownership of the Sherman. As remuneration, he would receive 75,000 shares—majority control of the company's stock. Ten thousand shares of the 150,000 would be held as treasury stock.

At opening, the shares were listed at $10 par. Dun was also to be elected president and given the balance of control. All lawsuits were to be discontinued, and Eben Smith was to be appointed general superintendent.[19]

The incorporation was contingent upon the vote of the stockholders in the old Caribou Consolidated Company. They ratified the agreement, but Dun would not consent to it until certain difficulties had been resolved. Foremost were the discrepancies in surveying that had caused much of the trouble in the first place. This matter was being taken care of by a surveying team that one of the groups had hired in early April to settle the claims and erect substantial corner monuments. Dun felt the Lehmer suit should also be settled. Long before the last echo of the Lehmer case was dismissed, however, Dun closed the consolidation. Finally, on June 25, the questions had been resolved to his apparent satisfaction, and he completed the merger substantially as it had been drawn in April.[20] Dun was now president of the expanded Caribou Consolidated, which encompassed the Caribou, No Name, Spencer, and Columbia mines.

After years of struggle both in and out of court, Dun had triumphed, but it might have been only a Pyrrhic victory. His original demand of nine-tenths, or at most four-fifths, of the merger had not been achieved. The Sherman, to be sure, was not included; this does not seem to have been a factor in accepting the lower amount, for the Sherman was being offered for sale at $50,000. Convinced, as shown in his letters, that Caribou prosperity rested upon No Name ore, Dun might have been swayed by the consideration that this solution was the best one possible at the time. He received the presidency and actual control of the company's operations, which could have been enough to sway him. Perhaps weariness and expense of the continued litigation prompted Dun to agree to terms, or he might possibly have felt that he could turn a profit by consolidation and end up in the black after all his troubles. Whatever the reason or combination of reasons that produced the merger, the prospects for continued profitable operation of all the mines looked better in June 1880 than they had since Chaffee's ownership.

The roles of Moffat and Chaffee in this transaction remain shadowed in mystery. Certainly these two were left with stock in the Caribou from the sale. As Moffat told Dun, he controlled 40,000 shares of stock with which he planned to break the price of the stock. Why he was willing to gamble this investment to help Dun and bring about consolidation is not so evident. Possibly the two had a plan in which

North Boulder, or Bates, Mill had a short and expensive career. Courtesy, Duane A. Smith

the transfer of control remained only a means to an end: unloading their stock, backed now by the Dun name, on the public. Both Moffat and Chaffee were experienced mining men, and they might have suspected that the hill was about "dug out"; if this were true, they could easily reason that their only chance to obtain a profit from their stocks resided in selling on the past reputation of the Caribou, plus the addition of the well-known R. G. Dun name. Dun's international reputation for integrity and his sound, successful agency certainly enhanced public confidence in the reorganized company. The price of Caribou Consolidated stock had fluctuated since the fire of the previous September, with a continuing downward tendency and an increasingly quiet market. It was their hope that Dun's name and reputation would act as a stimulus.

Another possible alternative is that Mottat and Chaffee aided Dun to protect their investment and develop the hill as a consolidated operation. Dun had money to invest and Dun's name, here too, would make it easier to secure needed American and European capital to meet the mounting costs of mining. Had they displayed the faith in the venture that Dun soon exhibited, this would seem to have been the correct assumption. As the situation eventually evolved, however, it appears that the first assumption is nearer the truth. At this late date personal motives cannot be ascertained with any degree of certainty, but there seems little doubt that both men were shrewd operators who planned carefully to come out with a profit. This is not to imply that shady or crooked dealings were involved; rather a well-planned manipulation of ownership and stock unfolded, with Dun left holding the bag.

A point of consideration in the Chaffee-Moffat story was the fact that at the same time they were promoting the Caribou sale they were even more heavily involved at Leadville in the same type of transaction. There they were promoting and selling the famous Little Pittsburg in 1879; then, in some quarters, they were heatedly blamed for its failure and collapse of stock price in the spring of 1880. At both Caribou and Leadville direct evidence is lacking to convict them of crooked—or at least shady—manipulations, but accusations flew thick and fast and the two operations together form a pattern.

Dun, in the meantime, seemed well pleased with the merger. Upon its completion, he left for one of his salmon-fishing trips to Canada. Although this particular vacation was cut short by business matters, Dun's correspondence for the remainder of the summer dealt only briefly with Caribou matters. Dun probably had never heard of an old mining adage, "It takes a mine to work a mine." His experiences so far had proven that one mine could not pay expenses; now he had several on which to try his skill.

The Sherman, still on the market, caused some annoyance, but Dun felt sure that either Minckler or Eben Smith would find a buyer. To show his faith in the Caribou Consolidated, in early September he told his broker to buy 5,000 shares of stock if the price slipped under $2, which it soon did. The low price bothered him and he instructed the firm's secretary, still John Graham, to send a circular to the stockholders telling them what was happening in Colorado and explaining why no dividends were being declared. Later in the month Dun and Graham traveled to Colorado to inspect their mining property, and during this period Dun made financial advances to the company, taking additional treasury stock as collateral. As a further private show of confidence, he gave his wife, on their silver wedding anniversary, a small silver brick from the Caribou inscribed with the facsimile of a 1,000-share Caribou stock certificate.[21]

Dun's great optimism was not founded solely upon wishful thinking, for the mines produced well in 1880. At long last it seemed he would be able to make a profit from the venture he so hesitantly entered five years before. Writing about the company to a stockholder, W. Schley of New York, on November 18, Dun confidently predicted, "As for myself I will only remark that I have great confidence in the future of the property and would not advise any stockholder selling at present quotation in the market."

Mines and Miners

Without Eastern or foreign capital and advanced engineering knowledge, Caribou mining would have been conducted on a very limited scale. This axiom, illustrated previously, does not tell the whole story. The men who went down into the mines and the underground operation itself are the core of the story. More than Dun or the Dutch capitalists, the local people staked their future and their very lives on the fortunes of mining. To them the mines meant more than stocks or investments; they represented a way of life. These pioneers generally worked for others; a few struck out on their own to become, for a time, small capitalists; however, only the ones with adequate financial backing survived to emerge independently wealthy. Mining made millionaires, but generally those with their own resources profited most from the opportunities offered. This requirement did not deter the multitudes, for no one knew when lady luck might smile benevolently and disclose a hidden bonanza.

At Caribou, mining evolved not only on a grand scale, as in the case of the Caribou Mine, but also on a "blast and prayer" basis—by one man or several, in a mine perhaps twenty to fifty feet deep. Whether means were limited or unlimited, the same problems faced both types of operation: everpresent water danger, snow and harsh winters, unknown depth and value of the ore-bearing vein, and the changing national and international price of silver. Each used similar mining methods. A shaft was sunk from the surface until it intersected ore, where work then developed along levels and drifts driven with the vein. Some mines produced from the very "grass roots," but most needed dead work before the ore body was exposed. In the larger mines the underground works were extensive, with numerous levels and winzes, or underground shafts. Each mine had to have cribbing and set-work to strengthen walls and ceilings to allow work to be carried on with some degree of safety. In the more elaborate operations mechanical means were employed to transport the ore to the surface, but the smaller operators utilized animal or human power and a bucket.

Descending into a mine in the 1870s, one's reaction might have resembled that of the man who described his experience in the Seven Thirty Mine. His tour was conducted by Gilbert Lehmer and his foreman, Samuel Richards:

> A current of cold, damp air came up from the mine below, and either that or something else produced a strange nervous twitching in the region of the back bone. I felt that this was a pathological symptom of an important character, but did not stop long to consider it. The ladder was wet and cold, and, as we descended deeper, the shaft grew darker and the ladder grew damper and colder, until each successive round felt more like my conceptions of a Greenland clan [clam?] than any thing else I can imagine. With three of us on one ladder at one time I could feel it trembling under me, and it was but an easy task of the imagination to transfer the movement from the ladder to the solid granite walls themselves. Back and forth they rocked until they seemed ready to fall and crush us all. Under such circumstances the first impulse was to jump and make an attempt to reach *terra firma*. Conscious that those walls are as firm as the eternal hills, it is yet with considerable effort that one restrain

himself under such circumstances. Down we went to the first
level, through a scuttle-hole, then down again and through
another scuttle-hole, and so on even unto the fourth, when slipping down a knotted rope we found ourself at the bottom—248
feet below the surface. I breathed freer. The solid rock was
under my feet, the walls had ceased to move, and I could look
around me with some composure. Curious places those underground caverns, with their dark, dripping walls of solid granite.
Down a gloomy hall twinkling lights could be seen, and men
were at work with picks and drills unearthing—rather unrock-
ing—the hidden wealth.

Following my faithful guide I was soon initiated into the
mysteries of shafts, winzes, foot-walls and hanging-walls, of sinking, drifting, stoping, &c. In passing along the various drifts on
our way up, I found that Mr. Lehmer, together with those who
worked the mine before him, had, at four different levels, run
4 drifts east and one west from the main shaft. The first at the
75-foot level is 100 feet long, the second at the 125-foot level is
212 feet long. On this same level a drift was driven 90 feet west
from the shaft, but the vein on this side is not so good, and so far
as developed will not pay at present. Both these levels had been
drifted and "back-stoped" before Mr. Lehmer took hold of the
mine. The third level is 185 feet below the surface, and the drift
is 122 feet long. The fourth, along which a part of the force are
now drifting, is placed at a depth of 235 feet. The crevice varies
in width from that of a few inches to more than a foot and a half,
and is well filled with sulphurets of silver, carbonates of copper,
silver glance, brittle silver and galena in small quantities.[1]

With evident relief this "miner" eventually returned to the surface,
for there was little that was pleasant or comfortable about the interior
of the mines.

Mining was an expensive proposition, with great rewards for a
few; moderate returns for some; but at best an even break, or worse,
a loss, for many. The cost of operation, unfortunately, cannot be accurately estimated. The only records known to exist are those of the
Caribou Mine for a short period early in the 1870s and 1876–1878 and
a scattering from the Idaho. The operating expenses of the former
during selected months of 1872 and 1873 ran from $622 to $2,993. A
fairly typical monthly statement—February 1873—showed expenses
of $1,410 and ore sales of $2,597, for a profit of a little over $1,100.

The most complete records still in existence of any mine cover
the period of Chaffee and Moffat's ownership of the Caribou, marred

only by the fact that no profit statements have survived. From November 1876 through October 1878, only three months are missing. For this span of time expenses at the mine and mill averaged almost $7,000. A steady increase is noted: for example, in November 1876 the company paid out $2,416, not much different from the expenses early in the decade; but by November 1877 they had risen to $7,089, and by the next October to $15,015. This of course reflected the increased scale of operation by the owners, not an inflationary rise in the cost of mining. To break these figures down further, June 1878 was selected at random. Expenses for the month totaled $7,845.74, of which the payrolls at the mine and mill, respectively, were $1,561.87 and $799.31. Eben Smith received $315.50. Other expenses were as follows: wood and lumber, $623.21; supplies (mine and mill), $875.43; freighting, $480; ore purchased from lessees, $465.35; contractors, $2,103.52. The Caribou Mine did the majority of its business with Central and Denver merchants.

Incidental expenses added a further burden to the management. In August 1877 Eben Smith paid the *Engineering and Mining Journal* of New York $125 for advertisements. Lawyers made money from mining disputes, of which the Caribou had its share. One man alone presented Chaffee a bill for $465 for work on his behalf from March to October 1877, and this was just the start of the legal entanglements. Considering these facts, it is understandable that Moffat and Chaffee willingly sold in 1879.[2]

Found in the operating budget were items that one might expect— rope, powder, fuses, picks, shovels, candles, freighting charges, and wages. Yet these did not encompass all the equipment needed nor the total costs. For example, the records revealed the following purchases and bills: horse blankets and brushes, hay, oats, doctoring and shoeing of horses to protect these essential beasts of burden; soap, whisky, cigars, and beer, apparently for the miners; coal, charcoal, lumber, sheeting, ore sacks, and a padlock for surface operations. In addition, the owners paid for maintenance of buildings, numerous construction projects, and even the grading of roads for ore and freight wagons.[3] One of the continuing expenses was milling the ore, which included not only the actual reduction charge but freighting as well. This proved to be one of the most expensive aspects of Caribou mining.

The *Engineering and Mining Journal*, August 11, 1877, in what remains probably the best single contemporary article on the Caribou mines, estimated that over six million dollars had been spent directly or indirectly in opening and operating the mines to the close of 1876.

This was broken down into different categories, some of which hold some interest here. Actual mining operations included 10,000 feet of shafting at $20 per foot; 18,000 feet of levels at an average of $10 per foot; 4,000 feet of tunneling at $15 per foot; and 15,000 fathoms of stoping (the act of breaking the ore above or below a level) averaging $25 per fathom for a total of $815,000. Another $375,000 was spent to construct surface buildings and mills and to purchase equipment. Ore reduction was estimated to have cost $920,000. Yet by far the largest share had gone to sellers, promoters, brokers, and the like—approximately three and a half million dollars. The Journal, which realized what had happened at Caribou, concluded with this comment: "It is a much larger sum than one would expect could be spent on the improvements visible, but as shown fully one-third was spent in speculative operations."

To cut down expenses and overhead, the owners tried several methods. In vogue in Colorado in the 1870s, the tribute system allowed miners to keep a certain percentage of ore mined, or its monetary value, instead of flat wages. This idea had originated in Cornwall, England, and was carried to America by the Cornish miners. Another procedure was to contract for the mining of a section of the vein by offering it to the lowest bidder. This system was especially popular in the smaller leasing operations, although the Caribou, for example, in 1879 employed seventy men on contract. Leasing a mine also avoided high costs, since the owner received a set rental and a percentage of the ore mined. Joseph Irwin reported in August 1877 that leasing was becoming quite the vogue, for "the miners can make the mines pay when companies cannot." Rather than using his own men, the employer occasionally asked for bids on sinking shafts, reserving the right to reject any and all bids. Usually the contractor had to furnish necessary materials, except lumber, and was required to build to meet certain specifications. During the early months of 1877, for instance, Eben Smith contracted for most of the work on the Caribou, paying a sliding scale, varying from $15 to $44 per foot. Work on the main shaft was most expensive, and that on drifting, minor shafts, and winzes correspondingly less.[4] This trend away from paying by the day was more noticeable at Caribou as the 1870s advanced. More flexible in approach, these methods allowed both the owner and the miner to be more independent in their dealings with each other and aided in spreading the risk and expense.

As the mines went deeper, the cost of mining rose correspondingly, a factor that precipitated consolidation and changing mining methods. No owner could hope to escape this inevitability, if he continued to develop his property. By the late 1870s this fact weighed heavily on all mining carried on at Caribou. Writing in 1875, T. F. Wagenen, editor and publisher of the *Mining Review*, warned against expecting unusual and unwarranted results from mining. Too often, he felt, in direct proportion to anticipation had come disappointment. This business was one requiring more than ordinary skill, while at the same time being one in which it was exceedingly easy to fail.[5] Caribou bore out his warnings.

Down into the mines in the morning went the miners, to emerge again only as the sun settled behind the Continental Divide. They toiled a long, hard day for their employers. Much of the labor was done by hand—hand drilling and picking into the rock depths of Caribou Hill, hand planting the explosives, hand shoveling the blasted waste and ore rock into cars to be taken to the shaft, where it was hoisted to the shaft house. Hand sorting of the ore on the surface, which was then shoveled into sacks or loaded into ore wagons to be sent to the mill, completed the process. Some machine drills and other labor-saving machinery appeared as the years passed, but the mines were developed primarily by the men with their own muscle, aided by picks, shovels, single and double jacks, and blasting powder.

Many of the miners had Cornish origins, or had come directly from Cornwall. In the 1880 census 60 percent of the miners reported they had been born in the British Isles, exclusive of Wales, Scotland, and Ireland; and another 4 percent had English parents. A sturdy lot they were, said to be the "best class for this business that could be obtained."[6] They, or their fathers before them, had toiled in the working environment of the mines of Cornwall; so the damp, cold, dangerous life at Caribou was not foreign. Hard work had become the accepted way of life to them.

The number of men working the mines is hard to estimate. In 1874 the Caribou, Sherman, No Name, and Poorman employed respectively 105, 15, 6, and 4 miners. One hundred eighty-seven men reported their occupation as miner in the census of 1880.[7] These two sets of figures serve only as an indication, for probably another 50 to 100 worked for themselves or in the smaller mines in 1874. In all years a continual group wandered in and out, finding only temporary employment or seeking a richer, more prosperous camp.

The daily wages received by the miners decreased in the 1870s, indicating the need for skilled men at first and a leveling after the initial boom. Records of the Caribou Mine from 1870 into 1873 show

A visitor likened this scene of the ore sorting room at the Caribou Mine to an "old-time New England farm house." Courtesy, Duane A. Smith

that the miners received $3.25 per day and the foreman $4 to $4.50. The men at the Nederland Mill were paid a lower wage—on the average of $3 per day. The miner was lucky, however, who was able to draw wages for every work day, because many times they were employed less than twenty days per month in a period before the five-day week went into effect. The length of the working day varied from eight to twelve hours, depending upon the company and the year, although the ten-hour shift came close to being standard. The No Name and Sherman, for example, paid $3.25 in 1874 for a ten-hour day. The same year Richard Harvey, Caribou foreman, complained that his $150 per month salary was less than other foremen received; he noted that the company now paid the men $3 per day. The miners' liens levied against the Caribou the next year listed the wages of the men who signed them. A sliding scale went from a low of $2 to $3.75, with the majority falling into the $2.75 to $3.00 category. Occasionally, an incentive was offered the miners for special effort. The Caribou Company, in the early years, gave the men a keg of beer for each shipment sent to the mill at Black Hawk. In 1879 an attempt to lower wages from $2.50 to $2.25 by several companies was stopped by a strike. By that year Caribou miners received less than

Caribou Mine crew, c. 1878. Courtesy, Garry Bryant

the state average of $3 per day and less than other Western states, such as Nevada's $4 and Montana's $3.50. This steady decline explains why contract and tribute work became increasingly popular, not only with the employers but with the men as well.[8]

The best picture of the labor situation for a given mine comes from the 1877–1878 records of the Caribou, whose owners in July 1877 employed twenty-seven men. Of these, seven were hired as miners, denoting a trend toward contract and tribute work. These men received wages of $2.50 per day, with three working twenty or more days and the others five or less. Also employed underground were three machine-drill men at $3 per day, one drill man at $2.75, three bucket dumpers at $3, one timberman at $3, and two rock passers at $3 and $2.50. Three machinists who received $3.50 and $3.25 and two brakemen at $3 per day operated the machinery and hoist. On the surface worked an ore sorter paid $2.75, a blacksmith and helper $3.50 and $2.50, respectively, and a carpenter $2.75. Overseeing the operation and receiving the sum of $4 per day for his responsibilities and experience was the foreman. Wages for the month totaled $1,550 for $514\frac{1}{2}$ days, or an average of nineteen days per month per man.

The mill had a much smaller payroll, employing only fourteen to sixteen men. Broken down, this figure included a foreman, assayer, engineer, carpenter, pan men, roasters, feeders, and roustabouts.

The wage scale ran from $2.50 for roustabouts to $3.25 for the carpenter in July 1878. The *Caribou Post*, in its March 10, 1872, issue, estimated it took, on the average, eight miners to keep one man busy on reduction; but the ratio dropped with the introduction of machinery.

The highest salaried official was Eben Smith. Smith, of course, supervised the entire operation and probably owned a share of the property. His salary varied from $218 to $516 per month, averaging $316 in the period from January 1877 to October 1878. Into this was figured also any personal expenses he incurred in the operation of the property.[9]

The prevailing wage trend, the continued long hours, and increasing absentee ownership resulted in discontent among the miners. No union local would be organized here, but spontaneous strikes were not unknown, and labor unrest mounted as the decade passed—a natural reaction to what was occurring.

As early as 1872 some of Breed's Cornish miners struck for a reduction of hours: from ten to nine for the day hands and nine to eight for night workers. Breed refused to comply with demands, and work nearly came to a halt. Threatened violence failed to materialize and a settlement of sorts was reached, with some going back at the old hours and others accepting a discharge in preference. Two years later the Caribou was again embroiled in difficulty, this time because of a reduction in wages. The newspapers remained vague about the difficulty, commenting only that it had been settled and work resumed.[10]

Absentee management's problems relating to labor were reflected in correspondence of R. G. Dun in November 1876. Dun had received letters from his worried manager, Harmon Minckler, describing the unrest of the miners over wages due them:

> I reckon there must be something owing them, but the fact is both Judge [Fullerton] and I have been too highly pressed to meet any more drafts on us. We must slow workers off as long as we can . . . but the laborers will certainly ultimately be paid every dollar due them—we want them to have a little patience.[11]

Such excuses failed to satisfy the men's demands and, according to Minckler, they threatened to attack if not paid. Finally, the money was secured and the back wages paid on December 1. Neither group really understood the other's situation. Without money the men could not live, which Dun realized, but he advocated patience for he knew he would eventually pay. The miners apparently did not have this confidence in Dun, especially with the recent failure of the Mining Company Nederland fresh in their minds.

The lowering of wages continued to be the fundamental dispute between management and labor in the following years. In May 1877 a small-scale strike against reduction resulted in the miners trying to organize for general cooperation. They discovered, after an "impartial scrutinizing," that they were comparatively powerless. Commented the *Colorado Banner*, "Why cripple the miner, the sole producer with all the burden? Why not take a little from superintendents, bosses?" Again in 1879 the miners went out on strike for a week, with better results this time, as mentioned, preventing a cut in wages. The following year miners of the Native Silver quit their jobs in dissatisfaction, shutting down the mine for the better part of a month.[12]

The most serious disturbance during the decade came in 1874, when the Mining Company Nederland attempted to introduce Chinese labor into its mine and mill. This had not only racial but economic overtones, for the cheap Chinese labor threatened to lower wages for all. The Chinese were not welcome here nor in most parts of the mining West. The company needed to reduce overhead expenses to produce the profits demanded by the stockholders, and apparently looked upon this method as a step in the right direction. News leaked out several weeks before, however, and despite the company's denial that it had any intention of using the "Celestials" in the underground workings, the miners and townspeople became alarmed.

The Chinese arrived at Nederland late in the afternoon of March 29. Citizens of both communities attended an "indignation" meeting, which resulted in a mob of about forty armed men taking possession of the Chinese camp and escorting the inhabitants out of town. No blood was shed nor property destroyed, although the local constable was unable to find men to deputize to protect the camp. Another group of Orientals later was reported on the way, but the company apparently thought better of the idea and no more was heard about them or the use of Chinese labor. A great deal of emotion was aroused by the Oriental threat, which led the *Boulder County News* to write a rabid anti-Chinese article, praising the action of the neighboring mining communities.[13] Caribou never again witnessed a demonstration like this, yet under the surface the potential for one remained, had the threat reappeared.

In this day before safety measures and regulations, Caribou had a relatively accident-free record. The most spectacular disaster hap-

Silver bricks, smelter crew, and young Maude Bryant at the office of the Caribou Consolidated Mining Company. Maude's father, William, longtime mill superintendent, kneels behind her. Courtesy, Garry Bryant

pened on the surface when nitroglycerine exploded in the shaft house of the Sherman Mine, demolishing it and the nearby Poorman shaft house. One of the owners of the latter mine was killed in the explosion. Underground accidents claimed four victims and seriously injured three others. Mishaps causing minor injuries, although more numerous, were not noted in the newspapers. Mining cannot be adjudged one of the safest occupations; but, considering all the circumstances, Caribou was safer than many other Western mining districts.

The total production of the Caribou mines during the 1870s is impossible to establish accurately. Peter Van Diest, who based his statistics on first-hand experience, calculated that from 1870 to 1875 approximately one and one-half million dollars worth of ore had been mined, while the *Engineering and Mining Journal* estimated $3,120,000 through mid-1877.[14] This latter amount seems too high for the period covered. The Caribou Mine had been the great producer, with over a million dollars to its credit. Using the most conservative figures for the other mines' production, one can probably credit about two million total for these years, not a large amount when compared to some of the great bonanza regions such as Leadville, Colorado, and Virginia City, Nevada, but a solid production.

Entering the 1880s, Caribou could look behind to a most prosperous decade. Despite some serious setbacks, advances had been made. The boom environment of the first year had died, but a more stable situation evolved. Consolidation—which replaced individual ownership—promised, if all went well, to improve the overall operation. The miners found wages declining, but the ambitious ones could always lease or work by contract to increase their incomes. Hopefully, the years of exploitation and trial and error had passed and a bright future lay ahead.

Businessman's Bonanza

In the spring of 1871 Caribou was nearing the end of its first year of community existence. The winter just past had not seriously dented the prosperity that came with the discovery period. Ahead loomed the most prosperous decade, although it was never to be so rosy as the most optimistic Caribouites would wish. If the miners had reason for rejoicing over their prospects, the townspeople had equal justification, for the community was growing and trade expanding as spring made its appearance.

The booming camp acted as a magnet in attracting the curious, especially the Eastern visitor who thought of this and its counterparts elsewhere as the "real West." Two who came wrote of their visit. In June John Tice went into the mines, and also examined the town. He was not particularly impressed with certain aspects, commenting that it had some 250 houses (which seems an excessively high figure), but, "The houses are frame, many two stories high, made of spruce and pine sawed by the mountain mills. Not a brush of paint had been applied to any of them when we were there."[1] In August the noted lecturer, writer, and domestic correspondent for the *New York Times*, Grace Greenwood (Mrs. Sara J. Lippincott), paid a visit—viewing the camp through the eyes of a romantic:

> Though nine thousand feet above the level of the sea, it is a broad, deep bowl-like valley, green and beautiful. Young as it is—scarcely a year old—there are evidences here of prevailing ideas of comfort and taste. It is compact, neat and home-like. . . . Beside almost every miner's cabin stands a tall pine, like a sentinel . . . and all the way up the valley . . . are lovely clumps of those steadfast comforters of a winter climate, and a "weary land." The whole place looked to me marvelously cheerful.[2]

Between these two descriptions the real Caribou could be found. Unpainted buildings were to be expected in the rush to complete construction and open them for business or dwelling. Elegance was lacking, but for those who lived there day after day, it was home. This camp was scarcely different from others in which many of the residents had lived or visited during a similar stage of development.

The most pressing problem that confronted the entire community was the lack of housing. As miners returned with the melting of the winter snows, the demand far outraced the carpenters' ability to supply it. Tice, in fact, reported seeing miners living in lodges made of a few poles laid over a gap between two large rocks, with pine boughs serving as a roof.[3] Not until the rush of this second season passed would construction match the need

The substantial frame homes that Tice mentioned—as did the editor of the *Boulder County News*, June 17—following his visit, testify to the faith of these early residents in their community. As sturdy in its affirmation was the growing business district. The merchant risked a greater investment, coming as he did to an unknown district, than did the individual miner, for he brought with him merchandise that must be sold before he could realize a profit. Caribou was fortunate in having, from the beginning, a class of responsible businessmen who gave stability to the transitory mining environment.

Even the business community was affected by the newness and the potential of the district. Businessmen flocked to Caribou, reaching their peak numbers during 1871–1872, the summer of the former year being probably the busiest of the decade. From comments and advertisements in the camp's young newspaper, the *Caribou Post*, and those of surrounding communities, there emerges a picture of the scope and variety of the business district.

The general store, a trademark of the mining West, was much in evidence. Patterson and Scott Bros., for example, dealt in groceries, provisions, hardware, mining tools, and the like, as did Van & Brother and Leo Donnelly, while the firm of Brodre and Tappan kept groceries and a bakery. The City Bakery also dispensed groceries, but the Caribou Brewery and Bakery claimed to have the best of both products in the community, wholesale and retail. The Capitol Bakery advertised a "full assortment" of groceries and liquors, as well as a lunch counter where a "good square meal can be had at all hours." Thompson and Co. was vague in its advertising but kept at least a stock of drugs; Fonda Bros. openly claimed a drugstore, while selling paints, glass, and fancy goods along with drugs and medicines. Herzinger and Co. (soon to become Herzinger & Harter) were general merchants but did not delve into the grocery business. Joseph Murphy had joined Pierce, and their market offered all kinds of fresh and salted meat products. Two blacksmiths, a boot- and shoemaker, a barber, and a jeweler added to the assortment. The camp also had a livery stable, assayer, mining engineer, and a photographic gallery, but no doctor or dentist.

For those seeking room, board, and entertainment, Caribou was not remiss in its responsibility. The Caribou Restaurant satisfied the culinary requirement, and several hotels and boarding houses provided both food and lodging. The exact number is unknown; the newspapers mentioned anywhere from seven to ten of these establishments, but the names of only five were given. The best known of the saloons was the Caribou Hall (Sears, Werley & Co.), which offered billiards and "choice wines, liquors and segars [*sic*]."[4] Other enterprises probably existed, either on a very temporary basis or, at most, for only a season.

The business district had expanded too fast for the available market and attrition soon took its toll of the less skillful or least lucky. Merchandising in a mining camp was no lark. It took practical experience, acumen in purchasing, a favorable location, and good fortune. The merchant who overstocked and was caught with a high inventory when the community went into a recession, or the one who proved too conservative and found himself running out of goods while his competitors prospered, did not last long. Obviously, some of the businesses mentioned came only because of the initial boom. Some owners quickly sold out and moved on to another area before the competition heightened. A few started later in the period, but the basic foundations were laid during 1871. From just a brief sampling of goods available, one can see that no large gap had been left.

The business district of Caribou was concentrated on two streets, each with wide boardwalks built in sections ascending the steep slopes. Idaho Street emerged as the main thoroughfare; however, during the early years, Caribou Street, running parallel to the north, put up a strong bid to gain the honor. On the former were most of the business establishments and the post office, a primary drawing card. Here people congregated to receive their mail, and the best locations were as near to it as possible, to tap the potential trade. The post office, next to Sears and Werley's saloon and in a building owned by them, received favorable comment in the October 7, 1871, issue of the *Caribou Post*. "Our new postoffice is a building not quite so costly as the New York City Court-house but really quite elegant for a mining town . . . the room occupied by the office is high, ample in size, well-fitted up, and, it is said, has the best finished case in the Territory." Frank Sears not only owned the building but served as postmaster.

Conspicuous by its absence was the bank. Caribou's more populous neighbors—Central, Boulder, and Denver—had banks and advertised in the *Post*; however none apparently ever ventured into the camp. This was not particularly unusual for a mining community of this size. Not only could the neighboring establishments provide credit and depositories, but a local store owner's safe served the latter function just as well. Bankers generally were reluctant to move into an unknown and risky camp unless exceptional potential was evident. Caribou's proximity to established firms made such a venture unnecessary.

By the summer of 1873, of the merchants who had come with the first excitement, only Herzinger, Harter, Pierce, Donnelly, Murphy, Sears, Werley, and the Scott brothers remained. Though others had replaced some of the departed, the number of firms declined steadily. Two years later the *Colorado Business Directory* listed two general merchandise stores, two livery stables, six saloons, four hotels, one fruit stand, a butcher, brewer, restaurant, and dry goods store. By 1879 Joseph Murphy operated the sole meat market; Herzinger & Harter and Scott Bros. still carried on their businesses, but Sears and Werley no longer operated their saloon. Leo Donnelly was a justice of the

Idaho Street business houses had a well-maintained appearance in the mid-1870s. Courtesy, University of Colorado Archives

peace and Peter Werley, temporarily out of the saloon trade, served now as town clerk. Some businesses dropped out noticeably, with only two saloons listed, along with one livery stable; no restaurant, brewer, or dry goods store was in evidence. To counterbalance this predicament, another general store and fruit stand had been added, and a new boot-and shoemaker, hotel, and milliner appeared.[5]

Besides the "old-timers" mentioned, a few other merchants had been in business for several years, including Sam Newell, who arrived in 1875 and operated first a saloon and subsequently a hotel. J. M. Reimer went into business the same year with his combination fruit, stationery, and news depot; in 1877 John Cosgrove opened his livery stable, but for the rest of the merchants the changeover had been rapid.

An important factor in the success or failure of a given enterprise was the ability of the proprietor to capture a large enough segment of the consumer market, limited as it was at Caribou. The older established firms managed to retain a loyal following, which had been built up through personal contact and service. This put any newcomer at a disadvantage until he could prove himself. Mercantile records have disappeared, but some indication of the amount of trade can be found in the newspapers. The *Boulder County News*, November 27, 1874, reported that Scott Bros. had grown in the past three years to about $60,000 per year; by 1877 it reached $70,000 per annum with a stock of about $25,000 on hand. Reimer's smaller store had an estimated $5,000–6,000 business per year by 1877.[6] According to the *Rocky Mountain News*, July 31, 1875, the monthly order business for the entire trade community was $10,000.

Only a fair percentage of a firm's business came from the various mining companies. Scott Bros., for example, in the period from March to December 1877, received payments totaling over $1,000 from the Caribou Mine. The existing records, however, show that most of this mine's trade was carried on with businesses outside the camp—such as Central and Denver—that offered greater selection. Of course this trade involved a certain amount of risk, for the businessman could never be sure when a vein might "play out" and a company go bankrupt, leaving uncollectable debts. Credit had to be extended, because much of the camp's economy was based on it, yet to offer too much was a decided leap in the dark. Herzinger & Harter tried to overcome this with the following warning placed on the letterhead of its statements: "All bills must be paid at the end of the month. If not paid then, credit will cease, and interest added to your account."[7]

Despite Caribou's isolation from the logical supply point, Boulder, the prices paid by the buyer in the camp were not much higher. For example, in mid-July 1871 in Boulder flour sold for $5.75 per 100 lb. sack, coffee for 25¢ per pound, and a pound of sugar from 15½–17¢; while at Caribou the amounts, respectively, were $6.75, 27¢ and 18¢[8]—roughly a markup of one to two cents per pound. Nor did the consumer suffer from lack of choice, for the money available in a mining district attracted a greater variety of stores and products than would be found in a correspondingly sized, one-year-old, frontier agricultural settlement. For the housewife doing her shopping in July 1871, the following items were available: fresh and canned fruits, vegetables, bakery items, dairy products, mountain trout, salted meats, all kinds of fresh game, and general groceries; for the mining man: blacksmithing, nails, rope, tools, blasting powder, chemicals, and such could be purchased locally. For the family, medicines, shoes, and clothes—or the material required to make them—were found in the shops. For masculine relaxation, liquors, wines, tobacco, and billiards tempted the pleasure seeker. By the next month a Caribouite could even have his picture taken at the local gallery.

The miner who supported a family would not have found much left from his daily wage to spend on luxuries, after the necessities had been acquired. Probably 75 to 90 percent of his earnings went for food, clothing, and other essentials. However, the single man—a decided majority in the early days—had money to spend on wine and women, and for him Caribou obligingly provided these divertissements.

It would be redundant to stress the interdependence of business with the success of the mines. The editor of the *Colorado Banner*, in the issue of July 31, 1879, succinctly summarized the relationship: "It is useless to say that the Caribou mine makes the town of Caribou. Shut down these works, and you drive a nail in the town's coffin." Bellwethers of the community's prosperity, the saloons were evidence of where the surplus money went. In August 1871 the number stood at four; increasing to six in 1875; slipping to five the next year; down to two in 1879; only to reverse the trend in the early 1880s. From 1871 into 1875 Caribou prospered, while the rest of Boulder County and most of the nation suffered from the depression of 1873. It advanced, moreover, to become the third-ranked mining region in the territory, behind Gilpin County and Georgetown–Silver Plume.[9] Then came hard times. Two reports, appearing in the *Colorado Banner* in the fall of 1877 and the next spring, paint a graphic picture of what had happened:

> Money is scarce, owing to the limited amount of mining being done. The hotel keepers manage to keep their heads above water these times, but it is hard work. They have been very kind to many of their boarders who are without money, trusting them until work is resumed in the now idle mines. [Fall]

> The looks of things have not changed materially since our last visit, many vacant houses and storerooms indicating better and by gone days. . . . I entertain not the slightest doubt but that business will revive a great deal this season. . . . While speaking of dullness, this camp is about as good as any in the country. [Spring][10]

During the depths of the recession, when the situation appeared blackest, a few people pushed for the organization of a cooperative store. The project lacked general support and died a-borning. In 1878 and 1879 the town experienced a revival of its previous prosperity. Business improved, stores reopened, and even some new ones were started. Caribou was fortunate in having exceptional hotels for a mountain community of its size and location. The first in the line was the Planter's House, which had opened by the time of Tice's visit; he spent the night there and described the proprietor, William O. Logue, as a former steamboat engineer and captain in the Union army. Logue had previously operated a hotel in Black Hawk. The imposing structure, two and a half stories high, with sleeping, sitting, and dining rooms, plus a ladies' parlor, earned a reputation for pleasant and clean rooms and serving a "bountiful" table. A visitor left this impression in 1874: "The accommodation and fare at this house exceeded my expectations. I found an ample supply of good things, well ordered and served, and no room left for complaint of want of attention and variety."[11]

The outstanding achievement in architecture and class was the Sherman House, built in 1874–1875. The pride of the camp, it rivaled the best that could be found in any Colorado mountain community. It opened officially on a rainy July evening with a grand ball that attracted sixty couples, in spite of the weather. Three stories high, the Sherman House had twenty-eight sleeping rooms, a reading room, parlor, and large dining room. Upon entering his quarters the guest found "carpeted floors, black walnut furnishings, and sheets, pillows and coverlets white as the driven snow."[12] The Sherman House quickly surpassed all its Caribou competitors, becoming noted for its sociable and comfortable atmosphere, as well as its "homelike" meals and—what must have been a godsend in Caribou's cold and windy weather—a cup of "genuine good coffee." It remained the social and visitor center for years.

Ownership and management of the Sherman House changed several times during the remainder of the decade, but William Donald, who entered first as a partner, eventually took over complete control and operated it into the 1890s. Donald in many ways typified the person who settled at Caribou. Born on Prince Edward's Island, he moved to Maine, then Michigan, and finally in 1860 to Denver, from where after a time he went to Gilpin County to prospect, without much success. For nine years he lived there, working as a miner and superintendent before being hired as foreman of the Caribou Mine in 1870. In the years that followed, Donald served as superintendent of the Native Silver and Seven Thirty mines and manager of the Spencer, a mine in which he previously had partial ownership before selling to Dun. He also owned the Grant County Mine. R. G. Dun thought highly of the man, writing in 1880 that he was anxious to get him out of the "hotel business and back to mining," for Donald was a "good man" with experience, just the man to be Dun's principal superintendent.[13]

Caribou reached its peak in the late 1870s. The schoolhouse, Sherman House, and other buildings were painted and the whole camp appears prosperous. Courtesy, Duane A. Smith

The Sherman House, however, took more and more of Donald's time, and he became respected in this endeavor as well as in mining. Unlike many others, he remained at Caribou during the declining days, confident that it would come back.

The merchant-miner was a common entity in the business community, although in Donald's case mining had come first and remained his principal occupation through much of his life. To illustrate the diversity of approach, William Logue had been an agent for one company, the Scott brothers leased part of a mine, and Herzinger was a partner in a mining operation. Some merchants grubstaked the prospectors for a percentage of anything discovered. The adventuresome and lucky businessman might make a fortune in mining, and no doubt many at least dabbled in it, if only on a limited scale.

Several factors besides those already mentioned had great impact on business developments—stable town government, a steady influx of outside capital, and a good transportation network. Lawlessness did not enrich the honest merchant's pocket; indeed, he tended to suffer in such an environment. It was essential, then, that he promote stability, and the businessman generally stood in the vanguard of the struggle for law and order and local government. The best possible year-round transportation system was also necessary to speed the delivery of goods, lower the expense of inventories, cut freighting costs if possible, and improve the community's image in the eyes of investors and prospective inhabitants. Once again the merchant stood to gain, and he avidly supported improvements. Advertising, not individually, but collectively, promoted the town, mines, and district and helped stimulate growth and investment—all essential to the permanency of any mining community. Although never organizing a chamber of commerce, per se, the business community united to provide a similar service.

From the initial rush, it had been easier to reach Caribou from Black Hawk and Central City than from Boulder, to the dismay of the latter's merchants. Caribou was situated logically within the economic and political orbit of Boulder County, but would not be there in actuality until a direct connection was completed. By following a roundabout route, it was possible to reach Caribou; but the shortest access went straight up Boulder Canyon, of which only six miles of roadbed had been finished—as far as the Magnolia–Central City road.

Not only were Boulder businessmen interested in breaking Central's hold, but their Caribou compatriots realized they would gain from the competition offered by opening another road. Boulder, an agricultural and mining supply center, offered more variety, direct access to needed farm products, and a less mountainous path to Denver. To meet this need, a group of energetic Boulder businessmen organized the Boulder and Caribou Wagon Road Company in late 1870 to build a toll road up the canyon. After some construction delay, it opened in the summer of 1871.[14] The road, snaking along the side of the canyon and crisscrossing the creek, required constant attention to maintain it in usable condition. It proved a costly venture for the company. The neglected repairs angered the Caribouites, causing the *Boulder County News* to warn on August 9, 1878, that it was in a "miserable and shameful" condition. The paper continued: "While the County Commissioners are the special guardians of public interests, they have allowed their sympathy for the road owners to influence their better judgment. The effect is to estrange the two sections of our county." Overcoming such problems, Caribou gradually oriented itself toward Boulder and Boulder County, as had been hoped, and the Boulder Canyon road became the chief artery of transportation.

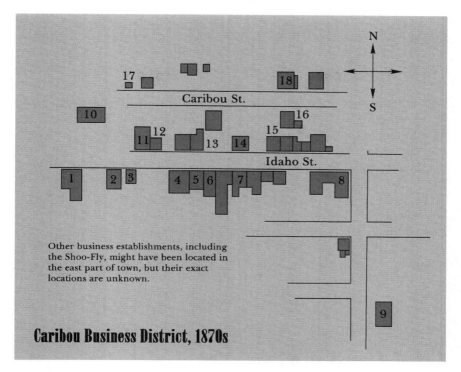

Caribou Business District, 1870s

Other business establishments, including the Shoo-Fly, might have been located in the east part of town, but their exact locations are unknown.

1. Brewery
2. Church
3. Telegraph Office
4. Murphy's Meat Market
5. Colorado House
6. Newell's Saloon
7. Dobson's Saloon*

8 Sherman House
9. School
10. Caribou House*
11. Werley's Saloon
   (Dr. Mann's office
   —2nd floor*)
12. Post Office

13. Scott Bros.
14. Herzinger & Harter
15. Reimer's Store*
16. Planters House
17. Jail*
18. Idaho House
*Presumed Location

Upon completion of the road, stages began to arrive regularly from both Central City and Boulder, carrying passengers, express, and mail. The Boulder-based Caribou Stage Company operated a line of Concord coaches during most of the year. In the worst season of cold, wintry weather, a sleigh transported passengers on the Nederland-to-Caribou run. During the height of the boom, stages arrived daily; then the service leveled off to three per week each way—sufficient to meet the needs of the camp. In 1871, after the residents requested the change in order to speed delivery, the mail route was shifted from Central to Boulder.

Even with the vastly improved situation, some people still were not satisfied. Only a railroad would answer the needs of Caribou; the idea enlisted supporters, especially when the district started to decline. The *Caribou Post* had been an incurable railroad booster, as the July 22, 1871, issue illustrates: "We wish every man in Caribou was brim-full and boiling over with railroad enthusiasm. Railroad men like to lay down their iron to places where the people keenly appreciate its advantages. This is the sort of community whose enterprise is sure to make business for the road." That year a route was planned, but it got no further than the drawing boards. In 1877 a Golden, Boulder, and Caribou railroad was proposed. Ambitious plans and surveys failed to bring the track within miles of Caribou, and the first of several balloons broke. On paper the railroad offered almost unbounded blessings: stimulation of mining, faster transportation, increased business, and general overall improvement.[15] In the 1880s and 1890s rumors persisted that a road would be built, and the camp anxiously awaited the coming millenium. It never came. Caribou was too small to lure it alone and too far removed from other mining districts to enhance the attraction for the railroad companies. Furthermore, the mines went too rapidly into decline to tempt a company to risk the expense of construction and maintenance.

Caribou had to grow or die and, like most young mining camps, it turned to advertisement to better its chances of survival. In this the mine owners and the businessmen cooperated, for each stood to gain and each needed the support of the other. Handicapped for most of the decade by the lack of a local newspaper, they were compelled to use other means to promote themselves. This dearth severely impeded their efforts, although never quite to the point that one pessimist claimed when writing to the *Central City Register*, January 8, 1873: "The citizens of Caribou do not own a paper filled each issue with absurd mining puffs, which, like sounding brass and tinkling cymbals, are empty and meaningless. Consequently, owing to our isolated situation and our distance from the press we are scarcely known abroad."

A good way to advertise was to enter rich mineral specimens at fairs and exhibitions—local, state, and national. Caribou, never remiss in this area, started in 1870 to send ore exhibits as far away as St. Louis, hoping to attract Eastern capital and produce favorable responses. The outstanding achievement took place in 1876, when ore was shipped to the Centennial Exhibition in Philadelphia. This event, on the one-hundredth anniversary of the Declaration of Independence, attracted displays from throughout the country and the world. Though Caribou mines were at a low ebb, they still won two bronze medals; the exhibit from the Idaho was the most spectacular—a sample worth $500.[16] The whole camp pitched in and a committee of mine owners and merchants organized and solicited funds to defray the expense of shipment.

The most grandiose exhibition was planned and perfected by Abel Breed, just at the end of his ownership of the Caribou Mine. President U. S. Grant, on his 1873 Colorado tour, had scheduled a visit to Central City. Following a wild ride from Idaho Springs to Central, Grant alighted in front of the Teller House and was confronted with a sidewalk paved with Caribou silver bricks. Somewhat incredulous at first, the president finally accepted the truth.[17] Caribou received free publicity, and Breed, with a flamboyant gesture, bowed out.

Although never so successful in luring tourists as mining capital, the Caribouites nevertheless did not completely ignore this possible bonanza. At a time when tourism was developing into something more than an occasional visitor to Colorado, the camp still had a progressive, lively appearance. Not one of the most scenic spots in the state, it held out a certain attraction, as a local resident described it in the *Boulder County News*, April 20, 1877: "with Arapaho Peak, only a very short ride from town to the falls of North Boulder Creek, the pure and invigorating air . . . a splendid view of the plains and snowy range . . . [and] also the surrounding parks." Tourists never came in large numbers, however, for Caribou proved to be too far from the main railroad lines and cities, and did not have a spectacular or unusual enough setting to overcome the disadvantages.

As Caribou grew in the 1870s, it spawned a number of villages around it, directly dependent on it or on mining. Nederland, earlier known by such varied names as Brown's Ranch, Dayton, and Middle Boulder, was the largest and most enduring; although it actually predated the discovery of the mines, the town grew as a result of the mill located there. By 1876 it had about 300 inhabitants, a small business area, and a school. Nearer to Caribou was Cardinal, about two miles east, supported by its own mines—especially the Trojan and the Boulder County. Described by Tice as a "hamlet of some dozen houses,"[18] it never achieved the fame of its neighbor. Eventually the site was abandoned, and those people who remained moved into the valley to the present location of New Cardinal. Batesville, previously described, had even a less distinguished history. Caribou and Nederland dominated the district, and the latter was unable to cut the economic ties between the two until the late 1890s. As Caribou itself was in the Boulder sphere, so did these camps find themselves dependent ultimately on this supply center.

"A Town Well Worth Having"

Caribou was more than three years old before it was incorporated and organized a town government. Nor was this unusual. Many mining communities, in fact, never established an official government. No outbreak of lawlessness or any other pressing problem forced this step, rather the demands of increased growth and the awareness of possible benefits to be derived from the action. Unfortunately, little was noted in the newspapers about the impending event; the fait accompli presented itself; the prime movers remain anonymous.

Municipal government thus established was controlled by an elected board of five trustees, one of whom served as president and acting mayor. The only other two officials, the town clerk and the constable–street commissioner, also were chosen by the people. The elections, held every year, commenced in 1874 and continued until 1899, although toward the last, interest waned and some years passed without any at all. Remaining records indicate that businessmen dominated the board of trustees. For example, in 1878 William Scott, Joseph Murphy, John Simmons, and William Donald were members, while Peter Werley served as clerk. Four years later Donald and Werley still held office, joined by George Scott and Joseph Lloyd. In each case they held a clear majority.[1] The demands on the city fathers varied. The need for money vexed them, especially as the camp declined, but in the 1870s this need, at least, was not so bothersome. A water works, sanitation system, and such minor matters as a surplus of dogs also had to be discussed, if not resolved.

Planning and construction of a municipal water works answered a crying need and demonstrated the progressiveness of the government, when all factors were favorable. The fire danger alone demanded it, but the camp also required a more constant and pure water source than that supplied by nearby springs. Started in the spring of 1878, the work was completed by late fall. The water, taken from near the Continental Divide and transported via the New Jersey Mining Company's ditch to a city reservoir, was then piped into Caribou. The town paid the company $200 per year in rental in addition to the initial cost of construction and equipment. This included five fire plugs strategically placed in the community and a fire hose.[2] The project, when completed, provided a further air of permanency and stability to the camp—a fact probably not overlooked from its inception. The clear, cool water and the very sufficient pressure provided no excuse for consumer complaint. Unfortunately, though, the pipes had been set too shallow, resulting in frozen mains during the depths of winter. Enough wells existed to provide an adequate supply at such times. Few people could fault this valuable and wise investment.

The sanitary precautions taken by the city fathers did not match the improved water system. Even with the natural sanitation advantages of sun, water, and wind, the situation got out of hand. Trash, garbage, and waste littered the streets and alleys, and outhouses were indiscriminately placed behind homes. Caribou became filthy, a menace to health. Nothing was done despite one person's pleas, "If there is any health officers would it not be a good idea to clean up the streets: If there is not, should not the town dads appoint one."[3] It took an epidemic of diphtheria in the summer of 1879 to jar some action into the lethargic community; a general cleanup session and

Idaho Street was crowded on this day. Werley's saloon is the first building on the left and Murphy's meat market has the balcony on the right. Courtesy, Duane A. Smith

Caribouites posing before Werley's saloon. Courtesy, Duane A. Smith

overall improvement resulted. As the *Central City Register-Call* of August 8 sadly noted, this happened only after "several darlings had been laid away in their last resting place." How many died will never be known: one of the gravestones in the Caribou cemetery listed the deaths of three children on July 5, 6, and 8 in the Samuel Richards family.

These two examples illustrate the progressive and inactive extremes of the local government. Far too often, the second was more typical of the nature of a mining community such as Caribou. The Caribouites did not become concerned about something unless it immediately affected them. Their attitude was why waste time and money when one could allow the situation to drift without undue suffering. This feeling, reinforced by the underlying and unresolved question of the camp's ultimate destiny, handicapped any effort of the board of trustees.

More typical perhaps of the type of problems faced was the overabundance of dogs. As one wit calculated, "The average as near as I can estimate, is not greater than three to each resident."[4] To meet this situation, the trustees passed a dog tax and ordered the town marshal to enforce it. Early reports of some success vanished as the wily dogs proved worthy opponents, matching the most ambitious efforts to corral them; the canines remained.

Despite the stereotyped image of the wildness of a mining camp, Caribou's government did not have to cope with any serious problems of criminal activity. This was not the wild frontier where a man felt naked without his gun. In fact, when a man did draw one to force an unruly intruder to apologize for his actions, a local paper became indignant: "Such conduct as this . . . at this state of civilization is uncalled for, as also is the carrying of deadly weapons."[5] Civilization was the key word, for Caribou looked upon itself as a respectable and civilized town; it could not, therefore, condone such actions. Throughout the decade comments appeared praising the law-abiding nature of the people. John Tice testified both to the "expected" image and to that actually found at Caribou:

> But it is due, before breaking off this narration here, to bear un-
> equivocal and unqualified testimony to the order and quietness
> of Caribou. . . . Liquor of every form is for sale here, but there
> are no drunken broils, rioting, wantonness or profanity. This
> is at variance with the common idea of the habits, customs and
> condition of society in mining villages.[6]

Crime of a serious nature was not unknown. Relatively soon after the rush, a miners' meeting was called in February 1871 to settle a claim dispute that resulted in a shooting and a bystander being wounded. Some stealing did occur and personal quarrels led to violence, but only one man died "with his boots on." This homicide resulted when a black man, supposedly the only one ever to live in the camp, was killed while attacking an Irishman over a dispute about food. The latter was acquitted. The following year, 1875, a dead baby was found; it could not be conclusively proved that the child had been murdered, although foul play was suspected since the infant was illegitimate. Two years later tremendous excitement was generated over the disappearance of 2,000 pounds of rich ore from the No Name Mine; most of it was quickly found hidden nearby. The guilty party was eventually apprehended.[7] Nothing in this "wave" of criminal activity supports an accusation of wildness.

A more general type of disturbance resulted from the overindulgence in John Barleycorn, because at this high altitude it quickly went to the head. The town jail, located across the street from the Caribou House, provided lodging for those who partook too freely. Occasionally, some individual was hauled before the police court for reckless riding or driving in the streets. The following Caribou news item appeared in the *Boulder County News*, August 4, 1876:

> The only excitement we have had for weeks was an impromptu horse race through the street last Wednesday evening. In the midst of the race, however, one of the horses encountered our muscular town constable [John Cosgrove], and a promiscuous heap upon the ground followed. The constable was the first to rise, and immediately invited the two race riders into the telegraph office, where the police court was in session. A small fine was imposed and since then no races have been run on Main street.

Then there were the humorous incidents, which gave the residents a chuckle if nothing else. Included in this category was the case involving a man fined for kissing one of the "young, handsome and respectable" married ladies; and the one that resulted in a jury trial over the ownership of two sows of similar markings.[8] It was, as the *Boulder County News*, September 25, 1874, commented, "a town well worth having."

City government provided a continuity and stability for Caribou that no other organization could have. It gave the potential investor and resident a sense of security that was sorely needed. The influence on the community was marked in some areas, almost unnoticeable in others. In the 1870s the administration functioned at its best and achieved desired results. That significant improvement failed to be effected in sanitation, for example, should not be blamed entirely on the Caribou trustees and residents, because other and older towns did no better. They did well for having started only in 1874. For the time and the place, the government was certainly adequate; too much governmental control was neither wanted nor needed.

Long before attaining the respectability of a city government, Caribou had gained another symbol of permanence, a newspaper. Almost all mining camps wanted one and felt deprived, as noted, if they failed to achieve the goal. The *Caribou Post* appeared in May 1871 to receive a friendly greeting on the twenty-seventh from the *Boulder County News* as a "large, well filled and neatly printed paper." The youthful paper itself exclaimed on July 22 that Nathan Meeker, late of the *New York Tribune*, considered the *Post* about "the best weekly in the territory"; and without modesty it commented, "Caribousters have thought so from the first." Printed in Central City by Collier and Hall, publishers of the *Register*, the *Post* employed Amos Bixby at Caribou as a semi-editor and writer. As initiated, this was a good four-page,

Caribou family dressed in its Sunday best. Courtesy, Duane A. Smith

seven-column weekly paper—a typical issue of which carried local, national, and international news. It also had miscellaneous articles on varied topics, specialty items such as poetry, or a story from some national magazine like *Scribner's Monthly*. A large segment consisted of advertisements from camp and surrounding merchants. Editorially, the *Post* discussed a multitude of topics including city improvement, agricultural versus mining land, and the Mormon "problem" (revealing the editor to be decidedly anti-Mormon). A subscriber could get the paper for three, six, or twelve months, invariably "paid in advance."

During the first months of publication, the local coverage proved particularly newsy, with the editor advocating many projects to improve the community. The *Post* also came quickly to Caribou's defense when some neighbor or visitor ventured to sneer. It received one letter that said in part, "Before returning east we would like to visit Caribou if you have anything attractive that way. . . . We cannot learn whether you have passable roads or such hotels as we find here [Georgetown, Colorado]." The editor angrily retorted,

> We do know however, that in this town, not yet a year old, are found, to the surprise of all who have good fortune to come this

way, well built and commodious hotels. . . . But it is more surprising that in a neighboring mining camp there should be any
ignorance of the fact of the excellent road from Black Hawk to
Middle Boulder. . . . But really we ought not to be surprised at
this indifference of our neighbors; although it is not pleasant to
have one's existence ignored. . . . This is the lesson: *We must take
care of ourselves.*[9]

Despite the fine start, the paper failed to continue its ambitious
program, declining until becoming little more than the *Register* with
the *Post* masthead and an occasional Caribou column. This aroused
criticism and the publishers felt obligated to defend themselves, but
the defense did not alter the obvious fact. Finally, on August 17, 1872,
the paper suspended publication, as they said, "for the present," with
this parting comment,

> We started it fifteen months ago, largely in anticipation of the
> future. While the inherent value of the mining region of the
> upper portion of Boulder county has been shown to be all that
> could be reasonably expected of it, and while we believe it is
> one of the best mining regions of Colorado, its development
> has not been as rapid as we had reason to hope and expect,
> and we have consequently been unable to make it a present
> financial success. While we believe we have given our patrons a
> good readable paper . . . we have not for several months been
> able to make it as good as we desired. That we are compelled
> to suspend at the present time, is not the fault of anybody, but
> rather the misfortune. When the mines of Boulder shall be so
> developed as to enable us to publish a paper . . . with financial
> success we shall resume.[10]

With all colors flying, the *Post* went down, promoting to the last. Its
editors had been overly optimistic, like so many of their contemporaries.
Caribou could not support a paper of its own, surrounded as it was by
Boulder, Central, and Denver newspapers, both daily and weekly. The
camp's population, at best slightly over 1,000, was just not enough. As
the editors had slyly hinted, the district had simply not developed as
they originally hoped. While active, the *Caribou Post* had contributed to
the community in endless ways, from advertising to reform. Its folding
prophesied more than the editors realized at the time, for despite their
optimistic hope it never resumed publication. The Caribouites had to
muddle along as best they could with occasional columns, items, and
letters in other papers.

There existed at Caribou a professional-business group, which included the doctors, teachers, agents of the larger mining companies, mining engineers, and the aforementioned businessmen. Strangely enough, considering the legal entanglements and the ability of other camps to attract them, Caribou did not have many lawyers; in fact, it passed most of the decade without any. Several doctors practiced here, but only one, Dr. William Mann, stayed any length of time. Born in Ohio in 1826, Mann came to Caribou as a mine owner as early as 1871, but did not open a practice in the town until mid-decade. He combined the two occupations with some success and was well respected by the people. To insure his remaining, in 1881 the miners agreed to withhold one dollar per month per man from their wages to serve as a retainer. This custom, not unusual for mining camps, made the practice that much more lucrative for the doctor who might be tempted by a larger town. Following his death in 1883, Caribou never again had a resident physician.[11]

Politics, which had gotten off to such a lively start in 1870, continued to move at a fast pace throughout the remainder of the decade. Every year either a local, county, state, or national election bid for the voters' attention. In 1871 once again a railroad bond issue was the critical question, with the county voters turning down the proposal. The Democrats captured the camp that year, but the Republicans dominated the rest of the decade. Indeed, the people remained conservative in the face of economic hardships and did not desert the Republican party. The Greenback party and its program of paper money failed to tempt the Caribouites, despite efforts in 1877, 1878, and 1879. The Caribou people, not surprisingly, chose to support hard money. According to one 1878 report, they listened to an hour-and-a-half address on the money question:

> The audience received the speech with great applause from the first to last . . . nor do they intend to be lulled to sleep by the sweet song of the fiat money party. The miners are too intelligent not to see that the worst thing that could come upon them would be the flooding of the country with irredeemable currency and the demonetization of gold and silver.[12]

The major support the Greenbackers found in the camp came from their nomination of Dr. Mann for state representative in 1878. He won the office, but lost out the next year in a race for county coroner and was listed in the returns as a Democrat.

Local people took an interest in running for office, and a year seldom went by without one seeking at least a county position. Mann was probably the most ambitious, but William Donald, Frank Sears, and others took an active part in meetings and rallies. A political meeting at Caribou continued to be a momentous event with speeches and entertainment, the latter frequently provided by the local band. Many people probably participated more for the sake of a change of pace than for any deep conviction or political concern. No assessment can be made of the individual interest in politics, for too many unknown factors have to be weighed. The number of voters (males only—women did not have the franchise) showed a gradual decline during these years, reflecting the population slump of the camp. The biggest drop occurred in 1876, even though it was a presidential election year. Hard times at Caribou accounted for this small turnout. They had two chances to vote that year—once to ratify the state constitution and statehood, which they did overwhelmingly, 173 to 2; and again that fall in the national election, in which 178 people participated. There does not appear to be any pattern between purely local and national questions insofar as numbers participating. In both situations the voters turned out in numbers ranging from a high of 272 to a low of 115.[13] It would seem that the people had a good voting record when the percentage of eligibles is compared to actual voters.

To sketch a picture of the general population of Caribou is extremely difficult; few sources adequately touch upon the so-called average inhabitant. The best remaining records are the original census returns, which, at least statistically, mention everyone. For Caribou in its prime, this means the census of 1880. The following reconstruction is based entirely upon the returns of that year, taken in June.

The Caribouites were young. In the age-group from 16 through 50, the median age was 30.4 years. If the entire population had been averaged, it would have gone deceivingly lower, for there were 174 children fifteen years of age or younger, and only eighteen people older than 50. Roughly 65 percent of the residents had not reached age thirty-one. No colored people of any nationality resided in the community.

A breakdown of the population of those over 16 shows a predominance of men. Surprisingly, the single men only barely outnumbered the married ones—138 to 126. However, not all married men had their wives and families with them, for only seventy-three listed them. Ten single women at least 17 years old resided here and of these but one had reached 25. Adding to this total of "eligible" women were five widows under 50. Divorce was extremely rare, with only two persons, one man and one woman, marking it on the form. In passing, it should be mentioned that the two oldest citizens—ages 70 and 73—were women living with their sons-in-law.

Some indication of the mobility of the people may be seen in the families who had children. For the people coming from Great Britain, the states of New Jersey, Michigan, and New York had been the most popular stopping places before moving on to Colorado. For instance, William Ternby's children had been born in England, New Jersey, and Colorado; William Firstbrook's in New York and Colorado; and William Todd's in Michigan and Colorado. Some Caribouites were quite mobile—Herman Williams having been born in Germany, his wife in France, and their children in Illinois, Kansas, and Colorado; and Epriam Vaughn—who had been born in Ohio—traveled to Colorado, back to Michigan and returned to Colorado.

The residents were fairly evenly divided between foreign- and native-born. Two hundred ninety-six, or roughly 54 percent, had been born in the United States; of these, 110 were native Coloradans, children of parents born outside the state. The next state after Colorado, and trailing badly with twenty-nine, was Ohio; then Missouri, New York, New Jersey, and Michigan. The Midwest, defined as states north of the Ohio River, west of Pennsylvania, and east of Kansas, had the largest representation—36 percent of the American-born. The states north of Maryland trailed with 22 percent. The South and the rest of the country had only negligible percentages. Caribou, then, did not serve as a safety valve for the discontented of the East; the percentage from that section would not have been so high without the immigrants' children born there. The Midwesterner moved into Colorado because he was of a pioneering generation and the new area was contiguous to his home. For him it did serve as a potential safety valve.

While only 46 percent of the population was foreign-born, the majority of adults had come from outside the United States. Altogether 215 people emigrated to Caribou from the British Isles, while an additional eighteen came from the British colonies; thus it may be seen that they dominated the camp. Twenty others had been born in Europe, Germany being in the forefront with thirteen. The remaining parts of the world were unrepresented. Finding a common language was no problem here, nor did any nationality tend to congregate in one section of the community. Caribou has been called a Cornish

Caribou women on an outing on the top of Caribou Mountain. Courtesy, Boulder Historical Society

camp and the assumption seems to be valid, although the census returns do not differentiate between the various sections of England. It would seem logical that a good sprinkling of those who gave England as their birthplace came from Cornwall, itself a mining center. Other evidence points to a similar conclusion. A study of the surnames shows many of possible Cornish origin. Several of the remaining headstones in the cemetery list Cornwall as the birthplace. Personal interviews with Harold Martin, Elizabeth Lee, and Rose Barnett—three who knew the people—further corroborate the presence of a good number of Cornishmen. However, just a single person listed Cornwall as his home—one of the local bartenders.

The birthplace of the men who gave mining as an occupation further supports the assumption that the Cornish appeared in large numbers. As would be expected, the largest single occupation was mining, with the majority of the miners being English. Ohio led the native-born miners, followed by Illinois and New York. Americans dominated the carpenter trade, teamstering, and common laboring, while the English monopolized the blacksmithing. Eight men listed their work as farming, which defies explanation. Farming on any scale at this altitude and with such limited tillable soil appears prohibitive.

The seventy-three families with both mother and father present had an average of 2.4 children, the largest being two families each with eight children. Girls outnumbered boys, one family having eight daughters and no sons. Surprising is the fact that with the large number of children, only twenty-three attended school within the census year. Illiteracy, however, was statistically non-existent, no one being listed as unable to read or write. Of the miners who filed liens against the Mining Company Nederland five years before, all except three signed their names. In thirteen of the marriages the wife was older than the husband, and in only two cases of the seventy-three was one partner younger than twenty years, though obviously others had married before this age. The median age of married couples, 33.9 years, was slightly higher than the rest of the adult community.

The professional-business class was small in 1880, although statistics can be deceiving, when a man such as William Donald lists mining as his occupation while operating the Sherman House. Two school teachers, a minister, and a doctor comprised the professional group. One of the teachers, Seward Merry, doubled as the town's barber. In this group should be included the mining engineers, although how many of the eight listed were self-styled cannot be known. As already indicated, for the businessmen an accurate figure cannot be determined; however, three merchants, two butchers, and a saloon keeper appear in the census records. These six averaged slightly over thirty-five years of age. The ratio of those employed in mining and related occupations to those providing services of one type or another was seven to one.

One hundred dwellings were reported occupied, which averages 5.5 people per house. This, of course, includes boarding houses for the miners, which boosted the average. After June 1, but before the census was started on the fifteenth, a child was born and six miners moved into town, only to be crossed out on the returns to comply with the requirements. This, then, was Caribou in 1880.

The number of people who lived at Caribou during the 1870s is a matter of conjecture. It was not 10,000 or even 5,000, as legends are wont to claim. Primary sources give no estimated population of over 1,000 for the entire decade, and the census of 1880 returned 549.[14] An estimation of the number can be devised from a ratio between the number of 1880 voters and the census total. Basing it on this calculation and using earlier election returns, the approximate figures would be: 1871, 964; 1873, 1,088; 1876, 712; and 1878, 600.[15]

Despite the decline, Caribou still ranked as the third largest town in the county in 1880.

The camp these people built resembled other mining camps architecturally, with frame construction dominating. Despite some agitation for brick and stone construction, for the permanency it would provide, the idea never went beyond the planning stage. The streets, too, remained packed dirt, with the problems of dust and mud in season discomfiting the Caribouites. Tice mentioned that the buildings lacked paint; this was not unusual—the rush of construction precluded such extras. The impression left with visitors varied with their experience on the mining frontier. Amos Bixby thought it well built, uncommonly so for a mining town; another examiner wrote, "A little town of log huts and cheap board houses."[16] The camp probably looked the best in the late 1870s, for by then paint brightened many of the business establishments and some of the homes and a few pine trees from the original stand remained to offer shade and pleasant greenery. Pictures taken in the 1880s show that by then most of these had been cut down. Despite the pride taken in their town by its residents, Easterners would have thought it crude, having few of the refinements they took for granted.

For those who rushed to Caribou, it beckoned with the seducing glitter of wealth, the silver bonanza at the end of the mining rainbow. Most of what became the mining West was developed under the same pretext. Promise, hope—call it what you will—kept the miners moving for over fifty years. Transitory, temporary certainly—what was the reason to stay when a new discovery elsewhere held out prospects of even greater wealth? Each new mining district lured miners from all the nearby regions and Caribou was no different. Proudly, a correspondent stated, "We have miners here from nearly every silver mining district in the world."[17] To keep the transitory populace there, however, proved to be another matter. As early as the winter of 1871–1872, a few families and a great many prospectors moved to more comfortable lower altitudes, some never to return. As long as Caribou remained young and promising, it could keep its people, but when it inevitably slipped, others would entice the miners away. Although never so burdened with the "drifting crowd" as larger camps, Caribou had its share, and as early as 1877 the Black Hills fever started to take its toll. Then came Leadville, followed by other booms, and the cycle had been completed within one decade, the older mining camp, Caribou, losing out to its younger rivals. Such was the fate of a mining community.

"Preaching Every Sunday, Shoo Fly Every Night"

The camp, the mines—the cold bare facts of history—existed by the grace of the people who spent a portion of their lives on a high, windswept valley and hill they chose to call Caribou. The men who toiled and aged in the dark recesses of the earth, the women who remained above, making a home for their families, and the children, who perhaps found the setting most enjoyable of all, have passed from the stage, but theirs is the saga of Caribou.

Life was never easy; the vacillation of mining insured that, and the environment reinforced it. Caribouites did the best they could to make living as pleasant and enjoyable as possible. Prosperous times eased the harshness and made the future seem almost unlimited. Good times prompted comments such as these in 1874: "Preaching every Sabbath day, and Shoo Fly every night;

no lawyers and few law suits, a sign of flush times which it is wished would extend to the valley towns," and "in fact all the lodes, and the town, and most of the young ladies are well worth having."[1]

Preaching had come early to Caribou and found the community receptive. The quiet, orderly nature of the people made a favorable impression on the two 1871 visitors already noted, Grace Greenwood and John Tice. The church found this characteristic a strong rock upon which to build. The first recorded minister, the Rev. Gay S. Allen, was appointed by the Methodist Church in 1871 to a circuit that included the Caribou, Ward, and James Creek congregations. The Presbyterians entered the scene a year later under the leadership of energetic Sheldon Jackson, and appointed a minister (the Rev. Lewis Hamilton) to serve the camp, Middle Boulder, and Boulder, with a recommendation of assistance from the Board of Home Missions to the local church. The Methodists, however, laid claim to Caribou and supplied ministers for most of the decade on a circuit rider basis, although as late as 1876 both denominations were active and jointly shared the schoolhouse for services. Even when no pastor was available, there were lay people prepared to conduct services, since this had been a common practice in Cornwall. A visitor to the community left this picture of a Sunday:

> I found the citizens were not wholly destitute of religious inter-
> est, consisting as they do of various nationalities. A kind and
> sympathetic feeling prevails, and though there is no resident
> minister there at present, yet I found a Sunday School in opera-
> tion, conducted by young men, all miners, where an interest-
> ing Bible class was being instructed. A service was held in a
> commodious school house, which was very well attended by all
> classes. A deep interest was expressed in the moral and religious
> welfare of the community, which speaks well for the citizens of
> Caribou.[2]

Not until 1877 did the camp obtain a resident minister and finally in 1880, a church. The Rev. John Stocks, the man most responsible for the latter, was born in England and served at Caribou for two years. Stocks picked the site, gathered the materials, and started construc-tion with the assistance of local businessmen and miners; his successor, the Rev. H. M. Law—apparently a carpenter as well as a preacher—completed it. Stocks, well liked by his congregation, utilized church suppers and sales, volunteer labor, and donations to raise the money and start the project. Though he was Methodist, the church he served was an interdenominational community one. The predominance of

The schoolhouse was braced for windier days than this one, which features scrubbed and well-dressed young scholars. Courtesy, Duane A. Smith

Cornish in the camp assured a good Methodist core, but others came as well. Writing some years later, Mrs. Mary Collins—who lived at Caribou—spoke of the way each member performed his or her share of the general work, from collecting funds for the minister's salary to janitoring. The church lacked an organ so one of the better singers "raised tunes" and the people joined in.[3]

There was nothing pretentious about the small frame building on the upper end of Idaho Street, but it had a marked impact on the community. It is easy, for instance, to picture the fine hand of the church behind the struggle to control saloons with a local licensing system. The matter came to a head in 1876, when a license slate won the town election. Many functions were served by the church. The building itself was utilized as a community and social center, the corporate institution a stabilizing influence and an important sign of civic growth. Finally, the church as a house of worship ministered to one aspect of the worshiper's life that no other could resolve; as one of the faithful inscribed on a Caribou tombstone, "The grass withereth, the tree fadeth. But the word of our God shall stand forever." The

Methodists predominated because of the prevailing convictions of the people and also because of their willingness to send ministers to the frontier. The Caribou church, typical of other frontier ministries, started with a circuit-riding preacher; then with the influx of permanent residents, especially women, it grew to hold a prominent place within the life of the community.

The activities of the church and public school complemented and occasionally paralleled each other. Both were community centers, with the latter used as the meeting house of the former until 1880. Both sought to educate youth, although in a different way, and each provided an acceptable outlet for social functions for young and old. Together they symbolized progress and permanence in the raw mining camp.

Located one block south of the Sherman House, the school had been built in 1874. The building, though not large, was comfortable and reflected the pride residents took in their school. The *Rocky Mountain News*, June 28, 1876, noted it was supplied with new wood furniture, blackboards, maps, globes, and "everything necessary for the instruction of the young." A local board supervised the institution and money came from the local school tax and the county. Pleas to delinquent taxpayers indicated that not everyone eagerly supported education, at least not in financial terms. Reports of L. S. Cornell, Boulder County superintendent of schools, illustrate, however, that the majority of Caribouites took an interest in education.

> It has been my privilege to visit this enterprising portion of our country, and among other things, to note the school interests. At Caribou I found the school closed for a day or two owing to the illness of the teacher Miss Isabella Backus. . . . Although they have had good teachers there, she is regarded as the best they have ever had. I hope she may be retained for years to come, and continue with the same marked success. The school records show an enrollment of 58 pupils. The enterprising School Board have taken great pains to furnish the school room with the best of seats and furniture.
>
> I had the pleasure of meeting all the School Board while there, and will say to their credit that they are wide awake to the school work. [1878]
>
> This school is one of the largest ungraded schools in the county, having a daily attendance of from 55 to 60 pupils, with 77 names on the roll . . . the citizens of this town are greatly inter-

ested in having a good school, and the present board tried to employ first-class teachers. [1879][4]

A schoolmarm did not long remain single, as in the case of Miss Backus, who succumbed to the courting of one of the "enterprising" school board members! Caribou was fortunate during the decade to have a number of fine teachers, both male and female. The term ran six months or longer with the basic subjects of reading, writing, and arithmetic being taught to the "willing" young scholars.

For a short time, Caribou had a private as well as public school. In 1877 a Miss Baumbaugh taught a private academy of about twenty pupils, using the public school building as headquarters. The term ended with a flourish, as students and teacher presented a program of songs and literature, followed by a free lunch furnished by the parents.[5] While there is no record of another term, for at least one year parents could choose to enroll their children in either a private or public institution. Obviously, the public school concept was much more popular and less costly. The means to support a tuition-paying endeavor did not exist.

The church and school were not the only institutions to promote social and intellectual activity. Occasionally, a lecture was presented, the topics varying from physiology to women's suffrage. The best-known speaker, Mrs. Lippincott, discussed the "Heroic in Common Life" and recited "Tom Flynn" on her visit to the camp in 1871. According to reports, she took hold of the miners with a "witty, eloquent" address, moving all to better purposes. How long the effect lasted may be questioned, but one of the lodes was promptly named the Grace Greenwood. Mrs. Lippincott remarked favorably on the intelligence of the miners; a later lecturer, speaking for women's suffrage, described her audience as composed of the "roughest and most ignorant Cornish miners."[6] Reactions may have differed, but in all cases the people turned out; the opportunity for this type of entertainment was too infrequent.

It should not be concluded from the foregoing statements that Caribou resembled a refined New England village. Though it might have been more sedate than the average mining community, it was still just that and no more. This was nineteenth-century frontier America, a time when the land was growing and Caribou with it; a season when the people measured themselves against what they accomplished when carving a settlement out of the virgin wilderness; an era as foreign to mid-twentieth-century America as it itself was to

Elizabethan England. Laboring long, the Caribouites still found life full of pleasures; they provided for and found their own enjoyment in and from life.

Of all the people who resided in a mining camp, children must have found its life most adventurous. Much of the hardship and privations would have gone unnoticed. Adventure could be unearthed in the community itself and also in its environs, where one found land for hunting, fishing, hiking, and picnicking in the summer, for sledding and skating in the winter, and family excursions year-round. The budding young capitalist who took a hike to gather raspberries and huckleberries found a ready market in town. The teenager matured rapidly; boys were expected to find employment after completing their education (eight years at most), or perhaps earlier if family circumstances demanded it. There was still time for recreation, such as the forty-five-foot swing that was erected in the fall of 1876. Practicing tricks to impress the town belles resulted in one young blade unexpectedly flying into a tree, emerging unscathed to find the seat of his pants ripped, much to the delight of his fellow acrobats.

For those who sought the strenuous life after a day's work in the mines, varied athletic activities were available. Occasional prizefights and wrestling matches tested local brawn and, no doubt, stimulated the betting urge of the spectators. Pitching quoits, a game similar to horseshoes, bowling, drilling contests (Caribou men entered both the double- and singlejack competitions at the county fairs), and roller skating provided further recreation. The last seized Caribou like a craze in the spring of 1877, when some of the young bloods organized a skating club. In spite of trouble in locating a place to skate, enthusiasm was not dimmed for this "healthful and moral amusement."[7]

A shortage of young women throughout the decade placed them in great demand, trying the ingenuity of the frustrated males. Dances, though extremely popular, were continually plagued by this vexing problem. As one reporter described it, "About fifteen ladies and thirty gentlemen composed the standing army; fifteen of the latter, not being wanted for actual services, formed the reserves, and were utilized as wall flowers."[8] This did not stop the locals. They danced on almost every possible occasion, particularly during the winter season when outside activities were curtailed. The two most popular spots were the Sherman House and Murphy's hall, above his meat market, where dances often lasted through the night, with a break for lunch about midnight.

At least one grand ball highlighted the community's Christmas celebration, the most active social season of the year. This being the slack mining period, the people had more time to relax and they took full advantage of the diversions. Starting with the Christmas festivities, the merriment continued through a New Year's Eve ball. The entire family joined in some activities, including carol singing, the community Christmas tree, and gift exchange. No child was overlooked, all receiving some kind of gift, and in prosperous times the large mining companies gave their workers a present, sometimes a turkey.[9]

The second camp-wide celebration honored Independence Day. It encompassed a series of events crowded into one day or, at most, the evening of July 3 and all day on the fourth. A patriotic speech was followed by toasts, some of which suited the occasion, others reflecting only an overindulgence in liquid refreshments. Describing the July 4, 1871, celebration, the *Boulder County News* listed the toasts offered, among which were found the following: "The ladies of Caribou—like any scarce article they are very dear," which prompted a half-hour speech on the subject. "Cleanliness is next to Godliness—with our close proximity to the snow capped peaks of the Rockies, and with streams of pure water in all directions, he would be a wretch indeed that would disregard this one of nature's best laws." Indeed! The main street, decorated with greens and flags, occasionally witnessed a small parade. Generally, a community picnic and band concert enlivened the afternoon (in 1872 a candy pull was the attraction), followed by a dance in the evening.[10]

On a more individual basis, picnics, small parties, and neighborly visits helped the time pass more pleasantly. A wedding was a special affair to be celebrated vigorously by all the newlyweds' friends. A charivari discomfited the groom until he paid the price.

After the ceremony a perfect battery of firecrackers was set off, and a rattling of tin pans kept up until the happy bridegroom appeared upon the scene and ordered a keg of lager beer, which seemed to satisfy the wants of the serenaders, who retired in good order.[11]

Most of the commercial entertainment offered was aimed at masculine tastes. Women had the church, quilting bees, dances, parties, and gossip to vary household routine; the men, single and married, had some of these and more. The saloon catered exclusively to masculine tastes. One of the oldest and best remembered establishments at Caribou was Pete Werley's, which started as Sears & Werley's billiard hall and saloon. Offering a chance to relax with one's friends in a congenial atmosphere or perhaps to gamble, partake in a game of billiards, or just pass the time of day, the saloon was a pillar of any camp's business district. Here the "boys" whiled away their leisure time, often inventing their own amusements, which included a mock trial to celebrate New Year's Day. Finding a willing victim, they organized themselves into a court and proceeded with "all the standard authors in English, Irish, Greek, Latin, Hebrew, Sanskrit, and Chinese" to attack the problem with a "brilliant array of legal talent." According to the later summation, "The peroration of the district attorney [Frank] Sears" reached unparalleled heights. "He piled up gems and gold, truth and beauty in radiant tiers. His speech was majestic crystal, brilliant in its noble bulk, and radiating from innumerable lines, facts, philosophy, poetry, ethics and religion." The jury, convinced by such eloquence, sentenced the defendant to treat the court. Another trial followed and another defendant, also found guilty, was ordered to pay costs, to be contained in "barrel staves, surrounded by hoops."[12] Thus the boys spent this day in the "realm of storms and snow."

Saturday was the climax of the week, when the outlying miners arrived in town during the late afternoon, and soon the "streets are as lively as a soldier's shirt—that is to say—provided the soldier has not changed for several months." Saloons were not the only attraction, for Caribou possessed a red-light district, where the demimonde, or "frail sister" (to appease Victorian sensibilities, she was not called a prostitute), carried on her trade.

Like the saloon, the red-light district was a weathervane of a camp's prosperity that received very little publicity in the newspapers or in any records, thus limiting the knowledge of its extent. Apparently, girls were present throughout the decade in varying numbers in the lower end of town. Caribou's chief claim to fame in this respect was called the "Shoo Fly." It flourished at least from 1872 to 1875, but two years later was being considered as a possible site for a roller skating rink. It was probably named after a well-known Central City establishment that had gained instant notoriety when it opened in 1870 with "pretty waiter girls," causing one irate citizen to write, "Anyone who has the occasion to pass the 'sink,' on any evening since it opened will bear witness that in shamelessness and size of the crowd, all other institutions are insignificant."[13] The Caribou Shoo Fly never reached such heights of infamy. It had girls, beer, and fights, but not, apparently, a "flaunty open exhibition of vice." The "frail sisters" also worked from individual houses or "cribs."

Despite a reluctance to admit that her "profession" existed and, along with it, de facto segregation in one end of the community, the prostitute provided a needed service in this male-dominated camp. The Victorian age observed a double standard with regard to women, placing the wife and mother on a pedestal, while at the same time tolerating and even encouraging brothels, a practice common not only to mining camps. Perhaps prostitution was more flagrant in the West, or this new land might have been less hypocritical; nevertheless, it received publicity throughout the country and helped shape the image of the frontier.

Another social outlet was available to Caribou men: the fraternal organization. Several were active at Caribou, including the Masons, Odd Fellows, Independent Order of Foresters, and reportedly a lodge of Redmen of the World; but no specific information remains on the last. The Foresters corralled some of the town's most prominent male citizens and became one of the most popular groups, followed closely by the Odd Fellows. Some joiners signed up with both. These organizations provided companionship with one's peers, lodge suppers, and meetings with grand ritual. They also held public dances and helped to sponsor community celebrations such as Independence Day. The Caribou encampment of the Independent Champions of the Red Cross, a temperance lodge open to both men and women, was active in mid-decade. What success it had is not recorded.

The married man whose family did not live at Caribou, and who did not care to join wholeheartedly in the bachelor activities was forced to create his own entertainment. The letters of one—Richard Harvey—remain, giving a glimpse of how this might be done. Newspapers, books (particularly ones on Cornwall), and magazines such as the *Harper's Weekly* helped pass many evenings, as did ordering catalogues from various business firms, scanning them, and occasionally purchasing some item. Harvey sold stereoscopic views to his neighbors as a side business and carried on a lively correspondence with friends and relatives. Generally, once a month he went home to see his family in Central.[14]

Harvey was Cornish and Cornishmen made a major contribution to life at Caribou. Nicknamed "Cousin Jennies and Jacks," they influenced life here far beyond their numbers. In the mines none were their peers, and they introduced into the industry the tribute system, the Cornish pump, and numerous mining practices. Seldom did the

Cousin Jacks join unions, although they did engage in strikes if they felt the situation warranted such a measure. No record remains, as mentioned, of a miners' union at Caribou. They lived in no special section of the community, but mixed freely with their neighbors. With the one exception of the Chinese, no racial violence erupted in this camp. The Cornish were distinctive in their customs and brogue, and were noted for their humor, wit, generosity, and independence, as well as their hard drinking, being especially fond of beer. They loved to celebrate and sing, traits that must have added up to some lively Saturday nights at Caribou.

Superstitious to the core, the Cornish left lasting legends in every place they worked. Little withered, dried-up creatures called "knackers" or "Tommy Knockers" lived in and roamed about the mines, the Cornish believed, bedeviling them. Hearing one forboded nothing good, although at times they warned miners of impending trouble. Woe be unto the poor miner who did not leave them a part of his lunch. Women in the mine meant bad luck; conversely, however, a rich strike was promised close to a spot in a tunnel where a woman made love to a miner. Rats in the mine were considered lucky, but a large gathering of birds seen on the way to work might cause the miner to return home. A sure way to scare away the ore in the underground workings was to whistle while at work. If a miner's candle went out three times on one shift, he had best hurry home because some other man was making love to his wife. All of these, of course, had variations. To protect themselves from such unseen terrors, the Cornish often recited the following short prayer:

> From ghoulies and ghosties and long-leggedy beasties,
> And from things that go bump in the night,
> The good Lord deliver us.

The Cornish were more than just fun-loving, superstitious people; they were solid citizens of the first rank. Accusations of illiteracy and weak wills where the opposite sex was concerned have been leveled against them, but A. K. Hamilton Jenkin, in his study of the Cornish in Cornwall, refutes this. He found them a people of high moral standards, with prostitution almost unknown in the mining areas of the country, and of a high level of intelligence. This latter fact was reflected at Caribou by the well-supported school and extremely high literacy rate. While prostitution flourished, it never reached the heights it did in other camps, thus reflecting possible Cornish influence. Although Jenkin noted in Cornwall that they had but a small interest in politics, in America they seem to have become involved in at least the local political scene with some zeal. Faithful religious people, predominantly Methodist in Cornwall, they carried this heritage with them to their new homes.[15]

The environment of the camp molded these people and they in turn molded it. What emerged was not a warmed-over Cornishman but an American, a product of the coming together of many nationalities and institutions that blended at Caribou and in a thousand communities like it.

Perhaps because of the Cornish liking for music, Caribou was famed for its band. The brass band, occasionally referred to as a silver cornet band, gave its first recorded performances at the Christmas and New Year's Eve balls in 1871, "a gay and enjoyable occasion for the lovers of merriment, music and dancing."[16] Continually popular for dances and parties, the musicians presented programs and enlivened serenades and weddings. Not content to stay at home, the band traveled to the surrounding communities giving concerts.

> The sensation of the week in town [Boulder] has been the presence of the Caribou Brass Band, on Tuesday and Wednesday. Many were the compliments bestowed, and much the pleasure given by their spirited playing. . . . The thanks of Boulder to the Caribou Band.[17]

For a town of its size, Caribou displayed a surprising interest in and support of its musical groups, for it also had a string band. These bands served as a cultural outlet and also as a social organization for their members. Practice sessions and concerts gave the musicians an opportunity to associate with friends of similar interests while relaxing away from work. While public programs might have been only incidental, they also offered a source of outside income. The camp stood to gain, as did the individuals who gave their time to play in a Caribou band.

More famous than the bands, though not regarded so highly, was the climate of the "elevated site, near the snowy range." Wind and snow impressed both visitor and resident, and even today one can appreciate the force of the winds when examining pictures of the community and noticing how many of the buildings were braced on the east side. Eben Smith, writing to David Moffat, warned, "Don't think of coming up without wiring me the day before so that I can let you know about the weather as some of the time a fellow cannot put his nose out doors on account of terrible winds."[18] Without much exaggeration the camp was nicknamed the place where the winds begin.

Mix the wind with a lot of snow and one has a fair idea of conditions that had to be contended with during the winter. It would snow for days and frequently weeks on end, isolating the camp in a white wilderness of great drifts that would "make a respectable showing at the north pole." It filtered into houses, through cracks and keyholes; drifted against cabins—a white dune nearly covering them; and at night piled against doors, forcing the occupants to shovel their way out in the morning. All in all, it could be a harrowing experience, especially for the uninitiated:

> I slept in the Sherman House, a good, substantial, well built
> house . . . but that night it seemed more like an old scow in
> a storm on Lake Michigan. I wanted to be down in the base-
> ment before the kitchen fire. How I envied the sleepers in one
> of those little cabins on the side hill, almost covered with drift-
> ing snow. It seemed like security and comfort compared with
> my position. Next morning I had a desire to see a mine. . . .
> I started, made ten steps and brought up in a snow drift any
> number of feet deep. Floundering out of this . . .[19]

The locals became adjusted to their climate; they had to, and eventually they were able to make light of it:

> Spring, always late in making its appearance in this elevated re-
> gion, is more than usually backward this year. . . . The snow in
> town is about five feet deep on the level; one house was seen last
> week coming through the snow that has not been seen before
> for three months, but the storm of last Friday shut it from sight,
> without leaving so much as the chimney for a monument to
> mark its final resting place.
>
> You can rest assured that none of the numerous claimants for
> the authorship "Beautiful Snow," will ever turn up in this dis-
> trict, unless they are hankering after a beautiful Caribou head.
>
> The almanac tells us it is the month of May, and, but for that
> timely adviser, we should certainly not know what season of the
> year it is. Snow, wind, and the tops of trees are amongst our
> instruments of entertainment. We believe summer is somewhere
> on the road, but whether its arrival will be celebrated this year
> or next, remains to be seen.[20]

While they might make light of a rugged environment, the people did not care to have it exaggerated at the expense of their community and

The pride of Caribou—its brass band. At one time it had thirteen members, six of them named Moyle, a good Cornish name. Courtesy, Duane A. Smith

mines. They frequently tried to set the record straight, but a reputation once acquired died hard.

Indeed, it was not so bad a winter as one might infer, because long spring-like spells often broke the snowy bonds. Spring was, and still is, a very pleasant time at Caribou, with an engulfing green mantle and wildflowers stirring gently in the dancing breeze. Summer waxed pleasantly warm in the daytime, complemented perfectly by a refreshing coolness at night. Vegetable gardens and flower beds blossomed during these months, adding variety to the menu and a dash of color to the camp, although the short growing season limited the diversity of plants that could be raised successfully. Nevertheless, even at its best, the weather remained subject to rapid changes that might produce snow flurries in any month.

Fall, a time of beauty with yellow aspens accentuating the green pines, could be a particularly dry and dangerous season with the surrounding countryside drying under the hot sun and relentless winds. The fall of 1879, in fact, was uncommonly dry and dusty. In spite of this, the people paid little or no particular attention to grass fires burning on nearby Arapaho Peak. Started apparently by careless campers, they burned for two weeks in September without endangering the community. On Sunday, the fourteenth, a smoky sky hovered over Caribou. That afternoon, a wind described as a perfect gale swept the fire up Caribou Hill where, despite the miners desperate efforts, it did severe damage. Checked, the fire abruptly turned north, raced over Idaho Hill, and blazed into town. Prepared as they were with their newly built water system, the Caribouites found themselves faced with a fire of unexpected magnitude.

> The wind blowing a fierce gale, high burning brands were driven over the upper portion of the town striking a point near the Sherman House and firing adjoining buildings. The East end of the place below the Sherman House was soon laid to ashes. . . . About twenty five dwellings were swept away, and nothing remains to show they were ever there, except the scattered ashes.
>
> The fire ran from dwelling to dwelling with such rapidity that women and children had to flee for their lives, many leaving every thing of value in their houses to be destroyed. Some went as far as Nederland, four miles below, not knowing where the fire would stop.
>
> The sight was a never-to-be-forgotten one. There were the angry flaming sunset skies, the rolling billows of smoke, and Caribou mountain with its hundreds of cords of wood burning on its top and sides.[21]

The water system more than proved its worth now, as the central portion of the camp was saved. The fight continued until late that evening, when the wind finally died, ending the immediate danger; the fire meanwhile continued to creep down the valley toward Nederland.

The damage was great; between forty and sixty houses and mine buildings were destroyed; fortunately, there was no loss of life. Many of the women and children fled to Caribou Park to wait out the holocaust; others rushed to Nederland.

September 15 dawned a gloomy, desolate day for Caribou. Smoke hung dismally over the valley as groups of tired, discouraged people returned to their homes to search the charred ruins for whatever might be salvaged. The prospect of chill, crisp fall nights out-of-doors made the task more dismaying for those who found their dwellings and belongings reduced to ashes. Somberly, they turned to rebuilding their town and homes.

Help was soon forthcoming, as Boulder, Denver, and Central rallied to the aid of the stricken town. Word of the fire spread quickly to these cities and donations of money, clothes, and provisions were rushed from Boulder and Central within a few days. Denver, a little slower, sent a committee to examine the damages that they estimated to be a total of $86,000. Relief eventually came from this source; but one Boulder paper grumbled that it was a lot of "useless rubbish" that "should have been sent to the rag mills."[22] Complaints aside, the neighboring communities had come magnanimously to Caribou's support. Still, the burden fell on the Caribouites themselves to rebuild and start again. In faraway Ouray, Colorado, editor and noted humorist Dave Day, in his *Solid Muldoon*, October 3, drew the following conclusion: "During the conflagration a woman carried a barrel of flour downstairs without bursting a hoop. In ordinary times it exhausts her to strike her husband twice with a poker."

This had not been Caribou's only fire during the decade, simply the most destructive. In 1871 a fire threatened the young camp and burned some nearby cabins. Periodically thereafter, small blazes flared, including one that destroyed Pierce and Murphy's meat market in 1874.[23] Such incidents as these had helped prompt construction of the water system that proved so invaluable in 1879. Without this and a wind that blew from the west against the advancing fire column, the main part of town probably could not have been saved.

Although the 1870s closed on a calamitous note, they had been generally prosperous. A sturdy, industrious population had established a community and maintained it; they had tamed a part of the passing frontier. Whether they would be able to bounce back after this last disaster would depend a great deal on the fortunes of their mines. The tenacity and the ability were present but there had to be some reason and need for the community's existence.

Hope Springs Eternal

The mines, as well as the town, suffered damage, but the former quickly rebounded; and Dun truthfully could be as confident of his mining property as he had written to his fellow stockholder Schley in November 1880. Reports circulating in Boulder and Denver papers painted a rosy picture, even allowing for local pride and prejudices. Under the direction of able Eben Smith the mine produced well, the main shaft now down nearly 900 feet, with various levels extending into the heart of the mountain. If 1880 was a good year, 1881 certainly equaled, if not surpassed it. That year, over $220,000 worth of ore was shipped through the Boulder express office, and chances seemed favorable that the Caribou Consolidated Company, now virtually in control of all the prominent mines on Caribou Hill, would continue to improve its record. New

Caribou Hill as seen from Caribou Park in the 1880s. Courtesy, Duane A. Smith

equipment, including improved rock drills, stimulated production and further testified to the confidence felt by the company.[1] Reflecting this improvement, the price of stock climbed back to $3.75 per share by July 1881.

To be sure, some trouble did occur. Water, that continuing impediment, prompted the installation of a new pump, the largest yet at Caribou, reportedly capable of raising water from 1,500 feet. If this indicated the potential extent of work, then the immediate future looked promising. In February 1882 the blacksmith shop burned, resulting in a loss of $1,000, but it was quickly rebuilt. Nothing stood in the way of the Caribou Consolidated.

Dun personally was having more trouble retaining his managerial team than with operating the mine. His brother Jim, because of his wife's illness, had to leave Boulder, and Dun did not have him to serve as his "eyes and ears." Arthur, too, now that he had been elected vice president, could no longer serve as Dun's attorney. Further dismemberment occurred when in July 1881 Eben Smith began to sever his relations with Dun and the Caribou, becoming only a general superintendent. George Teal assumed most of his old duties. For

A small operation with hoist, bucket, and shaft in the foreground. The roof of the Todd House is on the left of the hoist frame, and Caribou Hill sits in the background. Courtesy, Duane A. Smith

some months previously, Smith's letters had indicated that he was unhappy. He wanted a raise in salary, seemed to feel that Dun did not trust him (not the case at all), and in April had put his Caribou stock in Moffat's hands to sell.

Particularly in a letter the previous January, Dun had unburdened himself to Smith. He repeatedly reassured him that once he gave his confidence to anyone ("as I have to you"), it was not easily shaken. The salary would, he said, be advanced as soon as possible to five thousand per year, because Dun had faith in the property and reliance on Smith to "bring it out all right in the end." Only the gentlest of rebukes about not writing as often as Dun would have liked entered into this letter. It was to no avail, however, and in May Dun took over Smith's Caribou stock in trust. The next month he purchased it at the low market figure and wrote to Graham not to take unfair advantage of Smith but to keep the stock off the market. Although he was willing to sell it back to Smith, Dun was afraid he was in no position to take up the stock.[2] Smith's turning to other interests hurt the management, as well as the actual operation, and Dun lost a talented assistant. To make matters worse, he had purchased more stock, thus increasing his investment.

Despite the external prosperity, Dun was suffering some inward uneasiness. The price of stock stayed low and the company was in debt some $15,000 to $18,000, while the ore quality persistently ran at a lower grade than previously. Outwardly he remained optimistic, buying more stock for himself and his wife. Dun visited Colorado in the fall and felt that Teal was doing a good job and improving the situation; still, the company owed him personally $14,000 in advances.[3]

As the shaft went lower and mining was carried on at deeper levels, the cost of mining rose correspondingly, increasing water seepage being the principal villain. In 1880–1881 Dun could overlook such disconcerting facts, for despite his inner doubts, the mine continued to improve throughout the period. One still needed to weigh carefully the obvious changes occurring at Caribou.

Dun happily noted in January 1882 that the company had emerged completely from debt and even possessed a small balance in the treasury. This situation proved to be of depressingly short duration; in March he obligated his firm to make a temporary loan (the first installment being $8,000) to the Caribou Consolidated Mining Company.[4] That same month he wrote Teal requesting him to take charge of the Sherman, still controlled privately by Dun. Minckler had operated the mine until June 1881, when Dun ordered it closed.

The situation at Caribou receded from immediate importance when, in May, Dun suffered a personal tragedy with the death of his wife. For the remainder of the year Caribou matters were pushed into the background. Finally, in December, Dun wrote Jim, tersely commenting that prospects "are not very flattering." From all appearances, Caribou mining continued prosperous; as late as July, in a burst of enthusiasm, a Boulder paper called the mine the leading silver producer in northern Colorado.[5] Then came the first hint of trouble, and a strange quiet settled over the hill.

The miners stopped work for three days in August, demanding a definite payday on the fifteenth of each month and, according to reports, their wages, which had not been paid since June 1. Teal would not or could not bind himself to the first demand, and called the whole situation a misrepresentation of the truth. The company had paid the men each month for the past five years, and the superintendent blamed the agitation on the work of a few chronic grumblers, whom he refused to take back when the strike ended. Rumors of debts owed the men were stoutly denied by Teal.[6] Yet something must have gone wrong at Caribou to create the disturbance. This event would seem to support the conclusion that the men—at least some of them—did not have a great deal of faith in future prospects of the company, and wished to be paid regularly to insure against falling too far behind in their wages. Work continued, however, for reports of ore shipments appeared in the Boulder papers. The *Denver Tribune*, as late as September 30, commented that the mine again employed a full force of men and was being put in first-class order for work during the coming winter.

Suddenly on January 1, the mine was shut down, only to be started up a few days later, mining the richest ore to pay the most pressing debts; after several weeks it was stopped again, this time on orders from New York. An attempt to sell bonds in New York to raise money failed, to the consternation of that city's *Mining Record*, which confessed that it was more than a little puzzled over the sudden turn of events. The miners and other interested parties were just as mystified by the proceedings. The *Rocky Mountain News*, January 19, came to the conclusion it was "some sort of a freeze out game on the stockholders who don't happen to be inside the ring." Charges of stealing ore in their dinner buckets and clothing were leveled against some of the older employees, mostly Cornishmen. These men had been discharged before work resumed, but the new force did not have long to labor before they too were let out. Two of the men accused of "high grading" were tried in the district court, and found not guilty, lending some credence to the News's charge that it had heard the same story used before to justify dismissals and troubles within mines. The closure hit the camp hard. Unable to cash their time-checks with the company, a large number of miners reluctantly accepted seventy-five cents on the dollar offered by the county attorney, who also happened to be Dun's lawyer. Perhaps the malcontents indeed had a point in August. This turn of events created a great deal of ill will toward the firm and its operations.[7]

During this critical juncture, Dun's letters reveal little of what was happening in New York. In a letter to Eben Smith, now living in Ashcroft, Colorado, Dun painted a rather gloomy picture of a $30,000 debt and the failure to issue more company bonds. His friends and business acquaintances showed no desire to invest, seemingly willing to allow Dun to shoulder the burden alone. All factors considered, it appeared inevitable that the property would fall into the sheriff's hands. Dun still had faith ("the mine never looked better or more promising for a large yield"), hoping that he and Smith could buy the property if worse came to worst.[8] But within a year Dun's opinion toward Smith changed and on January 22, 1884, he stated, "I have lost all confidence in the man." The reason or reasons were not given, but the statement apparently was prompted by some scheme of Smith's concerning the Caribou.[9]

Unable to secure additional financial support, Dun's efforts were directed toward trying to relieve some of the pressure against the property. Neil D. McKenzie had brought a suit of attachment on the Caribou for failure to pay for ore sold the company. Dun wired $3,000 to satisfy this and the case was dismissed. Sometime earlier, in late December or January, Teal had been replaced; the new man had no better luck resolving the problems.

As principal stockholder and creditor of the corporation, Dun then moved to protect his interest by appointing Joseph R. Frith, manager of the Kansas City branch of R. G. Dun and Company, to act on his behalf in buying the property. Frith hurried to Boulder to gain control—for Dun—of all debts, in his own name, not Dun's. Dun, in turn, planned to form a syndicate with any stockholders who wanted to join with him in the purchase of the property after the assignment of claims. Dun advised, "get the claims at a discount—if so all the better—but you must get them anyway if you have to pay face and interest."[10] To work with Frith he retained a Boulder attorney, Sidney A. Giffin, who had written an enthusiastic letter to the *Mining Record* the previous May praising the Caribou's prospects. In a letter of February 7, Dun explained the changing situation to Giffin, who had originally been retained by the new superintendent, William Harris, and even offered him a chance to join the syndicate if he desired. The proposed syndicate never actually materialized.

Frith succeeded in securing damages worth approximately $60,000 and a judgment of the district court against the company for $61,275. As a result, the court set April 13 as the date for a sheriff's sale of the Caribou Mine and mill. The *Boulder County Herald*, reviewing the situation wrote:

> The Caribou mine is shut down for good and the company is heavily in debt. . . . The miners are unpaid and naturally want their wages. Dividends on stock are unknown. Everything has come to a standstill. . . . Things look exceedingly bad.[11]

Of the sum secured, some $32,000 was owed to R. G. Dun & Co. from loans, plus accrued interest. Eastern claims did not concern Dun at the moment. In fact, he did not know what they were, for Graham, who was sick, had been unable to discuss them with him. If he settled the claims in time, Dun planned to assign them to Frith to include in the suit.[12] On March 17 instructions were forwarded to Frith concerning the sale, Dun setting a ceiling price but hinting that if he could buy considerably more stock at the very low figure of "say five or ten cents a share," he would be willing to increase the bid. It was desirable, he believed, to get the property for as little over the claims total as possible.

On the day of the sale, Frith purchased the property for $62,645, sparing Dun the expense of going as high as the $150,000 he felt he might have to offer. Even though the deal was carried out in Frith's name as planned, the local papers noted openly that Dun was behind the move. At last in control of the mine, Dun realized that he had sunk more money into a venture that, at the moment, he apparently had no idea of working. In June he advised Frith that they had best not take the pumps out of the mine until the annual stockholders' meeting. "Why wait?" was another question, since the company was merely an empty shell. The next month the pumps were removed; the water flowed in at an estimated rate of fifty gallons per minute, flooding the lower levels of the mine.[13] The mill remained in operation to serve the needs of other mines in the region.

Dun, writing in March 1884, revealed the situation in which he found himself:

> I have an immense mining property on hand which has cost me
> (I am ashamed to say) some three hundred thousand dollars
> and I can't afford to have it lie idle. If I can't make a sale of the
> property, I'll have to work it, which will cost a considerable sum
> before any returns come back.[14]

Dun, to be sure, now had the mine free of debt, but only after further expenditures and, what was worse, needing still more to put the property back in operation. The ore reserves must have been virtually nonexistent or of extremely poor quality to warrant flooding the mine, for certainly operations would have continued had any hope existed. For the prospective operator, either Dun or some new buyer, the Caribou represented a decided gamble of known expenses against unknown ore.

Whether the resulting maneuvers that led to the sheriff's sale of the property were indeed a "freeze out" of all stockholders by Dun cannot be conclusively proven. Dun and Graham controlled the stock, Dun owning the largest percentage. What happened to Graham is unclear but he disappears from the story. Dun, while the mine was in the sheriff's hands, told Frith that if he were able to buy any considerable amount of stock for five or ten cents a share he could afford to bid even higher than the $150,000 previously mentioned. How much Dun may have purchased, if any, he never mentioned, although the company was allowed to continue its corporate existence after the sale, with Dun controlling its stock and serving as president. The company per se had no claim on the mine. The records of the court action brought by Frith indicate that he secured both large and small claims against the company. Unless the creditors sold their claims for less than face value, they lost no money.

Without evidence to the contrary, it must be concluded that Dun did not stage the whole affair to assume sole ownership. More likely it would appear to be another attempt to protect an investment already made, in a badly deteriorating situation. Further, the history of the mine after April 1883 does not support such an idea, because Dun hesitated to risk additional money to uncover new deposits. He was highly reluctant to send any more funds west.

The story of Dun and the Caribou for the rest of the eighties was the oft-repeated cycle of prospective buyers but no purchases—a dismal history for both the man and mining. An old face reappeared in the spring of 1884, when Dun gave Martin A. Smith a ninety-day option to sell the Caribou. Almost ten years ago Smith had sold Dun the No Name and Sherman to get him started, and now he thought he had a buyer for Dun, thereby bailing him out of the situation Smith had helped to create. Dun wanted $500,00 for the mine; much to his disappointment the sale failed to materialize.

Back in Colorado, there was continued suspicion of manipulation by certain stockholders, resulting in the closing of the mine. Dun was not being hurt, but water in the Caribou was rising steadily to the first level, prompting old-timers to estimate that it would take the profits of at least two years of successful working to put the mine in good condition. Men working over the dump was the only sign of activity.[15]

A year passed before Dun again mentioned Caribou. His remarriage and an extended trip to Europe obviously account for some of his inattentiveness to matters in Colorado. In November 1885, writing to Frith, he commented that the Caribou Company had collapsed and that Smith was sailing to London to try to negotiate a sale. That the company failed is understandable; that Dun still had his mine in Smith's hands indicates neither much effort nor interest on his own part. Again Smith's hopes disappeared and he apparently gave up trying, much to Dun's disgust. Having failed so far, Dun decided to open the mine at his own expense in the hope of attracting a buyer.

Supervision of his Boulder property was turned over to his brother-in-law, William James, who was sent out in November 1886 to start operations. The pumps chugged back into action, and within four months lessees went to work. Examining the mine in August 1887 Regis Chauvenet, principal of the State School of Mines, concluded that, considering the condition of the Caribou when the work resumed and the difficult pumping job required, its present condition was most flattering. Chauvenet expressed great confidence in its future. Although low-grade ore was taken to Philadelphia to be tested, no interested buyers came forth and Dun, in the late summer of 1888, ordered the closing of the mine. Lessees continued to work on the higher levels, but Dun's discouragement was evident: "I am so disappointed in not making a sale that I regard the whole property as a 'White Elephant.'"[16]

White elephant or not, Dun thought he had a buyer in 1889. Again Smith was involved, this time securing a lease preliminary to a sale. Dun now was willing to go further than previously to insure a sale: "Had I not been sick of the whole property I would have seen Smith in hell before I would have made so many concessions." As the year wore on, he began to suspect strongly that he would be unable to close the deal.[17] He was right.

While Dun was having his troubles with the Caribou, other mines continued to operate but were unable to take up the slack caused by the rapid decline of the "Queen." Indeed, for most of the mines, the 1880s were a dismal time.

The Native Silver Mining Company, reflecting the difficulties of the 1870s, proved incapable of sustained mining. Leased by Joseph Irwin, the Native Silver was worked in 1880 and 1881 with some success, despite water problems. Undisclosed labor trouble plagued Irwin in April of the former year, causing a temporary shutdown, before he brought in a new crew and resumed mining. Irwin also served as resident agent for the company. Even his experience and reputation as a miner could not keep the mine in full operation. Small leasing operations worked it sporadically the rest of the decade. In June 1883 R. G. Dun noted that John Graham was trying to buy Native Silver claims at a discount, to what effect he did not say. The water problem, higher mining costs combined with the decreasing ore value, and a declining silver price undoubtedly accounted for this lack of interest, although the company itself had never rebounded after the expensive failure of the mill. That colossal mistake sat idle the whole time.

The Spencer and No Name, two of Dun's properties, were operated only at intervals and then by lessees. The latter mine revived briefly in 1887–1889, when it was worked through the Caribou. The Sherman, which Dun kept separate from the merger, had no better success. It was over this mine and the Caribou that Minckler and he finally parted company.

Minckler, as mentioned, managed the property for the early part of the decade, though the mine was idle. Dun, who had repeated misgivings about the man, wondered, without evidence, if perhaps he was taking unreported ore from the mine. In February 1883 Minckler asked Dun for a lease on the property, which he refused, using the Caribou troubles as an excuse. Minckler pleaded that he was hard up, which prompted kindhearted Dun to enclose some money to help tide him over and finally agree to let him become superintendent of the Caribou operation under Frith. Having the "kindest" feelings toward the man, Dun nevertheless warned him he must "not get the big head and talk too much about affairs of the Company but act in a dignified way with all." Minckler must have been in financial straits, because Dun enclosed $50 to buy some decent clothes. In a letter to Frith, March 17, Dun commented without clarification that Minckler was not generally popular; he had a great many enemies, but Dun strongly felt that he was perfectly loyal. The three, however, quickly found themselves at odds, with Minckler being accused of stealing, selling Caribou property, and giving leases on the Sherman without authority. Dun's Boulder attorney, Giffin, supplied documents supporting the accusation. In May, Dun wrote Minckler, expressing disappointment about his failure to appreciate the position and warning him against further suspicious actions. By June, Dun and Frith had lost all confidence and the former felt that the "scoundrel" Minckler seemed to feel he was the injured man, but "I am glad we are rid of him and the gang around him." To Minckler he simply stated, "I wish to have nothing more to do with you, nor do I desire you to ever write me again. When any man abuses a confidence that I repose in him, I have nothing more to do with him."[18] Why Dun retained him so long remains a mystery, although it does indicate a predisposition toward leniency, at least with respect to Minckler. William Donald then took over the caretaking responsibilities of Dun's properties. Later in 1889 the Sherman also enjoyed a brief revival.

Gilbert Lehmer, who had done so well leasing the Seven Thirty and finally purchasing it in 1880, sold out the following year. Lehmer continued as superintendent, and the mine became one of the best at Caribou until 1883, when work suddenly ceased and nothing more was heard of it. The Idaho enjoyed spurts of activity from 1886–1890, remaining only a small producer. The Potosi, idle for years, reopened in 1889, only to be hindered by serious water seepage.

Typical of the promotional mining tried at Caribou during this period was the operation of the Northwestern Mine, located east of Caribou Hill. This property had been owned but scarcely developed by Dr. Mann in the 1870s, and sometime thereafter that ever-speculating Martin A. Smith had gotten his hands on it. In what seemed to be strictly a promotional campaign, an announcement was made early in 1885 that a vein thirty-two inches wide had been discovered. Smith placed Harmon Minckler in charge of operations, and glowing reports appeared in the Boulder papers until this terse comment in August, concerning the closing of the mine: "It had lifted hopes high."[19]

Only two mines lifted hopes high and kept them there for any period of time, the Belcher and the Poorman. The Belcher, which had done literally nothing the previous decade, was leased by one of the most active miners on the hill, Joseph Irwin, and his brother William, at least as early as 1884. Satisfied with what they uncovered, the brothers purchased it and then sold out in 1887 for a reported $100,000. The new owners and lessees continued mining the Belcher into the 1890s.[20]

The more important of the two, however, was the Poorman, which had never fulfilled the confidence Conger placed in it when he traded his Caribou interests for sole ownership of the Poorman. It had been worked in the 1870s without encouraging results. Neil McKenzie showed faith in it when he purchased the west half in 1876, mining thereafter with some profit. In the early 1880s he gained complete control of the mine and pushed work forward vigorously as a result. It became the big producer on Caribou Hill. A Caribou correspondent called the operation the neatest and best manner of working a mine he had ever seen.[21]

With the mine in such good condition and producing regularly, McKenzie sold it to the Poorman Mining Company controlled by Horace Tabor, Colorado's silver millionaire. Tabor, who purchased the mine for speculative investment rather than constructive mining, offered it for sale almost immediately through his Tabor Investment Company. While negotiations were being carried on, mining continued and McKenzie remained as manager. Tabor optimistically predicted that his recently organized Poorman Mining Company would, after June 15, 1888, pay dividends of $5,000 per month and double that after September. Such enthusiasm far overreached any previous record of the mine and was not matched by production during his control. McKenzie still owned a large share of the property, Tabor's role being more of a vendor than an owner.[22] Tabor had a well-known mining name, hence it is understandable that McKenzie took this route to sell his mine. Tabor's enthusiastic statements have to be weighed in this light, as well. Once again the big producer at Caribou was on the market and again the bait was cast, but no catches were made in the 1880s.

Mining at Caribou during this period went through alternate cycles of relative prosperity and stagnation; but the general trend was one of decline, with no repetition of the highs of the 1870s. The years 1880 to 1882 witnessed the comeback, started so well in 1879, continued by the reestablishment of the Caribou Mine. These were the best years; then came the rapid recession in 1883. For several years thereafter mining remained dormant. As the *Boulder County Herald*, August 27, 1885, described it:

> But alas! their strong life is drowning. We can see their dark
> smokestacks roaring high into the pure morning air, but showing
> no signs of labor. Their machinery is still. Water abides, where
> only labor is needed to make them well-to-do producers of silver.

A revival enhanced the outlook in the latter years of the eighties; there still existed a yearning for the return of the good old days, predicted by some to be just around the corner. By 1890 the situation was again deteriorating, as the brief spurt sputtered and died. The only major exception to this up-and-down cycle was the Poorman, which did increasingly better under skilled management.

This fluctuating, downward cycle prompted speculation as to why. The Caribouites themselves wrestled with the problem and seemed to skirt what must be the primary answer—the ore decreased in value as the workings went lower. These people must have understood this, but it was not easy to face the obvious, which confronted them with such serious implications for their camp. A team of government geologists, basing their conclusion upon personal examination and older records, wrote in 1957, "there was a definite, gradual decline in grade of ore as the mines became deeper."[23] This conclusion seems to be challenged, if not undermined, by the production of the Poorman and Belcher. However, it should be kept in mind that neither had been worked extensively in the 1870s, and were, therefore, still in the more miner-

The Nederland Mill was closed by the early 1890s. Courtesy, Duane A. Smith

alized zone. The same can be said for the Idaho and certainly for the brief flurries of some of the recently opened claims.

Alone, this decrease in value was not so sharp as to retard mining to such a degree. Together with other factors it explains what happened. Water, of course—the problem already described in some detail—was number one, the Caribou pumps being the key to its solution. "There is a bluish tint hanging over the mining interest of Caribou camp, owing to the shutting down of the great Caribou pumps, which will eventually close out every mine on that mountain below water mark."[24] Indeed, the mining cycle closely followed the working of this great mine, illustrating again its significance. Water made mining more expensive, and as the mines went deeper into the earth, other costs naturally rose. Logically then, the owner wanted to find not lower- but higher-grade ore to compensate for the increased overhead. This caught the miners in a squeeze of multiplying mining costs, pitted against lower-grade ore. An increase in ore quantity mined might have offset this disadvantage if a further factor had not intervened: the decline of the price of silver on the world market.

As Table 1 illustrates, the average price paid per fine ounce of silver in New York had been moving downward since the mid-seventies, reaching a low of $.93.6 in 1889. To maintain the level of mining in

TABLE 1—PRICE PER FINE OUNCE SILVER (NEW YORK) AVERAGE

1874	$1.27.2	1883	1.10.8	1892	.87.6
1875	1.23.8	1884	1.11.1	1893	.78.2
1876	1.14.9	1885	1.06.4	1894	.63.0
1877	1.19.4	1886	.99.8	1895	.65.28
1878	1.15.4	1887	.97.8	1896	.67.06
1879	1.12.0	1888	.94.0	1897	.59.79
1880	1.13.9	1889	.93.6	1898	.58.26
1881	1.12.8	1890	1.04.6	1899	.59.58
1882	1.13.8	1891	.98.8	1900	.61.33

The above prices taken from the *Miner's Register*, New York (1937), and the *Annual Report of the Director of the Mint*, Washington (1941).

the 1870s, the Caribou mines would have had to produce a larger amount of ore with a small profit margin. R. G. Dun, financially the best able to support such an endeavor, wrote in December 1889, "I have no doubt but that if 50,000 to 100,000 dollars were expended on the property . . . it would pay good dividends of one or two million dollars. Still I have not the money to spend."[25] Tabor had it on paper, but he was involved in many projects—his money dispersed—and he looked upon the Poorman for speculation, not for investment. As a result, mining as carried on at Caribou primarily involved small leasing operations with weak financial backing and little exploration and development beyond that which had already been done. By themselves, these efforts could not hope to regain or retain previous mining levels and in the end were fatally self-defeating, for they opened no rich veins to tempt new investment nor sustained large profits to encourage others to come and try.

Two rather contradictory trends dominated the Caribou mining scene. Optimism, as Dun expressed in his letter, was one; the other was the desire to sell a mine when it started to produce well. If the people had such faith and confidence in their properties, one wonders why so many persisted in selling when they could obtain a good price. Considering the known vicissitudes of mining, this course is understandable and epitomizes the general attitude of taking a profit and then pulling out. It also raises a fundamental question about the speculative nature of mine owners.

Optimism was nothing unusual; certainly at Caribou it had been around since the very beginning and had served a useful purpose. Now it sustained the people, promising so much, producing so little.

Caribou Mine looking east toward Nederland. Courtesy, Colorado Railroad Museum

Ben Franklin, speaking through Poor Richard, noted that he who lives on hope often dies of fasting. Such was happening here at Caribou. A few illustrations will suffice:

> . . . predict a future for Caribou far eclipsing its present and one freighted with possibilities for all who may have interest there. [1881]

> Throughout the section the silver veins are numerous, simply awaiting enterprise with capital to be made productive. [1882]

> That the question of conferring prosperity upon Caribou is but a matter of time is apparent to all thinking minds. [1885]

> You may form some idea about the future of Caribou from the number of mines being operated at this writing. The camp has a most healthy and prosperous appearance and is improving every week. [1889][26]

Such optimism helped sell a mine that at the moment happened to be doing well and boosted sagging spirits, without doing anything positive to reverse the trend.

Almost all the major mining operators remaining at Caribou took the opportunity to try to unload their property. Lehmer sold the Seven Thirty, as Irwin did the Belcher and McKenzie the Poorman, and as Dun would have sincerely liked to do with the Caribou. Some of them remained as managers or worked smaller claims, now having made their profit. In almost every case, the mine did not do so well under the new management, strongly indicating that these experienced mining men realized the hopelessness of the situation and got out at the most opportune moment. Poor Dun held on and was left with a very questionable, expensive property.

The big change during this decade involved leasing in place of large-scale operation. Men working for themselves or in small companies operated in every large mine sometime during these years. Statistically, the Caribou Mine still ranked as one of the deepest in the state, at over 1,000 feet, but in comparison Nevada had twenty mines over 2,000 feet. The district continued to maintain an extremely good safety record, with only one man reported killed in a mining accident.[27]

With the failure of the revival of the late eighties, it must have become obvious to many that Caribou would never return to its old preeminence, its days of real glory having passed. Perhaps not completely resigned to this development, but comprehending it nevertheless, a correspondent wrote to the *Boulder County Herald*, July 3, 1889, "There are few mines whose owners are working men that are standing idle, but the number owned by rich eastern capitalists are many." While comforting to blame it on Eastern ownership, albeit with a grain of truth, the growing reality of the situation could not be shunted aside.

"Times Ain't Quite as Lively"

The fire, which ended the 1870s on such a dismal note, damaged Caribou, but the camp retained the resiliency to rebound. Indeed, the community prospered early in the eighties as it had not done in recent years. Axiomatically, the same relationship between the mines and the camp's prosperity, which had charted the course of previous development, continued. In these last days before the start of the downward drift, Caribou enjoyed a moment of tranquility.

> It is one of the prettiest little mountain towns in Colorado. . . . Being the supply point for the district, it is well furnished with stores of all descriptions. The merchants are an enterprising, wide-awake class, fully cognizant of the great wealth that lies hidden in the hills surrounding them,

and imbued with confidence in its future. There are good
school accommodations. There is a church, and, in fact, all
the conveniences and luxuries that even a mountain town can
expect to enjoy.[1]

The business community remained stable in 1880, but changes
soon appeared as some of the old-timers left. In 1881 Herzinger and
Harter sold their grocery and general merchandise store to Joseph
Lloyd (there is some discrepancy in the spelling of his name; some
sources give it as Loyd), who had worked for them, and the next year
George Scott closed his business and went to the Black Hills. A count
of the commercial establishments in 1883 listed three saloons, one meat
market, a shoemaker, general store, grocer, barber, and toy store, this
last, something new for the town. Herzinger, Harter, and Scott had seen
the handwriting on the wall and pulled out before the slump hit, for
they had been around long enough to recognize the signs. By the end
of the decade only Lloyd and Joseph Murphy maintained businesses,
and William Donald kept the Sherman House open.[2] The decline had
been both marked and steady.

Other signs of the changing times also appeared. The Methodist
Church supported a resident pastor through 1883; after that, no
one, apparently, served solely this parish. Caribou again became
merely one stop on a mountain circuit. Mineral exhibitions no longer were sent abroad to proclaim the glory of Caribou silver. The
last major effort that was mentioned in the newspapers came in the
summer of 1882. Lack of financial backing, declining public support,
few good specimens—all caused Caribou to drop from the race to
promote itself.

The advent of the telephone was an event of major significance
for the town. A line was constructed between Caribou and Nederland
in 1881, and the Caribouites now found themselves availed of instant
communication with the outside world, helping to overcome somewhat
the lack of a doctor. Despite problems of line maintenance, Caribou, in
this respect, stood in the forefront of progress. Eight years previously
telegraph connections had been secured, so in the area of communica-
tions the camp was well supplied.

In many ways, life went on as usual in Caribou, though at a slack-
ening pace. After the disastrous fire, the threat of a recurrence was a
constant fear. A chimney fire managed to frighten some people nearly
"out of their wits" in November 1880, but the rest of the 1880s passed
without any serious repetition. One outbreak of diphtheria among

The Sherman House, once Caribou's finest, was showing its age by the 1890s. The New Jersey Mill looms in the background. Courtesy, Duane A. Smith

the children fortunately did not become an epidemic. Pupils appeared for the opening of each new school term in steadily declining numbers. The only schoolmarm who managed to attract the attention of a local reporter was one Miss Nichols, who, the boys said, "by all odds, is the prettiest school teacher ever seen here."[3] Samuel Merry, the town "tonsorial artist," also directed the young scholars for a while.

Mother Nature continued her wintry assaults. The winters of 1884–1885 and 1885–1886 were particularly hard ones, the local reporter for the *Boulder County Herald* noting on August 26, 1885, that a snow patch still existed within the city limits. Something new was added when, on November 7, 1882, Caribou was rocked by an earthquake; no serious damage was reported. Culturally, too, the camp was waning. Caribou retained its traditional community musical organization, at least into 1881, with a silver cornet band. Then nothing until five years later, when a string band and a so-called tree-toad band performed. The serious intent or actual musical talents of the latter group may be doubted. A dramatic club met in mid-decade to provide "mental improvement" and entertainment, only to run afoul of the Sunday school, which did not endorse its intentions. The two groups squabbled like small children over issues now lost, and even the local reporter failed to take note of the end result.[4]

Fewer students now studied at the school. The large number of adults must include a teacher and maybe the school board or parents. Courtesy, Colorado Railroad Museum

Temperance, a very necessary reform, according to certain residents, gained a foothold in 1886. Both its friends and its foes were surprised at the extent of its influence and amazed that it continued on into the next year. As "Brother Jonathan" himself, obviously a temperance man, wrote to a local paper, "Many thank God on bended knees for this timely help to the cause of temperance."[5] His warning, however, about a "few in Caribou who looked forward to the good old days" was well-taken. The 1888 business directory listed two saloons, double that of the previous year, so the question of lasting effects may be justifiably raised.

The mining and economic changes affecting Caribou help to explain the shifting of attitudes and loyalties on the political scene. The Republican party's dominance was challenged, if not overthrown. This can be most clearly shown in the presidential election returns: in 1880 the Republican candidate, James Garfield, polled seventy-two votes to his opponent's, Winfield Hancock's, thirty-two and the Greenback party's one; in 1884, despite a colorful campaign on the part of both parties, depressed Caribou could muster only forty-eight votes, twenty-five for the Republican James G. Blaine and twenty-three for Grover Cleveland; and finally in 1888, Benjamin Harrison defeated Cleveland's second-term bid fifty-three to thirty-eight. Although maintaining control, the Republicans' votes declined and their margin of victory narrowed. On the state level the same situation occurred in the race for governor, except in 1886 when the majority went to the victorious Democratic candidate, Alva Adams. In 1880 the Republican vote at Caribou went solidly down the line for the party nominees; but by 1890, of the thirteen state and local offices being contested, three went to Democrats and one was a tie vote.[6] Old ties were loosening and party alliances weakening, as a steadily worsening economic situation enveloped the community.

Locally, some hot contests evolved when such positions as constable and city council attracted qualified men from both parties. Such staunch citizens as William Donald, Neil McKenzie, Joseph Murphy, and Joseph Lloyd ran for local office; less frequently was a Caribouite nominated for county office.

No radicalism was apparent. Even though the choices offered by the major parties on the national and state scene offered no clear contrasts in political philosophy, third party movements attracted little or no attention. An air of unrest needed just a spark—in the form of a man or an issue—to explode it and completely rearrange the political pattern. On one of the more unusual issues on which they voted, local residents spoke overwhelmingly in favor of retaining the state capital at Denver. In this election (1881) Colorado voters were asked to choose between Denver as the capital or such towns as Colorado Springs (which received one Caribou vote), Canon City, Boulder, Niwot, and, of all places, Pike's Peak. Needless to say, Denver won by a statewide landslide.

These, then, were the outward manifestations of change at Caribou during these ten years. Internally, also, the situation was being transformed. Optimism, though soothing some of the troubles, could not produce a cure. As a reporter confessed, "It has been quite a number of weeks since the *Herald* had heard from the Caribou correspondent and we will have to say something . . . times ain't quite as lively as they might be, but we think before long we will see a change."[7]

In the year 1885 Colorado conducted a semi-decennial census. Caribou's population was 138, a sharp drop from the 549 of 1880, reflecting clearly what had happened to the camp. This year, the nadir of mining for the decade, might possibly have produced also the lowest total population. With the later improvement of the situation, the number increased slightly to 169 in the census of 1890.[8]

Some interesting changes are noticeable when this census is compared to that of 1880. The ratio of those employed in mining and related occupations to those providing services dropped roughly to two and a half to one. This change can be partially explained by smaller operations and by the fact that miners found it easier to move when hard times appeared than did businessmen, who had a greater investment. With the return of limited prosperity the ratio probably bounced up again. The median age of the residents from 16 through 50 jumped to approximately 35.25 years. Once again, if the entire population had been considered, the figure would have gone deceivingly lower, for there were forty-nine children 15 or younger and nine adults over 50. Although 57 percent of the total population had not as yet reached age 31, the people were getting older along with their town. Another statistic that illustrated the same trend was the percentage of citizens over 50, which tripled—from 3 to 9 percent in five years.[9] The younger people apparently found it easier to move.

The proportion of native- to foreign-born changed markedly. Ninety-eight, or 71 percent, had been born in the United States and 29 percent outside the country. Of the former, forty-four had first seen the light of day in Colorado, and of the ninety-eight, fifty-seven were first generation Americans, one or both parents having been born in a foreign country. The big change in the population of the camp was a startling decrease in the number of settlers from the British Isles. There were twenty-one, compared to 215 five years before, which indicates that the English-Cornish miners must have left in droves when mining declined. The 1880 census tends to confirm this possibility, for of the single men—the ones most likely to move first—54 percent came from England or English possessions. Of the remaining nineteen foreign-born, fifteen migrated from the British colonies, including ten from Prince Edward Island. Interesting is the fact that of the thirty-four men who listed their occupation as miner, exactly half were foreign-born, the rest American-born. Two men gave farming as their occupation, but neither was found in the section of the census describing county agricultural production. One man, at age 68, was probably retired; the other was one H. Minckler. If this were Harmon, one wonders why he should list this line of work rather than mining.

After the forty-four people who were born in Colorado, the number for any given state drops off sharply. Illinois with eleven and Missouri and Ohio follow with eight apiece, helping to boost the Midwest to approximately 45 percent of the total. Combining these with Colorado leaves only 10 percent for the rest of the United States.

Fire and declining fortunes started to take their toll by the mid-1880s. One of the few freshly painted buildings was the church at the upper end of Idaho Street. Courtesy, Duane A. Smith

The majority of the American miners came from the Midwest, led by four from Illinois and three from Missouri.

Men outnumbered women by twenty in 1885, although an interesting ratio appears when single men and women 15 years of age or older are compared. Those few fortunate women must have had the pick of the field, for they were outnumbered better than five to one. The four widows did not help measurably to relieve the shortage for only one was under 50. Divorce was slightly more common than in 1880, with two men and one woman listing it, compared to only two previously with four times as many people. Single men this time did not outnumber their married brethren, for they split evenly at twenty-seven each.

The twenty-one families with both mother and father present had an average of 2.4 children living at home. No marriages had been performed at Caribou during the past year, at least not among those still residing there, but five babies had been born. The median age of married couples, 38.5, again ranked above that of the rest of the community. Twenty-three young scholars attended the local school. Their age span ranged from 4 to 18. The boys outnumbered the girls, and the majority of the students had reached 10 years of age. No one admitted to illiteracy.

The professional-business class, on a percentage basis, was larger in 1885 than it had been at the last census. In the professional group were found a school teacher, an engineer, and a music teacher. The businessmen included a hotel keeper, merchant, tailor, butcher, shoe-maker, and three women who listed their occupations as milliner, dressmaker, and boardinghouse operator. There might have been two more merchants at Caribou that year, for the *Colorado State Business Directory* (1885) lists T. G. Trevarton as a grocer and P. J. Wesley, saloon owner. Trevarton appears in the census but did not give any occupation. Wesley does not appear, and who Wesley was (no P. J. *Werley* was listed either) is a mystery.

The thirty-four occupied dwellings held an average of just slightly over four occupants per house. This was an all-white community, no colored people being reported.

Age was starting to show among the men who had long been active at Caribou. William Donald was fifty-four and operated the Sherman House, probably doing a little mining on the side. William Todd, now forty-two, had changed his occupation to teamster from saloon keeper; Joseph Murphy at thirty-nine still operated his meat market. Only these authentic old-timers were left. Joseph Lloyd, forty-seven years old, had come later. Neil McKenzie, who first arrived in the 1870s, was forty-one; his brother Collin, thirty-eight. Leo Donnelly at 54, and Joseph and William Irwin, aged 43 and 33, respectively, were other experienced miners who had been around the camp for a number of years. Perhaps these people stayed because they had more faith or could still make a respectable living. Possibly they felt too old to make another move or had simply become too attached to migrate to new fields. Whatever their reasons, around them swirled the last vestiges of glory that once had been Caribou's.

According to one story circulating at that time, a Swede from Minnesota came to Caribou to work in the mines but soon quit, muttering that the region had nine months of winter and three months of late fall. Many shared that attitude but stayed while prosperity smiled, only to leave when the good times waned. The fading community could not hold them; but the faithful remained, and life went on with certain modifications. News of the camp appeared less frequently in the local columns; a void in information was thereby produced, which continued until the final demise of the camp. Fortunately, interviews exist, given by a few of the residents years afterward, that help to fill this gap; they were valuable for conjuring a picture of the times, even if not always so accurate as the historian might wish. Their story follows.

As the troubles of the 1880s descended on them, Caribou's residents drew closer together. Helping each other as much as they could, they shared what they had, often leaving fresh meat or other food at the home of a neighbor in need. Hunting and fishing were important sources of food; nearby Caribou Park provided plenty of trout. The large number of goats roaming the area during the early days had given that name to a nearby hill; eventually, they fell victim to the hunters' rifles. One goat even stalked into the home of William Todd, butting his wife while she was working in the kitchen. Youngsters contributed by gathering wild berries, mushrooms, and plants for the table. Many families kept a cow and some chickens to reduce expenses. The safety of the cattle was sometimes threatened by bears, especially near the local slaughter pen.[10]

The Caribouites' diet was "plain but plentiful." Women baked several times a week; the children were always eager to "help" for the reward of a few goodies. Cakes were a special treat, and one with a rich sugar icing denoted a special occasion. For a community celebration such as Christmas, the ladies would go all out to provide a bountiful repast. Two delightful women, daughters of William Todd, reminisced one afternoon with the author, recalling their happy Caribou childhood of the 1880s and 1890s.[11] With relish they savored the recollection of their mother's fruitcakes, which she would make in the fall. The whole family participated, the girls cleaning raisins. Stored until Christmas, these cakes were brought out to enhance the festivities, neighbors eagerly dropping in to enjoy a taste of this delicacy and join in the season's conviviality. Ice cream, a treat as well, was made only when snow was available—hardly a drawback some years.

Christmas parties were still held at the church. Each resident brought some dish to contribute to the potluck supper. There were always one or two trees hung with popcorn and cranberry strings and loaded with presents. Recitations or a play constituted the program, after which came the moment the youngsters had been anticipating— the arrival of Santa Claus, who called out the names on the gifts. Each child received one or more; occasionally, ill feelings were engendered when some got more than others. Another Caribouite, Heimer Murphy, daughter of the meat market owner, remembered the season as one of great rejoicing and deep religious feeling. Carols rang—the Cornish,

Light snow dots Caribou in this early 1880s scene. The 1879 fire destroyed the lower end of the camp. Courtesy, Duane A. Smith

particularly, delighting in singing the old favorites—and she praised "the big hearted hard rock" miners who spared no expense to make Christmas a happy time for everyone.[12]

The Todds, as did others, adjusted to the changing times. Shopping became more difficult as the number of local merchants declined. Their mother would go to Boulder in the spring for a week's visiting and marketing to augment Caribou's selection. On one trip the Todd brothers and sisters, who had never seen fruit displayed outside a store, thought they had found a free bonanza and dived in. Their embarrassed mother quickly separated fruit and children. In the fall, food was stored in anticipation of the long winter's sporadic transportation, which meant fewer varieties of meats, vegetables, and produce. The Todds stored their vegetables in the basement and the staple goods upstairs. Purchases were made in sizable quantities—jelly by the large crock and butter in tubs—but storage was no problem, as both ladies remarked, because one did not need a refrigerator at Caribou.

Clothes, simple and utilitarian, generally showed signs of patching and mending, as the people made the best of what they had. In the winter the idea was to keep as warm as possible; heavy woolen clothing took preference over all else. Gunny sacks strapped onto boots or overshoes made it easier to walk on the snow and ice. During the short winter days, the men went to work and returned home in the dark, not an easy task on those days when the wind-whipped snow cut visibility to near zero.

With no doctor available, the residents improvised as their skills allowed, William Todd on occasion treating gunshot wounds, setting bones, and helping to pull teeth. In serious cases a doctor was called. The trip from Boulder required the better part of a day, hence the need for local care of the injured and sick. One Boulder doctor's visits were fondly remembered, because he gave each child a piece of licorice. In the absence of a regular minister at Caribou, religious responsibilities fell to the constituents; someone always responded to take charge of the Sunday school class.

School occupied a large share of the children's time. Apparently, the terms varied from three months to nine, depending on the year. All eight grades were crowded into one room (double seats per desk), and the young children stayed as long as the older ones. Learning the ABCs, arithmetic, history, oral recitations, spell-downs, and copy books (which imparted such homilies as, "A good name is rather to be chosen than Great Riches") filled most of the days. School programs, with proud parents in attendance, were popular affairs.

For the children, life changed little from the previous decade, except, perhaps, insofar as the scarcity of money affected the availability of store-purchased toys. Sledding and sleigh rides were sources of great delight when weather permitted; most of the winter, however was spent indoors, involved in such activities as visiting, reading, games, and housework. The Todd girls had lamps to clean and fill, silver to polish, and mending to do. Books, always scarce, were often read aloud in the evenings so the entire family could share them. In the summer the outdoors held most of the attractions—fishing, picnics, homemade swings, marbles, and other games. Some youngsters became adept at amateur prospecting and spent their time looking for "floats" and ore samples. Another "prospecting" area was the main street's wooden sidewalks, a profitable venture for youths who crawled under them to recover a variety of items dropped by passers-by. Both boys and girls learned how to handle and carry firearms, the former using them for hunting. Valentine's Day was one occasion reserved for the young; comic valentines from unknown "admirers" often left the recipient in a quandary. Some of the verses were none too genteel, and sometimes caused bruised feelings for a short time. All in all, it was a happy childhood, even allowing for the romantic glow—imparted by passing years—that colors the memories of those who recall it.

Reminiscing with obvious delight about their experiences, the Todd sisters described how their home was heated by a potbellied woodstove, which necessitated their dressing by the warm stovepipe on the second floor on cold mornings. Extremely cautious with fire, their mother allowed only candles in the girls' room; coal oil lamps were reserved for the downstairs. On one mischievous occasion, they took a can of corn from the cellar without permission. Nearly being discovered, they quickly hid it in the stove. That evening the relaxing family was sharply shaken when the heated can exploded and blew the stove doors off their hinges. Two little girls were mighty relieved that it was nothing worse. Their remorse did not prevent a spanking. Calmer evenings were spent reading the paper or playing house or school.

During the summer, family or community picnics were popular, one of which was ruined by a blizzard on July 4. Sunday was a good day for a family walk or for pursuing the custom of visiting the cemetery to pay respects to the departed. The highlight of many a summer day was the arrival of a Jewish peddler, who brought his cart of dry goods and, for the children, a sampling of the world beyond Caribou. Even more exciting was the appearance of a traveling theatrical company, which played to young and old, who sat on boards placed across barrels in the room above Murphy's meat market. This makeshift theater provided entertainment as fascinating to the youngsters as any of the fancier theaters in the larger towns.

In these last years before adulthood robbed life of some of its joys, growing up in a mining camp was fun, mixed with a certain amount of danger. Sledding was thrilling, doubly so when one could coast all the way down to old Cardinal; one boy, however, lost control of his sled and was killed when he smashed into a house. Another group of boys, who should have known better, exploded a giant powder cap, which resulted in the loss of one eye and several cuts. Parents were also concerned about the continual danger of their children becoming lost in the mountains or confused during a storm and wandering off. Surviving such hazards and childhood illnesses, most Caribou youngsters lived to become teenagers and take on adult responsibilities.

Girls went to work early in boardinghouses or at similar jobs to augment the family income. Boys were introduced to mining by way of the easier chores of ore sorting or other surface tasks. Hours were long and pay small, but few complained—it was a part of life.

Entertainment and amusement for adults and children were primarily self-made. Hiking, horseback riding, and picnics retained their popularity. In the 1880s baseball grabbed a share of the spotlight; games were played on a diamond built in Caribou Park. Dances, generally held above Murphy's, often lasted into the early morning hours, three quadrilles or square dances being followed by a waltz, polka, or some other round dance. At midnight couples would stop for a lunch or dinner and then head back to the dance floor.

Men might spend at least part of an evening at the local saloon or general store, passing a congenial hour with their cronies and a pipe of tobacco. Gathered around a big stove, they talked about prospects and past events, using the stone- and gravel-filled container around the stove's base as a handy spittoon. Women called on one another, took care of the home and children, and held quilting bees. A warm quilt was a blessing on Caribou's cold winter nights. Weddings were big social events, although probably more so for the ladies than the men. Some adults also enjoyed tobogganing, skiing, and sledding as much as the children. Music continued to play an important role in the life of the community; many families had a piano, some even had home organs, and several music teachers were available to introduce reluctant pupils to the mysteries of music.

The shortage of women handicapped some social gatherings and prompted a reporter for the *Boulder County Herald*, on October 13, 1886, to write, "John McKenzie gave a 'stag' sociable at his cabin Saturday night and about twenty of the 'stags' congregated there and away they went—dancing, singing, preaching, roaring, shouting, and everything in the line of 'stags' of about 20 years old." On occasion, somebody might become rambunctious but generally quiet reigned.

The Todd sisters described it as a "good clean town," concluding that the people thought a great deal of each other. Isaac Beardsley, a Methodist minister in several mining communities (though not in Caribou), recorded in his *Echoes from Peak and Plain* that one Sunday morning an ordinary laborer of Caribou handed the local minister fifty-three dollars for missions.[13] Considering the wages of the period, this was a considerable sum.

Despite the inconveniences and hardships, the people seemed satisfied with what they had and with their jobs. Life was not easy; it involved long hours of physical labor and danger to make a living. They lived in dread of the mine whistle, signifying an accident somewhere in the depths of the workings. Yet this life had its rewards; Caribou to these people bespoke something alive and meaningful. They asked no more.

Waning Hopes

Caribou, twenty years old in 1890, had begun to show her age. Once shielded from outside economic pressures by the silver production of the mines, the district could no longer count on such protection. The rising cost of mining, the declining price of silver, and the decreasing value of local ore had seriously crippled production. A miracle was needed to restore prosperity; hope stubbornly persisted and complete abandonment was held at bay.

Money to promote mining and exploration seemed the most promising means for resurgence. Once again an outside source was necessary and two mines held the best potential, the Poorman and the Caribou. R. G. Dun offered his property for sale at what he considered the right price; Horace Tabor had more success with the Poorman. Trying to sell in 1890, Tabor only fitfully worked the property—a situation that hurt the entire camp because this mine was now the major producer. The next year his efforts were rewarded when he found a buyer, a group of Scottish investors.

The new owners, incorporating themselves as the Poorman Silver Mines (of Colorado) Limited, paid 105,000 pounds. Although the price reported in the press was $650,000, the actual amount was nearer to $510,300. The company's expansive objectives included operation of the Poorman, exploration and development of all property belonging to them, purchase of mines and land, construction of new buildings, and acquisition of the newest machinery. Leonard Gow, a Glasgow shipowner and merchant, headed the group, which contained basically Glasgow men. The company wisely retained Neil McKenzie as superintendent.[1]

That Tabor did not buy the mine, acting only as the vendor between McKenzie and the Scotsmen, was shown by the fact that McKenzie received 87,700 ordinary shares (value one pound each) in the new company, out of the 91,000 paid to the Tabor Investment Company. In comparison, Gow had only 1,000 ordinary and 1,000 deferred shares of stock. As late as 1906 McKenzie still retained 67,000 out of 103,000 ordinary shares issued. Even with this amount, he did not control the company because the ordinary shareholders held no voting power or voice in the management, which remained in Scotland. The original stockholders were a diverse group from Scotland and England, including merchants, accountants, engineers, a music teacher, and an ironmonger, as well as those who simply listed themselves as "gentlemen."[2]

McKenzie moved rapidly to drain the flooded mine, and it appeared that Caribou verged upon the injection of another economic stimulant, courtesy of foreign investors. The Scotch, though, were not the Dutch of the 1870s. They worked their property conservatively under the guidance of McKenzie, and in 1892 the mine produced over $150,000 worth of silver.[3] This did not prove to be enough to cope with the mining problems that were faced, and by the next year all the effort was going toward working enough ore to pay the expenses of pumping out the water.

The Poorman Silver Mines Limited retained nominal control and operation of the property until 1908, when the company dissolved itself. The mine ownership then reverted to Neil McKenzie, to whom it had belonged, in reality, for years. In a telling letter to the Registry of Joint Stock Companies in February 1908, the last secretary of the firm wrote:

The property has not been worked for many years, and it was some years ago taken possession by parties in America who had advanced monies on account of the property. The Directors would have put the company into liquidation a considerable time ago, but they hoped that the price of silver would improve, and that probably some arrangement would be possible with the parties now in possession of the property for its being restarted, or that it might be sold on terms that would admit some reversion to the shareholders.

He went on to say that the recent fall of the price of silver and difficulties surrounding the mine made this impossible. No assets were left "on this side," and none of the shareholders bothered to attend a meeting called to liquidate the company; on which note the harassed secretary concluded, "I find it quite impossible to obtain the necessary quorum to pass the resolution for voluntary liquidation."[4]

Thus dissolved the last major attempt to revive Caribou's rapidly waning fortunes through foreign economic transfusion. In better times the Scottish owners might have been able to make their speculation profitable; but their total capital of 130,000 pounds did not leave them a large surplus with which to work, after subtracting the purchase price and the cost of resumed operation. They bought the best remaining mine on the hill and still could not maintain operation after one fairly successful year—a poor omen for Caribou.

Dun, meanwhile, worked with somewhat restrained vigor to dispose of his Caribou mine, mill, and other properties. As 1889 drew to a close, he had written, "[I] still have great faith in the value of this group of mines, but the property being so far away from me and with no practical experience in mining am desirous of selling it." The year 1890 proved disappointing, when suddenly prospects brightened after the end of the year. In a January letter to his Boulder attorney, Sidney Giffin, Dun optimistically reported that a conditional sale had been made to a Boston group. Within a month the prospect vanished, as the parties could not agree on unspecified conditions. A second prospect appeared, this time in England. Writing to Thomas A. Richardson, manager of R. G. Dun & Company in London, Dun explained that he had given an option on all his Colorado mining property to George Purbeck, an advertising man and broker of New York City, who thought he could sell it in Great Britain. "I have great faith in the amount of silver that could be taken out," he wrote, continuing that large dividends might result from a capitalization of "say two million," but, "No one can see beyond the end of a pick in any mine."[5] Dun admitted he could no longer work the mine and wished Richardson to help Purbeck or his agent, George Tewksburry, as much as possible.

By November Purbeck had returned from London, certain that a sale would be forthcoming. One obstacle stood in the way—the condition of the mine. Purbeck wanted the pumping resumed and the property drained, Dun underwriting the cost, which he promised to repay whether or not a sale was consummated. Dun agreed and Purbeck hurried to Boulder to reopen and reactivate the Caribou.

While all this had been transpiring, Caribouites lived on hope and rumor. A year before, on December 17, 1890, the *Boulder Herald* concluded that, "Every week for the past six months reports have circulated that the Caribou mine will be started up soon, but from present indications there will be no effort made in this direction." Not convinced that the property deserved such a fate, the same newspaper pointed its finger at Dun, blaming him for not putting up sufficient capital. Then came the reopening, and while reacting cautiously at first because of the known expense involved, the editor soon anticipated full operation.[6]

Undoubtedly, no one awaited the event more eagerly than Dun, for again he was spending money attempting to recoup past investments. By April 1892, with the water pumped out below the 740-foot level, another $12,000 had been expended. Giffin now informed Dun that one McKenzie—probably Neil—had made an offer on the property, which at the moment obviously could not be considered. Dun wrote back that he had doubts that the English sale would materialize and wanted Giffin to sound out McKenzie. Confidentially, he told his lawyer, if he had not been "tangled up with this English party," he might have entertained McKenzie's offer. Unfortunately for him, his doubts again proved well-founded, and McKenzie removed himself from further consideration. What he had offered and why the sudden change of heart is not known. The headline of the Camera cried, "Caribou Murdered," when Dun ordered the pumps stopped.

> Poor old Caribou! Boulder's peerless Silver Queen, long suffering and faithful, is again smitten to earth just as she was about to rise once more. The gold bugs have scored another triumph and yet we are asked to continue to submit in silence.[7]

The local paper estimated it had cost more than $30,000 to take the water out; Dun himself admitted he lost over $40,000 when Purbeck defaulted on his promise. The costly promotion did little to advance

mining. Apparently, English mining experts had visited Caribou in
the summer and their unfavorable recommendation weighed heavily
in the decision to terminate negotiations. The ore mined, and subsequently milled at Nederland, failed to realize enough to reimburse
Dun.

Work came to a dead halt. Dun, in his late sixties, wished only to
sell. Finding buyers was another matter during the panic and depression of 1893–1895, and Dun's letters contain only references to property taxes. In 1896 he thought he was on the threshold of completing
a deal for the sale of the Nederland Mill but again was destined for
disappointment. In February 1897 he thanked Giffin for obtaining a
reduction in taxes, commenting that, as the property "stands idle and
going to rack," he hoped Giffin would continue to hammer down the
taxes.[8] Dun and the Caribou had come a devious, discouraging road
together since the 1870s.

Hopes were not completely dashed in the district; there were
those optimistic people who felt the corner had been turned in 1899,
when a rumor circulated concerning the pending Caribou-Poorman
consolidation. Nothing came of it. A few lessees worked spasmodically
on the dump, shipping the ore that earlier had been considered too
low grade to consider. The "Queen" had fallen a long way. In New
York, Dun, seriously ill, could no longer be called upon to provide the
financial support for the mines and camp. He died in November 1900,
and the Caribou property passed into his estate.

As mentioned in a preceding chapter, Dun admitted in 1884 that
he had invested $300,000 in his Caribou enterprise. Twice in the suc-
ceeding years he reopened the mine, which entailed increasing expense.
Add to this the cost of taxes, which, after Giffin's 1897 reduction,
amounted to $554 per year; the expense of caretakers at the mine and
mill (the evidence is not clear that Dun hired any, but a businessman
of his caliber certainly would have protected his property); and such
financially minor items as Giffin's retainer; and it is obvious that the
total investment must have gone over $400,000, perhaps nearly half
a million. No record remains of the profits Dun received from actual
mining.

Dun had been the major benefactor of Caribou mining for a long
time. He stood alone in this respect, and his death closed a chapter of
the story. In retrospect, Dun's misfortunes illustrate what frequently
happened, albeit on a smaller scale, to Eastern money sent in search
of elusive silver or golden wealth of Western mines. Continued investment followed the original purchase price into an increasingly

expensive property. In the end, with neither profitable ore nor a buyer in sight, operation came to a halt, to the dismay of the owner and local employees.

Dun's contribution involved more than just his adventures with the Caribou and other mines. The salaries he paid, the leases he gave, the mill he operated—all stimulated the camp and the district's economy. Dun's name lent prestige to Caribou, although he himself worried about a potential misuse that would reflect adversely on his firm. For Dun, a rather hesitant initial investment turned out to be a continuous worry and even a financial burden. Not until near the end did he really seem to lose heart; perhaps this conservative, well-established, Eastern businessman had caught a case of mining fever. In spite of some rather shady manipulations around him, Dun remained above them and maintained a respected mining-business reputation. Regardless of some sour comments in the local newspapers, Dun did a great deal more to benefit Caribou than he ever did to damage it.

Caribou's general mining conditions reflected the individual ones of the Poorman and Caribou mines. Water, which had been pumped out by the system installed in the Caribou, flooded every mine, forcing smaller properties to remain idle. The year 1890 slipped dismally away, its plight summarized by the terse statement, "It certainly is high time for Caribou to make a start if she expects to class with the mining and productive camps of the county. Up to date little mining has been carried on up in the Cloud City, only talk that terminated in wind and gas."[9] A slight revival by some of the smaller mines in 1891 rejuvenated hope; however, only a few men found work in each. Conditions improved somewhat the next year, only to collapse in the panic of 1893. The one new trend worth mentioning was the shift to gold mining in some of the district's marginal mines, but not in those on Caribou Hill.

Typical of what transpired was the Potosi Mine, which went through a flurry of activity in late 1890 and into 1891, but suspended operation when an apparent stock promotion failed. Exploration was not being undertaken in the mines. The *Boulder News*, October 19, 1893, carried a Caribou item portraying how far the deterioration had gone: that relic of past expectations, the New Jersey Mill, was refitted for use in the treatment of ore from the Caribou dump.

Deterrents to Caribou's revival consisted of internal matters, including the increasing cost of operation and the decreasing grade of ore, and external matters, which centered on the depreciating price of silver and the silver versus gold struggle in international finance. So pressing was the crisis that unless something could be done, Caribou would, in the words of the local press, sink into oblivion and soon be ancient history.[10]

The issue, for the Caribouite, held immediate and personal significance. Free silver might have been ranked among "the heresies with free love" in the Eastern view, but it provided some solace to the man out of work or faced with a small reward in return for his labor. It might seem oversimplistic to demand a rise in the price of an ounce of silver to ease the nation's economic woes, but the rationale of a mine owner or miner was guided by a different perspective. No one could deny that the price of silver had plummeted from $1.27 in 1874 to $.63 in 1894. Why this ensued and what to do about it aroused an impassioned debate, first in the West, then carried by Western congressmen to Washington, and finally spread throughout the country. By the summer of 1896 Bryan's ringing statement of crucifying mankind on a cross of gold struck a responsive chord in the depressed, disillusioned, and rapidly diminishing Caribou residents.

The origin of the crisis went back to 1873, when Caribou, then enjoying youth and prosperity, watched Breed sell his mine for $3,000,000, ignoring President Grant's signing of a bill to abolish the coinage of the silver dollar. To be sure, the world price of silver was better than that offered by the United States treasury, and the official silver-to-gold ratio, sixteen to one, resulted in the hoarding of silver coins. This abolition did not hurt the silver miners, since they had not been selling their bullion to the government at the offered price. Nothing had been done in secret—later charges to the contrary—nor at the moment was abolishment considered the "crime of 1873." William H. Harvey, the pro-silver propagandist, might rail against the act twenty years later, labeling it a crime because it made thousands paupers, tens of thousands tramps, "because it brought tears to strong men's eyes and hunger and pinching want to widows and orphans," and placed the nation on the verge of ruin,[11] but he would have received little audience at Caribou in 1873.

The whole matter might have rested there except for an unexpected swift change in the international silver market. Huge outpourings of silver from Western mines in the 1870s, combined with diminished demand throughout the world—as commercial nations replaced silver with gold currency—started the price tumbling; and within two years it had slipped under that previously offered by the treasury. Silver miners turned with alacrity to the government for a better price, only to find to their dismay and astonishment that the treasury no longer was in the market. Pressure on Congress as early as 1876 resulted two years later in the passage of the Bland-Allison Act, over President Rutherford Hayes's veto. Temporary exultation over the fact that the treasury had been ordered to purchase two to four million dollars' worth of silver per month at market prices and coin it at a ratio of sixteen to one soon died, as the price continued to fall and the secretaries of the treasury purchased at the lower sum. Adding insult, the newly minted silver dollars were backed by gold and could be redeemed at any time for gold.

Though some Caribou interest was manifested in the events in far-off Washington, as yet the local situation did not warrant great concern. Recovering from the Caribou Mine failure in the mid-seventies, the camp saw a promise of greater days just a step ahead. The *Boulder County News*, however, entered the lists as a defendant of silver as the honest money. It charged that the people had not been alerted when demonetization was threatened, nor had the members of Congress been entirely honest when they pretended that the clause was not in the bill. Unable to believe that such a thing could have happened in America, the paper readily blamed the English and a "conspiracy of moneyed men throughout the world operating in concert through the governments of their respective countries."[12] Prophetically, the editor warned against those who said demonetization would not affect Colorado, for, he reasoned, Colorado "is not out of the world" and needed money for development—money that would not be available in the ruined financial system of a depreciated silver market.

Caribou recovered and prospered despite the fluctuating, ever-downward silver price. Then came the closing of the Caribou Mine in 1883 and the end of prosperity. Caribouites immediately became acutely aware of the silver question. Western mining men in general (for much of the region mined silver) were becoming disenchanted with the Bland-Allison Act at the same time, because it had not operated as they fondly expected it would, nor had silver been placed on a par with gold. By mid-decade open agitation for the free coinage of silver had resumed.

Colorado's Senator Henry Teller, speaking in January 1886, foreshadowed Bryan when he said, "silver is adapted by nature to supply the wants of the human race as money."[13] Free coinage would, in his estimation, bring back the price of silver before "it was discredited and degraded"; stimulate commerce, trade, and industry; open closed factories; provide more and steady employment and good wages.

This was certainly a large order and he was somewhat vague on specifically how it would be achieved. The issue was taking on new meaning, attracting debtor classes that expected cheap money to produce relief through inflation. At Caribou any larger issue took second place to the immediate one of price increase, for a better silver price would open another Caribou era of widespread and steadier employment.

Throughout the eighties, rumblings of discontent appeared in *Boulder News*papers. Neither major political party, however, picked up the silver banner. Finally, in 1890 a third party, the Populist, arose and offered an alternative, even though it did not encompass all that the Westerner might want. For the moment, however, Caribou retained its old party loyalties, voting Republican, probably because of the passage of the Sherman Silver Purchase Act the same year.

The swelling Western demand for free coinage of silver paid dividends in 1890, when the Republican party found itself with an uncomfortably small majority in Congress while facing a stiff struggle over a higher protective tariff. Western Republicans, not particularly enamored of a higher tariff, found themselves in a strong bargaining position. Out of this situation emerged the Sherman Silver Purchase Act, which required the treasury to purchase at market price 4,500,000 ounces of silver per month, to be paid for in treasury notes redeemable in gold or silver. Again it appeared that Western demands had been met, for the amount purchased per month was calculated to be the total United States production. With a ready market at hand, the price of silver jumped to over a dollar per ounce for the first time in five years. Excitedly, the *Boulder County Herald* on June 18 forecast: "it would be no surprise to us if all the mines of Caribou were started up again. Caribou is certainly one of the richest silver camps in the western world."

Despite cheering promises, little measurable results could be found at Caribou, although this act might have helped sell the Poorman. The failure of government fiat points clearly to the conclusion that something besides a guaranteed purchaser and a better silver price was needed. Here, and to a degree with the Bland-Allison Act, the only noticeable result—evanescent stability—was purely negative when weighed against expectations. Only one glimmer remained: the free coinage of silver and a correspondingly higher price. As frail as this hope might have been, it seemed to point to salvation.

Desperation forced the Caribouites to switch political parties. Disenchantment with the older parties' policies produced a complete revolt, and the Populist party emerged triumphant. The new organization promised reform in a variety of areas, including the eight-hour day for labor, a graduated income tax, and, most significant to Caribou, the free and unlimited coinage of silver at the sixteen-to-one ratio. Such staunch old-timers as William Donald and Neil McKenzie went as delegates to the county Populist convention to demand unlimited coinage. The Populists ran a national and state ticket in 1892. Caribou responded enthusiastically by giving the Populist candidate for president, James Weaver, a landslide forty-nine-to-three victory over Benjamin Harrison, and the Populist Davis Waite, candidate for governor, a forty-six-to-seven edge over his Republican opponent.[14] Although Weaver lost nationally, Waite won and—with the support of the silver Democrats who captured control of their state organization—triumphed over the state's conservative Republicans, who attempted to straddle the fence on the silver issue. Not only for Caribou but for the entire state, silver was the most important element in the economy. Over half of the total production of the United States came from Colorado mines.

Caribou became a symbol of the issue in the 1892 Boulder County contest between the Democrat-Populists and the Republicans. The Republican *Boulder County Herald* questioned whether the low silver price hurt the camp, and asked two penetrating, key questions: Was there any truth to the assertion that the pumps were pulled out of the mines because of the low price of silver? Had the Caribou Mine paid a dollar dividend or even expenses for the past twelve or fourteen years? Replying more emotionally than directly, the Camera answered that the Caribou had been "swallowed up in the greedy maw of the avaricious gold bugs," and overwhelmed in the great battle against silver. Concluding its pre-election arguments on November 3 with a story headlined "More Men Discharged," the paper hit a vital issue:

> No mine can afford to take out ore, no matter how rich it may be and sell it at ruling prices. Silver at 84 cents means 70 cents to us, by reasons of the percentages off and the losses. We simply can't stand it.[15]

Indeed, the temporary revival of 1890 completely collapsed and the price fell to unexpected lows. Democrat Grover Cleveland, who had defeated Weaver and Harrison, took office just in time to confront a severe financial panic, then a nationwide depression. Along with many Eastern conservatives, Cleveland blamed a single major factor, the Sherman Silver Purchase Act; the panacea would be its repeal. In

Caribou looked its age in the 1890s. Courtesy, Duane A. Smith

June 1893 the president called a special session of Congress expressly for repeal, and despite valiant efforts by Colorado and other silver state representatives, the measure was pushed through and signed by Cleveland. It did not cure the nation's economic ills, and the price of silver sagged the next year to $.63.

The repeal of the Sherman Silver Purchase Act was the final blow to many of those who still attempted to live and work at Caribou. The Todd sisters movingly described how this and the panic hurt the camp. Most of the people, they said, did not have money reserves to see them through the hard times. Everyone attempted to help the less fortunate as best he could, and simply tried to make what he had go as far as possible. One particular picture etched itself in the sisters' minds—the broken-hearted men coming down from the mines when operation finally ceased that summer.[16] Many people moved; no invigorating omen tempted them to stay. Businesses closed. Finally, only a melancholy shell, a few diehards, and the persistent wind remained.

Only twenty-seven voters cast ballots in the 1894 state election; populism retained its hold. The next year a county election gave further testimony to the support the Populists had secured. The year 1896 found a prostrated Caribou. The few miners who continued to

work stored their ore against a rise in the silver price. Not yet completely despairing, a few optimists predicted a recovery of greatness
and prosperity once silver regained its "former just vocation as the
people's medium of exchange."

One illusive hope was held out: if only the free coinage of silver
could be adopted as a major campaign promise by one of the parties.
A steady drift of the electorate toward free silver appeared encouraging. Ever since 1893 a flood of speeches, articles, and pamphlets
had preached silver. None was more popular than William Harvey's
"Coin's Financial School," which explained the question in simple
terms the average American could grasp without much intellectual
struggle. The arguments, though not new, were freshly presented.
The bankers, England, and the selfish few wanted gold to secure
more wealth. Silver, by contrast, was the money of the poor, and
its integrity and identity were respected by the Founding Fathers.
The demonetization cut in half the foundation of the United States'
financial system, causing stagnation, falling prices, and paralysis of
business; but debts had not shrunk with all other values.[17] These
arguments, though oversimplified and emotional, were nonetheless
effective; and Caribou silverites must have cheered this national presentation of their desires.

The Republican party did not welcome such heresy and converted
itself completely to the single gold standard, despite a walkout of
thirty-four convention delegates, including Senator Henry Teller. To
head its ticket, the party nominated William McKinley. In contrast, the
Democratic convention found the silverites in control and a platform
unequivocally demanding "the free and unlimited coinage of both silver
and gold at the present legal ratio of sixteen to one." The dramatically
presented and emotional "Cross of Gold" address by William Jennings
Bryan swung the delegates to his nomination, and he went forth to
battle for silver. The Populist party, its program gutted by the Democrats, followed their lead and nominated Bryan, although picking a
different vice-presidential running mate.

In the campaign of 1896, the American people had a unique opportunity to air their grievances on the money question, as the "battle
of the standards" took precedence over all other issues. Bryan took his
program to the people in a whirlwind, whistle-stop campaign, which
stood in bold contrast to McKinley's sedate, nebulous, front-porch approach. Caribou proudly raised its silver banner, and fervor here was
as high as that described by Vachel Lindsay.

I brag and chant of Bryan, Bryan, Bryan,
Candidate for the president who sketched a silver Zion.
The one American poet who could sing outdoors.
He brought in tides of wonder, of unprecedented splendor.
Wild roses from the plains, that made hearts tender,

July, August, suspense.
Wall Street lost to sense.
August, September, October,
More suspense,
And the whole East down like a wind smashed fence.[18]

Bryan's appeal stirred visions of a "silver Zion" at Caribou and other silver-producing areas. For indeed it seemed to them that "the gold standard has slain its tens of thousands," and they lifted their voices wholeheartedly to his ringing "you shall not crucify mankind upon a cross of gold." It is not hard to imagine that Caribouites contributed to the campaign from their meager resources, but it would be extremely doubtful that R. G. Dun made such a donation.

November came, and with it, decision. Caribou's determination remained steadfast to the last, thirty-four votes cast for the "silver-tongued orator" to two for McKinley, curiously close to a sixteen-to-one ratio. Boulder County and Colorado gave him roughly a six-to-one majority, but the national victory went to McKinley and gold. Caribou voters, without looking backward, switched parties, abandoning the Populists and rejoining the Democrats. They maintained their interest in silver, which the Democratic party now took up as one of its main issues. The money question was paramount in the campaign and it had been settled. The American people, having fought a passionate contest, did not take up the standards again. The silver issue was dead, its tattered banners never to be raised again as they had been in the summer of 1896. Caribou was left alone.

Could a Bryan victory and resumption of free coinage have saved the camp? While the answer will never be known conclusively, it seems highly improbable. It might have helped restore confidence and arouse interest, but it could not have produced a high-grade ore or checked the rising mining costs. A brief revival would have done nothing to reverse permanently the drift toward abandonment. Caribou's mines had been operating for over twenty years, a long time for a mining district as small as this one. Other and newer camps had surpassed it in volume and richness, which dimmed any Caribou chance to find another benefactor of the R. G. Dun mold. It had ceased to advertise its merits long before, and the only major mining transaction since 1888 had depended as much on Tabor's name as on Caribou's fame. A tantalizing prospect had been held out; too tantalizing, for it gave the local residents only a desperate, blind hope and left nothing except a bitter aftertaste.

Enough resiliency remained to expend one last effort to recapture the fading past. It was cruelly ironic that gold spurred the few remaining miners into action. The St. Louis Mine, located east of Idaho Hill, and the Belcher led the 1898–1899 excitement. The Belcher created considerable interest, located as it was on Caribou Hill. As prophesied, none of the big mines was reopened. Local newspapers, of course, spawned enthusiasm. Even the Nederland Mill, after years of idleness, was refitted and put into operation. Some visionaries talked of constructing a tunnel 500 feet below the present workings to drain the hill and open up an estimated "immense ore body in the Caribou and other mines in the district."[19] Water, low-grade ore (gold or silver), increased costs—all these old problems remained unresolved.

Feebly, the camp revived. The number of merchants increased, and the *Boulder County Herald* estimated 300 people in the place and "all of them at work" in June 1898. Enough newcomers arrived to organize a Sunday school and hold sessions in the church. The only other indication of the population comes from the number voting. In 1898 one hundred sixteen persons cast votes to only thirty-eight a year later. As late as 1899 a slate of nominees for town trustees was nominated, promising if elected to put the water mains in good shape, as well as accomplish a number of other needed improvements. The pattern now emerging, which would continue on beyond the demise of the camp, was for people to move in during the spring, work during the pleasant months, and leave before winter settled. "Old Caribou, once the silver bonanza camp of North Colorado, is now a busy hamlet."[20]

"Old Caribou"—the name implied more than the writer intended. As the century ended, Caribou was only twenty-nine years old—young for a town, but old for a mining camp. It had held its own the past two years; then fate dealt a cruel blow. On Tuesday morning, December 26, 1899, fire broke out in Ritchie's general store. The cause was unknown; an overheated stove might have been the culprit. The wind, according to reports, was blowing a gale, quickly spreading the fire to adjoining buildings. No fire-fighting equipment remained, and the town's water works had long since fallen into disrepair. A volunteer

False-fronted, weathered buildings—one even braced—and empty lots tell a tale of faded hopes. Courtesy, Duane A. Smith

fire bucket brigade, utilizing the town pump, managed to save the structures on the south side of Idaho Street but the north side was razed. Peter Werley's unoccupied establishment was one of the first to go, and Werley, who now lived in Boulder, also lost another building. Among the other landmarks reduced to ashes were the shaft house of the Potosi, the Planter's House, and all the store buildings on the north side of Idaho Street.[21] Only one of them—Ritchie's—was occupied at the time.

The newspaper reports concluded that the buildings saved afforded enough space to accommodate the business of this "once prosperous and considerable town." No rebuilding was planned, apparently. The brief boom was over; the Gay Nineties drew to a close five days later.

No Tomorrow

The chorus of the popular sentimental ballad of the 1890s, "After the Ball," closes with these lines:

> Many a heart is aching,
> If you could read them all;
> Many the hopes that have vanish'd
> After the ball.

For Caribou the ball was ended, actually long before 1900; now even the hopes had vanished. The previous decade had not been the Gay Nineties of folklore and legend. They might have been gay somewhere, but not in Caribou, and the twentieth century promised even less.

The federal census taker made his decennial visit and could record only forty-four people for precinct 12, which embraced the camp. In the summers a few more came in to augment those hardy souls who braved the winters. Writing some years later, a visitor to the camp in November 1900 remembered only one store—which served as a combination post office, drug store, and restaurant.[1] Not until 1902, however, would a state business directory list any trade establishments here, for the first time since 1899. Then, and for several years afterward, it was a general store that sold drugs and groceries and functioned as a post office.[2] The population during the period remained fairly static, around forty.

The year 1900 was a presidential election year, the Democrats again turning to their silver-tongued leader, William Jennings Bryan. The Republicans nominated William McKinley for a second term, producing a rematch of the 1896 contest, with one major difference from four years before—silver was no longer an issue. Caribou again faithfully gave Bryan most of its votes, this time twenty-three to eight, and favored the state fusion ticket over the Republican nominees. Nationally, the vote went against their choice and Bryan went down to another defeat.

Life went on routinely in the years that followed. The decline had gone about as far as it could, short of complete abandonment. In September 1903 an earthquake rattled the region, including the neighboring towns of Eldora and Ward. The local papers neglected to interview anyone in Caribou, which must also have felt the tremor. Obviously, news of Caribou was no longer sought after.

Two men, who were young boys in the camp after the turn of the century, fondly remembered their youth when interviewed sixty years later. Charles Smith had been taken to Caribou in 1896 as a year-old baby, and Eugene R. Trollope's parents moved there in 1902. School for the children was in session only the three summer months. Teachers willing to come to Caribou for $45 per month were hard to find. Eventually, the salary was raised to $65, over the heated objections of some, who complained about the increase in taxes. A minister occasionally visited the community, holding services in the schoolhouse. The same building served as a movie theater when the traveling show arrived, for this entertainment also followed a mountain camp circuit.

Trollope remembered that many of the old miners were simply caretakers, looking after mining property for a small monthly wage. Both he and Smith agreed that the St. Louis Mine was the biggest one still in operation.

The Sherman House, the grand landmark of other days, was "pretty well beat up" by the time Trollope's parents leased it, forcing

The Sherman House looked better than most Caribou buildings, but few visitors came anymore. Courtesy, Colorado Historical Society

them to purchase a building up the street and convert it into a hotel and eating establishment. Their hotel served as a social center, especially for the Sunday afternoon meal. Snow and wind continued to plague the residents, as did animated creatures. Smith particularly recalled the great number of house flies that alighted on any food left out where they could reach it. "Mountain" rats were nearly as numerous in the abandoned and still-occupied buildings. Their eyes shining in the dark, and the haunted sound of their scurrying back and forth on the wooden floors in the quiet of the night, left a vivid impression on Charles Smith.[3]

Mining conditions fluctuated from bad to worse. The price of silver, which had crept back to $.61 per ounce by 1900, stayed around that level for the next five years. This was not enough to overcome the low-grade ore and the expense of pumping; that bothersome water problem had yet to be resolved. The *Boulder County Herald*, November 15, 1905, commented that for a time after 1893 Caribou was little more than a memory, but "of late it has picked up again with brighter prospects ahead." The revival was destined to be slight, not needing a camp to support it. All that was required were a few buildings to provide shelter and perhaps a store or hotel. Caribou no longer had any justification for existence.

The fire that destroyed Caribou on November 14, 1905, mercifully ended the prolonged agony of abandonment. This one, like that of 1899, broke out in a store, and was probably caused by a defective flue. The wind again played havoc with attempts to fight the fire, which rapidly spread to adjoining buildings, the dried wood serving as perfect fuel for the flames. The Sherman House, the church, Murphy's meat market, and other relics of a bygone age soon lay in ashes. "The structures were all wood and none of them had been painted or scarcely repaired for 20 years. It is not known what the loss will amount to . . . to replace the destroyed structures would involve quite an expense."[4] The south portion of town, which had survived the two previous fires, was almost totally destroyed. Smoke, seen in Nederland and Boulder, testified to the tragedy; no help could possibly have arrived in time to save the doomed buildings.

Sparks ignited some of the small shaft houses around the community, though fortunately the major mining buildings were not damaged. Whatever mining would be carried on in the future would center around these, the miners and their families living in the few homes still standing on the site of Caribou.

As a cold, cheerless November evening silently settled upon the scene, a smoky haze drifted over the debris, reddened by the glow of the coals in the smoldering ashes of what once had been buildings. Etched starkly against the darkening night sky stood Caribou Hill. A red sunset, a long night, but no dawn would come for Caribou.

Pushing aside the smoke to peer into the future, one would see no town reemerge from the rubble. A few people would continue to live on the site, the numbers steadily declining with the passing years. By the time of the 1930 census, Caribou's precinct would be absorbed by Nederland, its former satellite mill town. Those who did stay worked in the mines, received their mail addressed to Caribou, and for another ten years were able to trade at a small general store. The post office, which had been established in January 1871, would continue to exist until March 1917, when this last relic of earlier glory closed. Then any resemblance to a community would end.

Ironically, that long-cherished dream, a railroad, finally came within a few miles of Caribou. The Colorado and Northwestern went through New Cardinal in 1905 while constructing a line to the gold mining camp of Eldora, located across the ridge to the south of Caribou. The great ambitions of the railroad promoters of the 1870s and

The wind was taking its toll on the Caribou Mine buildings. Courtesy, Colorado Railroad Museum

1880s failed to materialize, however, because the price of silver simply was too low, and the cost too high, to revive Caribou mining. A three-decades-old dream evaporated, and few were left to mourn its passing.

Boulder did not completely forget its "cloud city" neighbor. In 1919 it sponsored a semi-centennial silver jubilee to honor the original discovery of the Caribou Mine. On September 1 a parade was formed, including eighty-four floats and four bands, with twenty of the floats directly related to Caribou, the others portraying varied topics. The celebration honored all of the Boulder County pioneers, and two of the more hardy ones present knew a great deal about that event fifty years before; they were William Martin and Samuel Conger. Additional festivities competing for the spectators' attention were rock-drilling contests, baby shows, children's games, a tug-of-war, and a baseball game (Boulder versus the miners). The celebration was supposedly filmed to be shown around the country.[5] While the silver jubilee helped bring long overdue recognition to Caribou, the remembrance was brief. The 1920s turned the public's attention elsewhere.

Some mining continued in the district, but no important discoveries were made. The crash of 1929, the depression years, World War II—all came and went. A few more buildings collapsed in the now completely abandoned site, and tourists came to gawk and pry around the remains, wondering and speculating about their past.

The atomic age descended rather abruptly on Caribou in December 1948, when Look magazine, in an article titled "Atomic Ore Discovered in Colorado," announced the discovery of pitchblende in the workings on Caribou Hill. The camp was not revived during the nearly ten years miners again worked in the heart of the hill. This venture, too, faded away—not completely perhaps, but at the moment no visible effort is being made to continue operation.

Few cared on November 14, 1905, what the future might bring. Only the shell of Caribou had burned—the people and the mining that had given it life had long since left. Born of a mining rush, the camp outlived its usefulness. Ignored (for no second article appeared to tell the reader of the aftermath of the fire), Caribou's saga ended.

Requiem

Caribou—the camp—is dead now, completely gone except for a few wind-battered, crumbling relics. Soon these too will disappear. Even the mine dumps scarring Caribou Hill and Idaho Hill are being gently masked by the fast-growing aspen; nature is reclaiming her own. Only the cemetery remains as physical evidence that a generation of people once resided here.

Caribou survived for thirty-five years against an adverse environment and fluctuating economic conditions—a short era when measured against Eastern cities or centuries-old European villages. For a mining camp, it was a better than average span in terms of years and productivity. Leadville and Cripple Creek, Colorado, for example, went through similar cycles and within thirty years had declined considerably, though each struggled on in a much reduced capacity. Throughout the Rocky Mountains are numerous camp sites occupied and abandoned within a shorter time than Caribou's.

Like the majority of these camps, Caribou became a ghost town. The fires alone did not decree this melancholy fate; an isolated location, backed against the Continental Divide, proved equally fatal. Unlike neighboring Central City, Caribou did not become the trade center for surrounding camps; nor, as they declined and disappeared, did it pick up population remnants to boost its own sagging fortunes. Never was Caribou able to free itself from the economic orbit of Boulder and, to a lesser degree, Central City. Relying solely on mining, since no agriculture and only little ranching could subsist in its altitude, climate, and soil conditions, the camp had no real reason for existence after the 1890s. Nor was the climate or scenery such as to induce tourism or encourage people to stay.

A product of the times—the Western mining frontier—Caribou lived out its life amid the generation spawned by this excitement. Fire mercifully ended its existence before complete abandonment, but already it subsisted as a relic of another age. A new chapter in the annals of Colorado had unfolded; Caribou would not be a part of that story. Quickly forgotten, the camp passed into the saga of the settlement of the trans-Mississippi West.

In the years of its existence Caribou evolved through the complete cycle of mining. First had come the prospectors who made the discoveries but lacked the financial resources to develop their claims. Then came the individuals with money to buy or finance operations, who converted their investments, via incorporation, into companies that eventually dominated the district. Corporate mining did not prove to be the final answer and, as the mines declined, it was replaced by leasing; finally small operators came, scavengers who picked over what was left on the hill. In the end all ceased and only the scars remained.

Exploitation of natural resources was carried forward in a massive assault paralleling similar developments in other industries throughout the country in post–Civil War America. Industrialism reigned, conservation went unheeded; streams were polluted, resources squandered, and the landscape marred. So compelling were the short-term rewards, though, that no loud continuing protests were raised.

Caribou was a frontier mining community, a fact that shaped its entire existence. Yet it was not of the same genre as Denver in 1859 or Virginia City, Montana, in 1863. When Caribou was born,

it was surrounded by settlements established for at least a decade
and no Indian danger ever threatened it. Nor did it depend on long
lines of communication to settled regions. Colorado was no longer
a virgin territory. During the same months in which the Caribou
rush started, a railroad connection with the transcontinental Union
Pacific was being completed; within six years statehood would be
gained and in seven a state university opened in nearby Boulder.
Agricultural products from the Boulder valley and elsewhere along
the mountains appeared almost with the miners, so there were no
food shortages. Mining experience and knowledge could be found
near at hand, although they were no guarantee of success. As a result, Caribou passed through its first pioneering stage rapidly and
with relative ease.

The camp faced certain typical frontier problems such as shortages of buildings, transportation connections, and financial capital,
but within a year, except for the last, these had been solved. Even
women, initially conspicuous by their absence, quickly swept in, and, if
not satisfied by the local belles, a young man could always visit neighboring communities to find his lady. Though it passed through this
first stage, Caribou never rose beyond the classification of a frontier
mining camp. Prosperity's bloom faded swiftly, and the subsequent
decline became too deeply ingrained to provide the economic balance
necessary for permanent settlement. By the late eighties the camp
looked far older than its years. The settlers had wanted more than
this; they struggled to give Caribou an air of durability. To a point
they succeeded: a business district, church, and school arose, but the
economy failed to go beyond its mining start. No railroad came, nor
did a steadily increasing population swarm into the camp and surrounding district.

In a compact urban settlement, with people crowded together
in a small valley, problems appeared that had to be resolved; they
were tackled by the community as a whole or by chosen representatives. Some of the solutions were accomplished in the easiest possible
manner: surveying a townsite, then organizing a local government
to establish ownership of land and a governing body for communal
control. The philosophy of "grow or die" charted the course, reflected
in the 1870s by the people pulling together to advertise Caribou's distinctive features. A community spirit matured, lasting far longer than
the decade of the seventies and helping to sustain the residents when
fortunes changed. A church building was needed and many cooperated to erect it. Better transportation arteries were essential and from

2341. CARIBOU from the WEST.

*As the twentieth century dawned, few remembered what Caribou once had been.
Courtesy, Duane A. Smith*

the start the people pushed for improvement. First and last, they
wanted a railroad; in this they failed, but did succeed in securing road
connections to Central City and Boulder.

These events, not radically different from more individualistic
frontiers (farming, for example), were changed in their timing by the

urbanity of the circumstances. Self-sufficiency was not encouraged by the rush to riches and the very numbers of people involved. Individualism was allowed, although held within limits established by the communal whole in order to protect itself and individual members. Caribou skipped much of what had been the usual slow growth of a frontier settlement by jumping from wilderness to camp virtually overnight. Such speed permitted the residents to bypass some problems, only to intensify others by sheer newness and lack of social cohesion.

An urban settlement from the start, Caribou was part of the Rocky Mountain urban mining frontier. Growth had been astonishingly rapid: almost instant birth, followed by a year's swift development into a community of about 1,000 residents. In rapid succession came a series of ups and downs, the first decade of existence ending on an upward swing. The pace then slackened and gradual decline settled fatally over Caribou. The cycle here reflected similar patterns in other Western mining communities, with varying time spans, but contrasted markedly with the slower agricultural regions.

Many people and forces molded the history of Caribou. The businessman played a significant role, appearing early to help establish the camp and staying there until the end. Literally pillars of the community around whom swirled so much of the camp's life, they helped promote and advertise it, certainly not for completely unselfish motives, but everyone gained. Gambling as much on silver as the miners, they sought to develop something more than just a mining community, since their profits rested on permanence, not transition. At Caribou this goal remained unattainable; nevertheless, the striving generated progressive community momentum. Men like Donald, Murphy, and Werley entered into many phases of Caribou's life, from business to politics to mining, and were recognized leaders; this group provided the leadership on all but rare occasions.

Initially in the booming camp, the general merchants and their more specialized counterparts found their services in demand, then gradually the former came to dominate and by the nineties were all that remained. They worked hard because they had much at stake. A few grew old here; but like their customers, most moved on to more prosperous camps before Caribou's demise.

The speculator came to profit from the mines, not to build a town. Caribou had its share, from Breed to the ill-fortuned Dun, and they played a significant role in Caribou mining. Without their financial aid, mining would have stagnated or developed extremely slowly. As long as money flowed into Caribou, it prospered; when this reservoir emptied, Caribou's fortunes deteriorated. These mining speculators did not personally control the camp nor did they even visit there for any extended period, but any action they took affected the mines and community. Caribou was never completely free of their influence, except in the initial rush; for better or worse, they guided its destiny.

Of them all, Dun was the most consistent and did the most for mining. Breed developed and advertised and, had he stopped there, could have been a major positive factor; but the cloud that surrounds his Caribou sale darkens his contribution. Chaffee, Moffat, and Tabor never really placed their full attention here. The former two came out ahead, just in the nick of time—paralleling their activities elsewhere, and probably dumping the Caribou into Dun's lap as part of the bargain. Tabor speculated briefly, and only as the middle man, so had little impact. Bates's activities, however, provide an almost classic example of promoting a property and then selling out at the right time. The Caribou careers of these individuals and other lesser lights, when compared to those of mine promoters, owners, and speculators at, say, Virginia City, Nevada, pale in comparison. Yet the impact was similar, albeit on a smaller scale, and Caribouites' hopes rose and fell on their activities, just as much as did their Virginia City contemporaries.

Corporate mining, under their guidance, gained dominance over the major mines, and the small-scale operator was forced to lease or move into the marginal properties. Unionism, however, did not influence laborers for the purpose of counteracting the exploitation of management. The few strikes at the camp seemed to be spontaneous reactions against pressing grievances rather than union-masterminded demonstrations. Several things prevented the start of unionism. Leasing and contract mining offered openings for individual initiative and money for anyone with ambition, and the opportunity always existed to move to a new, prospering camp where wages were higher. The labor force was never large when compared, for instance, to the ones at Leadville or Butte, Montana. Finally, the major mines fell under the control of powerful syndicates or Eastern ownership, agents far too strong for the slender resources of the Caribou miners to challenge successfully. By the mid-1880s the mining situation was so bad that striking would have gained the few hired miners nothing except the probable closing of the mines and the termination of their jobs. In the nineties, when unionism was making progress in many Western mining districts, Caribou had long since passed its peak and offered no opportunity for organization.

A few so-listed farmers settled in the camp, but they could not have carried on agriculture in the surrounding area. Except for a little friction at first over the railroad bonds, the mining camp got along quite well with its neighbors on the plains. The farmer wholeheartedly came to the support of silver in 1896, although with more diverse purposes in mind than the Caribouites.

The silver issue was strictly an economic one. The local residents had not been political reformers nor inflationists prior to the 1890s, clearly voting down an earlier appeal by the Greenbackers for paper money and inflation. When the price of silver dipped to what appeared to be a fatal low, they became emotional. The personal appeal of silver as a cure-all for the country's ills remained secondary. Upon the rejection of silver in 1896, they retained their faith in Bryan, but by a smaller margin in 1900. Free silver would not have helped Caribou, as some of its more enthusiastic promoters prophesied. Caribou was too far beyond redemption to find salvation in this solution, or any other advanced at the time.

If free silver would not have redeemed Caribou's sagging fortunes, neither can it be said that the government's repeal of the Sherman Silver Purchase Act of 1893 ended silver mining in the district. It hurt when the price collapsed, but peak production had passed more than a decade before and little fresh capital was infused to spark exploration. The decline in the intervening years was marked and accelerated. It seems safe to say the end would have been similar regardless of the silver issue of the 1890s. A continuing high price of silver from the 1870s would have postponed the inevitable and continued the "good years" a little longer.

Despite the predominance of men, women made significant contributions. The problems they faced were no different from those of their pioneering sisters, though partially modified by the more settled period and region in which Caribou had been established. The appearance of women and families closed one frontier phase, and here it happened quickly. They brought with them refinements of culture and society that were not found in a masculine environment. The school and church reflected their subtle persuasion, as did the general improvement wrought by the appearance of families. The failure of prostitution to gain a foothold and the absence of lawlessness should be partially attributed to the early appearance and continuing residence of the entire family unit.

Even as summer neared, snowdrifts still lingered at Caribou. Courtesy, Denver Public Library, Western History Department

Caribou does not fit the stereotyped conception of a lawless frontier mining camp; in fact, it was extremely quiet and passed through no wild era of rowdiness and red lights. Other than an occasional drunk or disturbance of the peace complaint, little disturbed the residents. Caribou was not a large camp nor extremely rich and therefore failed to attract the transient crowd. No big groups of single men were needed to work the mines and serve as ready clientele for bawdy amusements. The Cornish, who dominated the camp, did not openly support the red-light district, which had caused so much trouble in other communities. Finally, Caribou was quickly overshadowed by wealthier boom camps that proved to be much more promising attractions for the gamblers, girls, and the assortment of people who "mined the miners." The situation at Caribou—surrounded by settled towns and with an organized territorial and county law force available—helped prevent lawlessness. Conversely, it also offered an easier opportunity for the lawless to migrate from the older to the newer, but this did not happen to any great extent.

Caribou's law-abiding nature was not an exception to the general situation; it would appear to be more of the norm than the better-known and more flagrantly rowdy Deadwood, Leadville, and

Tombstone. The people of the mining camp presented a much better image when they acted more like a civilized community. All camps needed outside investment, population, and business; lawlessness in no way promoted these goals.

Except in degree and timing, Caribou in most aspects typified other camps, although, as Bancroft hinted, none can be referred to as typical. Wealth quite often begets notoriety—for example, Virginia City and Leadville; in this area Caribou achieved little. Yet this camp was nearer average than its larger sisters, because for every Leadville there were scores of smaller camps. Indeed, to study them gives the historian more of a composite picture, since life went on here without extremes of wealth or publicity.

The Cornish, particularly active at Caribou, which became known as a Cornish camp, left a distinctive mark on all aspects of Caribou's history, especially on the memories of old-timers. The "Cousin Jacks and Jennies" lent substance, color, and social charm. Caribou, and other camps in which they resided, helped Americanize them and educate their children in the culture of their new home; they assimilated easily. Their impact on mining and folklore was significant, but their identity as a group disappeared. Upon leaving the camps they dispersed, making the necessary transition, and the second and third generations retained only memories, Cornish recipes, and stories.

Two important elements of life at Caribou were the church and the fraternal lodge. While symbolizing the settlement's maturity, they provided a gathering place in which to find companionship and people of similar interests. In the largely impersonal life of a new camp, such things were needed; each helped strengthen community bonds and hold the people together. Caribou did not face the problem of group-lessness and lack of social cohesion of the magnitude found in larger mining towns, additionally illustrating why lawlessness failed to gain a head start.

The people of Caribou were not unique. They came to the camp in hopes of improving themselves, making a fresh start, or for the sheer adventure of it. The editor of the *Caribou Post*, in the September 30, 1871, issue, took it upon himself to answer the charge of the "unstable, lawless, coarse, repulsive character of the new mining towns." If one discounts local prejudice, it is seen as a fine job. To the charge of unstable, he answers, "not true." The original discoverers were displaying a remarkable tenacity to hang on and the same could be said for others. Lawless, "not so"; squarely the opposite was true. Echoing the sentiments of Grace Greenwood and John Tice, the editor denounced the idea that the Caribouites were coarse and repulsive in character. Quite to the contrary, the "intelligent and generous bearing of the miners inclines them to settle disputes amicably and honorably." Not to be outdone, he took a jab at the East:

> Our people come from Christian communities, and, in due time, will found here the institutions of learning and religion. But the freshness and freedom of a new country tend to a less regard for the outward show, to neglect of conventionalities, and disgust of the affectations so common to the civilized east.

The polemic closed with dismay over the "want of true appreciation of character—the tendency to judge by appearance only," which led to such uncharitable judgments.

Ray Billington's interpretative examination, *America's Frontier Heritage*, presents pertinent conclusions relating to the significant role of the frontier. Some of these are particularly relevant when compared to the experience of one mining camp.

Billington found the frontier a democratizing influence during the nineteenth century, because it vested greater control of government in all the people. The opportunities in a new land made men equals, for no one knew when fortune might favor him. On the local level at Caribou this seemed to be the situation; no group dominated the political scene and all men had the franchise, with the obvious exception of the Chinese. W. Turrentine Jackson, in his study of the White Pine, Nevada, Mining District, *Treasure Hill*, concluded however that from the very beginning class lines, social status, and economic position prevailed and that even the democracy of the political process broke down. Although documentation is sketchy, it seems unlikely that Caribou displayed such marked evidence of these factors, although, as Jackson noted, the miner could be politically passive unless a vital interest was at stake.[1]

Municipal government, born in the boom days of the seventies, struggled until the end of the century, declining with the camp. It could not maintain needed services, as the tragic case of the water system illustrated, but the fault lay equally with the people themselves, the mining situation, and the city fathers. The government that evolved was what the community wanted, and apparently did not suffer financial misfortune until the eighties. Initially, support was generated spontaneously for providing the framework of local government, and throughout its history the city fathers tried to answer all needs adequately without overburdening the taxpayer.

Some of the mine owners at Caribou exhibited a decided willingness to promote innovation in mining and smelting.[2] Although the varied processes tried at the New Jersey, Nederland, and Bates mills did not always work, they offered conclusive proof of variety in approach and the influence of expediency. In mining, new machinery was introduced and multimodes of production, from paid laborers to leasing, were used to put the operation on a more profitable basis. In other areas, including acceptance of the telephone, the Caribouites were ready innovators, in hopes of making their lives easier.

The potential for upward economic and social mobility offered at Caribou may be questioned.[3] The initial rush presented to everyone a similar, yet long-shot, chance of finding a silver bonanza. This chance became more remote as corporations gained control of the richest mines. Opportunity on a smaller scale remained throughout the entire thirty-five years, if a miner were willing to lease a property and with hard work and luck make it profitable. The few men who made a small fortune in the district should not obscure the number who barely made a living from their claims. Social mobility was always possible; social class lines were not tightly drawn when almost everyone worked at the same occupation—mining. In this microcosmic frontier society a man succeeded on his own merits; to achieve social prominence, he had to move to a more populous community such as Boulder. The continued absentee ownership of the large mines prevented the appearance of a social elite, and the mine managers apparently made no attempt to substitute themselves for the owners, socially. By the mid-1880s Caribouites, with few exceptions, were equal financially—the equality of declining profits and prospects.

Individualism, so often described as a primary frontier characteristic, did not chart the course of Caribou development. Individual initiative helped spur people to come to the camp and perhaps sustained them while searching for their bonanza. But the original Caribou Company came together to pool resources for underwriting the initial expedition, and even then did not have enough capital to develop their property adequately. In every case, the discoverers of the major mines sold out or went into partnership to finance the mining operations. Mining did not encourage individualism unless supported by abundant resources.

Nor could a Caribouite express militant individualism and hope to remain in the settlement, all having to give up certain freedoms to live within the community. As society became more complex, a spirit of cooperation manifested itself in many matters, including road building, camp promotion, and church construction. This spirit became even more necessary as the camp declined. In certain areas such as housing and recreation, the Caribouite could exercise his individuality within the possibilities available; though even in a small settlement such as this, the majority ruled in community matters, leaving the dissatisfied the choice of abiding or leaving the district.

Caribou, as previously discussed, did not serve as a safety valve for the discontented in the East and only possibly for the Midwesterner. As Jackson pointed out about the White Pine District, however, the mining camp served as a safety valve for many men in the West.[4]

In 1870–1871 miners, merchants, and others came to Caribou from surrounding depressed or stabilized towns, thereby easing the labor and economic pressures in the older communities. As would be expected, the greatest numbers came from nearby counties and towns. The previously mentioned article in the *New York Times*, September 12, 1870, clearly illustrated this tendency when it noted that the men came from Central City, Black Hawk, Georgetown, Denver, and such farming communities as Evans and Greeley. From outside the territory they came from as far away as White Pine, Nevada, and nearer Cheyenne. Richard Harvey is a good example of a miner who came from Central City because of better opportunities in the new camp. Examples of merchants who moved to Caribou have already been cited.

Optimism, opportunism, materialism, and the fleeting essence of the mining West kept the mining frontier shifting and stampeding for better than half a century. Caribou held out fresh opportunity as did every new mining community. This kept the mining frontier moving and, at least in the instance of Caribou, served as a safety valve for the nearby depressed or stabilized camps, such as Central City, Nevadaville, or Ward. While older camps were, in a sense, hurt by this drain, it also lessened the chance of a discontented, economically deprived element fomenting trouble, such as that which occurred in Colorado after the closing of the mining frontier in the 1890s.

When Caribou started to decline and no longer offered so good an economic opportunity, the emergence of new bonanzas drained off her now-surplus population. The Black Hills took some in the 1870s; a casual study of Leadville papers will show that more went to this silver metropolis. Caribouites drifted to the San Juans and into other Colorado districts that boomed in the 1880s, as a result helping to prevent serious labor strikes or general unrest at Caribou. Only those with investments or great faith were compelled to stay. Without question, Caribou served as a very real, yet at the time unrealized, mining camp safety valve.

In a sense, Caribou's pioneers stand indicted on charges of wastefulness and exploitation. They gutted the wealth of Caribou Hill and wherever else they found it in the surrounding area. Nothing remains of this effort except waste rock packed on drab mine dumps, seen by all who visit the site and its abandoned internal workings. They exploited vigorously what they discovered, then left—a neat conclusion, but far too simple.

The mineral wealth of Caribou helped build Boulder County, and its profits went into the pockets of men from Denver to Europe. Indirectly and in a small way, it stimulated the national and world economy. The potential prospects of the district advertised Colorado and promoted investment, both of which the struggling young territory needed to gain maturity. As the local press readily admitted, outside investment was the key and, despite the repeated failure to make a substantial profit, mining lured dollars to Colorado. Merchants, retailers, transportation, and freighting companies in the three supply towns of Boulder, Denver, and Central City reaped direct benefits from the Caribouites and their silver. As they prospered, so did their communities. Finally, Caribou's wealth substantially aided Boulder County for over a decade, with taxes, advertisement, investment, and a diversified economy based upon mining in the mountains and farming along the foothills. The ruthless exploitation of the silver stimulated a wide area, though it left behind only gutted remains at Caribou. In the long run, the success of the surgery overshadows the disfigurement of the scar.

It may be charged that a wasteful expense of time, effort, talent, and money went into building a community that disappeared within thirty-five years. Nothing concrete remains, so in this sense it is true. Final judgment must be based on a deeper significance. Caribou served as home for a generation of Americans who helped change Colorado from a frontier territory to a settled state. Here they tamed the land, passed from youth to old age, and struggled to provide a better opportunity for their children than they themselves had been given. The Caribouites encouraged education and nourished and transmitted their cultural heritage. These intrinsic factors, unweighable in dollars or hours, are essential parts of the camp's inheritance.

These people were not self-sufficient and relied on outside producers for almost all their food, clothing, and other items needed to

Only the cemetery now marks a generation of folks who had called Caribou home.
Courtesy, Duane A. Smith

sustain their settlement. They provided a ready market for farmers' produce and the wares of local manufacturers, thereby encouraging a more permanent, diversified county and state economy. They supported better methods of transportation, and the camp's existence was responsible for several new roads that have served as important transportation arteries. Advertisement was an important contribution, as previously discussed, but not only in the sense of mineral wealth and materialistic opportunities. Although not conspicuously successful in attracting tourists, Caribou made efforts in this direction and was one of the many to advertise Colorado's natural beauties. Not originally intended to do so, the site and mines continue to attract a small flow of the curious.

Caribou was but one segment of the whole mining frontier in Colorado; as such it played a role in the frontier saga of this state. Its significance, in all fairness, cannot be appreciated by examining what remains. Certainly the story of the struggle against the environment may be sensed by seeing the location and feeling the biting wind off the Continental Divide. That there is more to the story the reader should now be aware.

Caribou is gone and will not, like a phoenix, arise out of its wind-blown ashes a young and beautiful city. The heritage of Caribou is the heritage of the American frontier. It is the legend of the people who lived and worked, succeeded and failed, were born and died, at this place. At Caribou a generation's struggle to plant a lasting settlement failed; this does not dim the glory of what they did, or tried to do. The inscription on Mary Webster's tombstone again comes to mind:

Remember friends as you pass by
As you are now so once was I.

Epilogue:
"No Risk, No Gain Is Our Motto"

Caribou, the town, died on that cold November 1905 day, but the district and the legend lived on. The latter, indeed, managed to grow as the decades went by and public interest in the mining West expanded.

Mining continued in the district, in a rather haphazard manner, and a few people lived there. Very few stayed year-round. The *Colorado State Business Directory* for 1910 listed only one general store, a postmaster, and a population of twenty-five. The same problems that bedeviled Caribou at the end of its active career continued. The low price of silver, the high costs of deep mining, and the lower-grade ore being mined kept this district, and many others, from reviving to "good old days." As a Colorado Bureau of Mines report (1902) admitted, "Mines in the Grand Island District have not progressed as expected years ago."

Denver mining man W. G. Swart visited Caribou in November 1909 to look at the "old" Caribou Mine "owned by the R. G. Dun Estate." His reaction to the site probably reflected many others. "This mine lies practically on the 'top of the world' up on the main range where winter set in last September and where spring will show up next June." He did not recommend to his client that they become involved in the plan to work the low-grade material in the dump. The group currently leasing the dump was having a "very poor" time saving the silver.

Such troubles did not stop the ever optimistic. In 1914, for example, a 100-ton cyaniding mill was completed at Caribou to treat ores from the dumps of the Poorman and the Caribou mines. It is interesting to note that Horace Tabor had helped promote one of the early processes that used cyanide to recover gold, but like the Poorman Mine, his 1890s financial condition proved too precarious to grant him success. Cyanide, in a weak solution, dissolves gold and silver, which allowed low-grade deposits to be worked profitably. It also allowed dumps to be reworked to recover precious metals from the low-grade ore that previously could not be profitably milled and had been thrown out on the dump. The process provided a real boost for mining in the early twentieth century and prolonged the lives of declining districts.

It did not prove a lasting salvation for Caribou, however. After working for most of 1915, apparently without much success, the operators changed to a different process the next year—flotation-concentration. The remodeled mill still closed within the year. Reworking the old dumps, rather than mining, showed the district had markedly declined.

The hopeful did not give up. The *Boulder County Miner*, May 9, 1918, predicted a revival, "Caribou Coming." "It is not exactly a boom," the article went on, "but a steady setting in of the tide." At "Caribou-by-the-timberline," mining is "rising from ashes" in its "great unfathomed mineral veins." In the July 4 issue the reporter noted, "the camp is attracting many visitors with a view to capitalizing and getting busy."

The aging dowager, the Caribou Mine, attracted the most attention, as she always had. Veteran miner Jack Clark took over the property in 1918 and leased various levels. This well-known Boulder County mine operator had made his "stake" in the Nederland tungsten boom of the World War I era. During the next five years, about $300,000 "is said to have been taken out." That, of course, encouraged the *Miner*, which reported "wide veins" and high-grade ore. The mine, meanwhile, was unwatered to the 1,000-foot level. Throughout the 1920s, work continued. Hope sprang eternal at Caribou. One break came when electric lines reached Caribou, easing a longtime power problem, but not reviving mining.

It was not to be; hope proved fickle. The State Mining Bureau reported that not one Caribou mine operated in 1930. As the Great Depression settled in, Caribou slipped into silence. A few attempts were made to reopen this or that property, but neither investor nor rich ore appeared. A report for the years 1930–1938 gloomily stated that activity "was limited to sporadic attempts by individual operators to reactivate certain mines."

Caribou and other districts were also hurt when the Denver and Pueblo smelters closed, forcing them to ship ore to Leadville. This, noted a Bureau report, "necessarily resulted in the cessation of operations of nearly all, if not all, of the low grade mines" in Boulder, Clear Creek, and Gilpin counties. The solution, an "up-to-date, modern metallurgical reduction plant" at a central location, never rode to the rescue.

Except for occasional mining efforts, Caribou lay quiet until 1945. Old-timers dreamed that if silver reached $1.50, "Caribou would come back." That hope was reminiscent of one of Franklin's admonitions: "he that lives upon hope will die fasting." Yet it was just that hope, not reality, that had kept the mining West moving for nearly a century.

As World War II came to a stunning end amid the dropping of two atomic bombs, Caribou gained a fresh lease on life. In this new atomic world, uranium ore was found on the old Caribou dump. Suddenly, Caribou arose from its sleep and joined post-war America.

Work on reopening and lengthening the old Idaho Tunnel (3,700 feet long), which ran under Caribou Hill, started in 1946 with the hope of economically draining all the old workings above it. The Caribou Mine was again drained, reconditioned, and mining began in 1947. The Consolidated Caribou Silver Mines Company went into operation. Soon ore trucks rumbled down the road, carrying not only uranium ore. Some of that ore was worth mining for lead and silver.

Lead-silver ores went to the company's mill at Lakewood, five miles east of Caribou, then the concentrate was sent on to the Leadville smelter. During the next decade more than $500,000 of lead-silver came out of the Caribou workings.

Big news came in December 1952, with the announcement that a uranium vein had been discovered at the 1,000-foot level. Some pitch-blende was found in the Caribou, but primarily "the uranium-bearing veins do not differ in mineralogy from other lead-silver veins" in the area. In the midst of the Cold War, this appeared to be big news. Exploratory work, under contract with the Atomic Energy Commission, went on. Except for one vein, however, only trace amounts were found. Uranium mining continued on and off, but, unfortunately for Caribou, the ore proved low grade.

Current Caribou owner Tom Hendricks, in a November 5, 2002, letter, shed further light on these years.

> I spoke with many of the miners who worked in the Caribou
> Mine for the AEC during the late 40s and early 50s. They only
> brought out seven small train car loads of high-grade silver
> ore that contained pitchblende. The black sooty-looking pitch-
> blende ran several hundred to several thousand ounces of silver
> per ton. Most was kept for specimens.

When reopening the Caribou in 1984–1985, pitchblende occurred at only one spot on the 1,030-foot level. "We were unable to find any uranium ores or occurrences anywhere else in the mine."

Further, the uranium rush in the four corners region—New Mexico, Arizona, Colorado, and Utah—discovered larger, more accessible, and richer deposits near to new mills, all under the guidance of the AEC. Caribou could not keep pace, and the excitement and headlines soon faded.

The mine and mill shut down in 1955 and the mine flooded again by 1957. The old Caribou Mine suffered the indignity of being sold at public auction for delinquent taxes that same year. Once again quiet settled over Caribou Hill.

In the years that followed, plans appeared to revive the "historic Caribou Mine." Hopes and dreams produced little ore when they encountered reality in water-filled mines and collapsed tunnels.

Meanwhile, Caribou itself quietly disappeared into a fading yesterday. The few buildings still standing slowly collapsed under unrelenting snow and merciless wind, then disappeared back into the earth, ebbing like a dream. The Todd House, once a fixture for several generations of visitors, collapsed, and the last member of the original Todd family, who had long ago called it home, died in 1981. The remaining links to a pioneering generation had now joined those who had gone before. Caribou folk had, like their community, caught up with their past.

All was not gone, however. Like a phoenix arising from its ashes, Caribou mining revived in the mid-1970s. An article in the *Boulder*

Caribou's present and future, Tom Hendricks, standing at the port of the Cross Mine. Tom has mined thirty-one years at Caribou, longer than anyone else.

Camera (October 9, 1977) heralded the event: "Mine at Caribou Reopens After 38 Years." The Hendricks Mining Company opened the Cross Mine just slightly east of the original townsite. With the distinctive enthusiasm of Western miners since 1848, young, twenty-eight-year-old Tom Hendricks, the company's president, predicted a mining industry comeback. "Mining is going to boom in the West. It is going to happen."

The Cross dated back to Caribou's heyday but, like its neighbors, shut down with the collapse of the price of silver. It had reopened in 1928, operating until 1939. Like so many mines, its sporadic production history did not offer a great deal of promise, except to an enthusiastic young mining man.

An eight-year Caribou resident, Hendricks had started negotiating for the Cross five years before. He worked alone at first, then eventually added a crew. By 1977 the mine was producing thirty tons of ore per day from four levels, averaging six to seven ounces of silver and one-quarter ounce of gold per ton.

In a February 11, 1979, story in the *Rocky Mountain News,* Hendricks explained the problems facing a small mining operation. It takes at least six permits, an intimate knowledge and compliance with safety regulations, and at least $100,000 to open a small mine. A mill has to be available within a reasonable distance and ore has to be "worth about $80 a ton." Miners' wages could be a problem too: "A miner can make up to $100 a day."

Caribou had not changed one bit in winter, as he jokingly pointed out. "We have to shovel our way into the mine so we can shovel all day, then shovel our way out again." He gave this advice to those planning on opening a small mine.

> Plan on working sixty to eighty hours a week until the mine is profitable.
> Don't have an office staff bigger than the mine crew.
> Buy good used equipment and find a partner willing to stick through the thin times.
> Learn to sample ore correctly. It's easy to get excited over a rich pocket, but to make profits there has to be a good level of gold in all of the ore.
> Use selective mining techniques for best efficiency.

These constituted his mining tenets for the years ahead.

Times had changed greatly since Caribou and Colorado mining had been in their prime. By the 1970s environmental issues had raced to the forefront, and Boulder County stood on the cutting edge of the movement. To mine in Boulder County took an environmentally sensitive miner, something rather rare in the industry in those days.

Tom Hendricks matched that challenge. "Even though you have environmental restrictions, you can still work within them and produce," he believed, adding, "we are making money now." In the years that followed he proved that he was committed to an environmentally sound operation, along with reclamation. For example, dumps already on the site were backfilled into the new operations. Water coming out on the property was treated before it ran down Coon Trail Creek. Ongoing research continued, as Hendricks sought to find even more advanced water treatment methods. "We have more fun with this thing. We are not under tremendous pressure. We are striving for consistency and a good working environment."

Times had changed in another way. No longer was the too often used nineteenth-century philosophy of "rape, waste, and run" acceptable. Tom's philosophy reflected a new era and a new awareness of the role of mining. "Mining is not a get-rich-quick scheme anymore. Those days are over. But with hard, dedicated work, you can operate one mine as an ongoing business."

Just to be able to successfully operate a Boulder County mine in the late twentieth century indicated clearly that Tom Hendricks lived up to his credo. He represented one of the best of the new generation of small miners. Precious metal mining had become an endangered species in much of Colorado.

Not only that, Hendricks had gained a deep and lasting appreciation for Caribou's heritage, as well as Boulder County's mining legacy. His work to preserve this history served as an example for the industry as a whole. One outstanding effort was to try to preserve the old Caribou cemetery, which souvenir takers had vandalized almost out of existence.

His interest in mining's legacy goes far beyond this. He has opened his Cross Mine to tours, including many school groups. Like others in the industry, Hendricks has worked hard to overcome misconceptions of the industry's role in today's world. While this is neither the time nor place to sermonize, the old "rape and run" ideology has long ago seen its era pass. Its heritage persists, however. In particular this has involved environmental questions, which include mine drainage, dumps, old smelter locations, and superfund cleanup sites. The legacy of the industry has not always been good, even if judged by standards under which the old-timers worked.

Also, Hendricks became a guardian of this fragile mountain environment. Sometimes this led to a confrontation, as when a witless Denver disc jockey decided that Caribou Park would be a perfect place to let dull-witted, four-wheel-vehicle drivers and other misguided enthusiasts tear up the environment.

Over the decades the Hendricks mining company suffered problems that many a nineteenth-century miner would have readily understood. A fire burned several of the surface structures; the price of silver, and now free market gold, leaped and dipped almost at a whim; and operating money sometimes proved very hard to come by. Investors, too, languished few and far between.

Still Caribou operations produced 200,000 ounces of silver from the old Idaho Mine from 1977–1985. Mining operations were carried on through the reopened and renovated Caribou Tunnel. The Cross Mine during the same years yielded 5,000 ounces of gold and 250,000 ounces of silver, plus lead, zinc, and copper. Mining then slowed, affected by the fluctuation in precious and base metal prices. Exploration with core drilling continued and the Apache vein, right underneath the old Caribou townsite, opened.

In 1984–1985 Hendricks dewatered the Caribou. A "good deal" of money was spent at this time testing water and veins throughout the mine for radioactivity and none was found. This exploration did "allow for the discovery of several new high-grade gold/silver veins."

Without wavering, Hendricks continued on in the following years at Caribou with his Cross Mine and his faith in the district. He moved steadily to consolidate nearby claims, along with his property, into the Consolidated Caribou Mines project. Now it is all part of the Calais Resources Inc., with Tom as CEO and general manager.

The company in 2002 controlled a 3.5 square mile area in the district that contained both patented and unpatented lode mining claims. This included all the old major mines—Caribou, No Name, Poorman on Caribou Hill—and property almost down to now vanished Cardinal, once Caribou's small neighbor, and also the entire Caribou townsite.

Like miners of old, exploration and development plans look to the future. These include surface and underground core drilling, backed by that modern mining technique, the computer. Commented Tom Hendricks in November 2002, "Now after completing over 140,000 feet of diamond core drilling throughout the district, we have located seventy veins that hold over 500,000 ounces of gold and 20,000,000 ounces of silver."

Right next door to the Cross sits the Caribou Mine's 500-level buildings with its tunnel that taps back into Caribou Hill and the old workings. On the hill itself, the company has surface facilities where once the Caribou Mine and its neighbors held sway.

Looking back over the 133 years since Sam Conger and his friends discovered an outcropping of silver ore, nestled near Colorado's snowy range, Caribou has told the story of the dreams and disappointments, lives and times of generations of ordinary Americans. Few are remembered today, and like their town, they have left little note of their passing. Their dreams, however, have not died, as witnessed by the continued search for the elusive mineral wealth that brought them there in the first place.

Ralph Waldo Emerson wrote, "This time, like all times is a very good one, if we but know what to do with it." This serves as an excellent tribute to the people who called Caribou home, who persevered under some very trying conditions to make the very best of their time.

They knew what they planned to achieve with their efforts. That they did not always achieve their goals represents no failure.

Dell Merry, writing a long letter to her sister from Caribou (covering two days, April 23–24, 1889), discussed family matters such as the sisters' recent babies, the weather, and her family's "awfully cute little she dog about as big as your fist." She planned to "go below in another month for a few days" and would have a picture taken of her Clarence "and send you a specimen of a Rocky Mountain boy."

Commenting on the times, Dell spoke for miners and their families everywhere. She captured the essence of an age as well as anyone and, better than most, displayed the spirit and spunk that kept Caribou alive for decades and the mining industry continuing on into the twenty-first century.

> Times aren't very brisk here but might be much worse. Frank is leasing now but so far hasn't made much but we miners are always looking for something big whether we get it or not. No risk, no gain is our motto. We have enough to live on and that is more than a good many have so we ought to be thankful.

"Caribou Will Live Again!!"
A Photo Essay

As much as Caribou illustrated a great deal about its contemporary mining communities and districts, so did the years stretching into decades, that came after 1905. Mining, having declined in many districts and camps, became ghost towns where visitors wandered and wondered. New mining methods, new technology, and new ideas changed mining forever. As was written nearly twenty-four centuries ago by the Greek philosopher Heraclitus, "Nothing endures but change."

Well, maybe not all change! Caribou's winter weather remained eternally familiar. Observed "Miner Tom from the Hills at Caribou" in November 2002 amid another onrushing winter:

> I'm ready for another 32 years up here. The long
> winters at Caribou are more bearable as each year

passes, because you get used to 120-mile-per-hour winds, white-out snow, and sub-zero temperatures. It takes a few days for the wind to stop blowing to realize it has actually stopped blowing. I used to walk out of the mine building and throw the international mail into the air, so it would reach its destination on time. I had a pin-sized crack in the west wall of my cabin at the Cross Mine. In the morning after a driving blizzard, I would have a snow drift in my cabin from the kitchen through to the east wall of the living room. I used to keep the upper road open to the Comstock mine with a Cat D 7. By the time I got to the top of Caribou Hill and turned around, the bottom was completely snowed over again.

Miner Tom Hendricks, with the spunk and spirit that typified those Caribouites who had gone before, closed the letter with a resounding affirmation "Caribou will live again!!"

The few houses remaining in Caribou in 1911 easily sheltered the small population. Courtesy, U.S. Geological Survey

Mostly the dumps were being reworked in 1917, although some miners still held out hopes. Courtesy, Duane A. Smith

Winter still held a tight grip on the old buildings in the late 1920s. Courtesy, Garry Bryant

A few buildings calmly waited on Caribou Hill in 1939 to remind visitors what once had transpired there. Courtesy, Special Collections, Tutt Library, Colorado College

By 1952 only a handful of buildings survived the elements and tourists wandered about a ghost town. Courtesy, Duane A. Smith

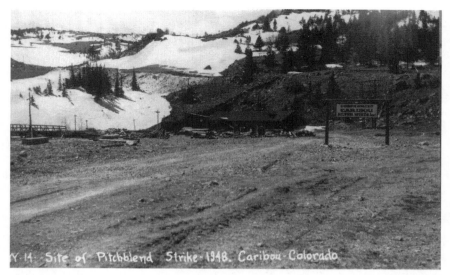

Uranium excitement briefly called attention to Caribou, but it passed as quickly as it had come. Courtesy, Special Collections, Tutt Library, Colorado College

As the 1970s opened, the remains of the 1920s stone buildings marked a town now gone. Courtesy, Duane A. Smith

A slow June day in 1980 at the Cross Mine. Courtesy, Duane A. Smith

Not much is left of the cemetery now; vandals have removed most of the grave stones in this photograph. Courtesy, Special Collections, Tutt Library, Colorado College

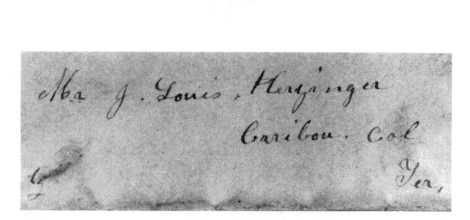

Of the people who once lived in Caribou, only memories remain and a few reminders such as this address on a faded envelope sent to Caribou, Colorado Territory. Courtesy, Duane A. Smith

Caribou's site on a bleak December 2002 day. Courtesy, Tom Hendricks

The Cross Mine as 2002 draws to a close. Courtesy, Tom Hendricks

Caribou lives on as Tom Hendricks takes a sixth-grade class through his gold mine. He has taken more than 38,000 people through his mine in the past thirty years. Courtesy, Tom Hendricks

Notes

Introduction: Silver Clarion

1. Hubert H. Bancroft, *California Inter Pocula* (San Francisco: The History Co., 1888), p. 381.

2. Mark Twain, *Roughing It* (Hartford: American Publishing Co., 1872), p. 304.

Rush to Riches

1. Interview with Samuel P. Conger, October 15, 1921. Mss IX-15, Colorado State Historical Society. Conger weaves in and out of the history of the *Grand Island Mining District*. He was involved in the Nederland tungsten boom in the early 1900s.

2. Those sources supporting Conger include Amos Bixby et al., *History of Clear Creek and Boulder Valleys, Colorado*, (Chicago: O. L. Baskin & Co., 1880), pp. 426–427 and the *Boulder County News*, July 28, 1876. Presenting an opposing view were the following: interviews with Hugh McCammon and William Martin located in the Bancroft Manuscripts, University of Colorado Western History

Collections; *Central City Register*, July 9, 1873; S. S. Wallihan and T. O. Bigney (eds.), *The Rocky Mountain Directory and Colorado Gazetteer for 1871* (Denver: S. S. Wallihan & Co., 1870), p. 414. Interview with Harold Martin (son of William Martin), July 19, 1960. Still another version is found in the *Central City Register*, July 9, 1873, and the *Boulder Herald*, Dec. 1, 1886. One tale that can be completely discounted is the story of Conger and the beautiful Arapahoe princess (see John and Doris Buchanan, *The Story of the Ghost Town Caribou*). No one involved in the original discovery, including Conger, mentions it. It definitely would appear to be a product of twentieth-century romanticism.

3. Filing notice of Carriboo [*sic*] Claim, Dec. 23, 1869, and Poor Man, March 26, 1870, pp. 181 and 187, respectively, of Boulder County Miscellaneous Record, Book H. Boulder County Court House. Interviews of McCammon, Conger, and W. Martin. Spelling of both names changed after this initial filing. Poorman became the accepted usage. Mrs. Alice Weber in a letter to the author, July 1960, noted that the group had very good reasons for not wanting Conger in the company. What these were is not known.

4. Material for this section was found in P. H. Van Diest, *The Grand Island Mining District of Boulder County, Colorado* (Denver: Mining Review Publishing Co., 1876), pp. 6–7. F. V. Hayden, *Seventh Annual Report of the United States Geological and Geographical Survey* (Washington: Government Printing Office, 1874), pp. 300–301. Joseph T. Singewald, "The Titaniferous Iron Ores in the United States," Department of Interior Bureau of Mines Bulletin 64 (Washington: Government Printing Office, 1913), pp. 126–128. F. B. Moore et al., *Geology and Uranium Deposits of the Caribou Area, Boulder County, Colorado* (Washington: Government Printing Office, 1957), pp. 522–523.

5. *Weekly Central City Register*, August 24, 1870. Hereafter referred to as the *Central City Register*.

6. *Daily Central City Register*, July 24, 1870.

7. *Central City Register*, June 22, 1870.

8. *Colorado Banner* (Boulder), July 31, 1879, and *Central City Register*, June 29, 1870.

9. Wallihan and Bigney, *Gazetteer*, p. 217. See also, W. Martin interview; *Central City Register*, June 22 and 29, 1870; *Daily Central City Register*, June 17, 1871.

10. Mill Records of the Caribou Company, Oct.–Dec. 1870, Harold Martin personal collection. *Daily Central City Register*, June 17, 1871.

11. *Caribou Post*, quoted in the *Daily Central City Register*, June 17, 1871. *Boulder County News*, June 22, 1870.

12. *Rocky Mountain News* (Denver), Sept. 23, 1870.

13. Boulder County RePlat of Plat Book 2 in 2 volumes. Vol. 1, p. 62. *Weekly Colorado Tribune* (Denver), Sept. 14, 1870. *Rocky Mountain News*, Sept. 23, 1970.

14. *Colorado Banner*, Feb. 23, 1876.

15. *Boulder County News*, Aug.–Sept. 1870.

16. *Central City Register*, Oct. 26, 1870.

17. *Central City Register*, Oct. 26, 1870; *Weekly Colorado Tribune*, Dec. 7, 1870.

18. The *Rocky Mountain Directory and Colorado Gazetteer for 1871*, p. 415.

Queen of Caribou Hill

1. John Tice, *Over the Plains and on the Mountains* (St. Louis: "Industrial Age" Printing Co., 1872), pp. 119–120.

2. *Caribou Post* (Caribou), Jan. 27, 1872. See also *Daily Central City Register*, May 19, 1871. *Boulder County News*, Dec. 22, 1871. *Caribou Post*, July 29, 1871. The *Caribou Post*, March 10, 1872, estimated that it took eight miners to keep one mill hand busy with ore.

3. Thomas Egleston, *The Metallurgy of Silver, Gold and Mercury* (New York: John Wiley & Sons, 1887), v. 1, pp. 233–238 and 350–353. *Caribou Post*, Jan. 27, 1872; *Boulder County News*, June 13, 1873; and Rossiter W. Raymond, *Statistics of Mines and Mining in the States and Territories West of the Rocky Mountains* (Washington: Government Printing Office, 1873), p. 291. Raymond's report of 1875, pp. 308–310, and Frank Fossett, *Colorado* (1876), pp. 383–384, carry detailed reports after it had been in operation.

4. *Boulder County News*, Sept. 8, 1871, reported the sale. H. Martin interview, July 19, 1960, gives the date of the deed as August 25, 1871.

5. See *Central City Register*, Jan. 11, 1871; *Boulder County News*, July 1, 1874; *Mining Review* (Georgetown), May–Aug. 1874.

6. See *Caribou Post*, July 8 and 22, 1871; *Boulder County News*, Nov. 21, 1871, Jan. 5 and Nov. 1, 1872, Feb. 28, 1873. *Rocky Mountain News* (Denver), May 21, 1871. *Weekly Colorado Tribune* (Denver), Dec. 7, 1870.

7. Breed to Martin, undated and April 10, 1872. Caribou Mine and Mining Company Records.

8. *Boulder County News*, March 14, 1873.

9. *Mining Review*, May 1873, pp. 31–32. See also *Boulder County News*, May 2, June 6, and June 13, 1873. *Central City Register*, April 30, 1873.

10. Eben Smith to H. Orahood, April 2, 1878. See also Eviction Notice, April 13, 1878; D. B. Miller, Cincinnati, to Henry and Willard Teller, Nov. 1, 1877, and March 26, 1878; and Nov. 2, 1875, Teller Papers. Following the sale of Caribou, Breed gave presents to the miners; at least the foreman received an engraved gold watch and his wife silk for a dress. Mrs. Catherine Burris to author, Feb. 1. 1961.

11. "Records of the Myncompagnie Nederland," Ministerie Van Economische, The Hague, Netherlands. The author has the records on microfilm.

12. *Mining Review*, May 15, 1876.

13. *Mining Review*, May 15, 1876; *Denver Republican*, Nov. 30, 1881; Fossett, *Colorado* (1876), pp. 381–382. For bullion records see *Central City Register*, April 9, 1873, and *Boulder County News*, March 14 and 28, 1873.

14. P. H. Van Diest, The *Grand Island Mining District*, p. 7.

15. *Daily Register*, July 7, 1870. Moses Anker, *A Hurry-Graph of Colorado and Its Silver Mines* (Baltimore: Jones Brothers, 1870).

16. Richard Harvey to De Bruyn Prince, Aug. 28, 1874; Harvey to John Moyle, Aug. 7 and Sept. 15, 1874; and Harvey to William Downing, March 31, 1875. Richard Harvey's Copying Book, Colorado State Historical Society (also printed in *1958 Brand Book of the Denver Westerners*). Harvey was foreman of the Caribou Mine from January 20, 1874, to November 1874. Hereafter cited as Harvey Col. Raymond, *Statistics of Mines* (1875), p. 206, levels a charge of dissension in the company.

17. Harvey to L. S. Nyburg, March 22, 1875, Harvey Col.

18. Van Bosse to S. S. de Pinto, Sept. 18, 1874, "Records of the Myncom-pagnie Nederland," translated copy in author's possession.

19. Unnamed Dutch journal quoted in *Boulder County News*, May 7, 1875.

20. In the case of *Augustine Langford vs. Mining Company Nederland* . . . (626), Boulder District Court, the court ruled the property would be foreclosed and sold. See also *Jerome B. Chaffee vs. the Mining Company Nederland* (628); *Moses Anker and M. A. Shaffenburg vs. the Mining Company Nederland* (629); *Moses Anker vs. the Mining Company Nederland* (633). There are numerous other cases on record in the Boulder District Court archives.

21. *Rocky Mountain News*, June 2, 1876.

22. For information regarding this whole episode, see *Central City Register* (daily and weekly), Dec. 8, 10, 13, 14, 1875, and April 12, 1876; *Boulder County News*, Dec. 17, 1875, and March 24, 1876; *Mining Review*, May 15, 1876; and *Colorado Banner* (Boulder), Feb. 3 and March 2, 1876.

23. Quoted in the *Boulder County News*, April 7, 1876.

24. *Central City Register* (daily), Dec. 14, 1876. *Rocky Mountain News*, July 19, 1876, and Jan. 2, 1884; *Colorado Banner*, Feb. 3, 1876. *The Denver Inter-Ocean*, March 14, 1880, claimed the Dutch experts had too much champagne while on their visit.

25. Harvey to Nyburg, March 22 and April 13, 1875; Harvey to Downing, March 21, 1875, Harvey Col. See also Regis Chauvenet, *The Caribou Silver Mines* (Golden: n.p., 1887), p. 6. *New York Times*, July 28, 1877.

26. *Engineering and Mining Journal*, March 8, 1879.

Eastern Investors Try Their Luck

1. Tice, *Over the Plains*, p. 112. Tice does not define a well-paying mine.

2. For further information on the two mines, see *Boulder County News*, April 8, 1871, Nov. 29, 1872, May 30, 1873, Aug. 21, 1874; Raymond, *Statistics 1872*, p. 292; *Central City Register*, Jan. 8 and Nov. 26, 1873; *Caribou Post*, Sept. 16 and Oct. 7, 1871; *Denver Tribune*, June 30, 1874.

3. *Colorado Banner* (Boulder), Feb. 3. 1876. See also Raymond, *Statistics 1875*, p. 307. *Boulder County News*, April 23 and July 23, 1875, Feb. 18, 1876; *Mining Review* (Georgetown), May–Sept. 1875; *Central City Register*, April 12, 1876. *Colorado Banner*, July 13, 1876, and May 29, 1877. *Engineering and Mining Journal*, May 6, 1876.

4. Levi M. Bates to Henry Teller, Dec. 14, 1875, April 2, Sept. 20, Oct. 28, and Dec. 19 and 27, 1876, Jan. 13, 1877. M. A. Smith to Teller, June 7, 1875, and Nov. 18, 1876. Found in Teller Papers, Western History Collections, University of Colorado.

5. R. G. Dun to J. Dun, July 15, 1872. W. Fullerton to D. Moffat, March 8, 1877. The quotations from and, in some instances, complete copies of the Dun and Fullerton letters were furnished the author by Owen A. Sheffield, former corporate secretary of Dun & Bradstreet. The original letter books are in the archives of Dun & Bradstreet.

6. R. G. Dun to J. Dun, Nov. 18, 1875. R. G. Dun to J. S. Brown & Bro. (Denver), Nov. 24, 1876.

7. R. G. Dun to J. Dun, Aug. 17, 1876.

8. R. G. Dun to J. Dun, Nov. 10, 1876.

9. R. G. Dun to W. Fullerton, Nov. 16 and Dec. 13, 1876. R. G. Dun to W. Dun, Aug. 17, 1876. R. G. Dun to J. Dun, Nov. 10, 11, and 28, 1876.

10. R. G. Dun to J. S. Brown & Bro. (Denver), Nov. 24, 1876.

11. R. G. Dun to J. Dun, Nov. 28, 1876.

12. *First National Bank of Denver vs. Sherman Mining Company and the No Name Mining Co., Boulder District Court* (802), Oct. 17, 1877. Other cases filed in Boulder District Court relating to these companies were in order of their appearance: *George Scott and William Scott . . . vs. Sherman Mining Company* (705); *John J. Ellingham vs. Sherman Mining Company and No Name Mining Company*; *John Best vs. H. Mincler [sic], the Sherman Mining Company, and the No Name Mining Company* (794); *Wm. M. Roworth and Richard C. Lake . . . vs. H. Mincler, [sic], the Sherman Mining Company, and the No Name Mining Company* (793); *Charles F. Hendrie and Wm. Hendrie and Henry Bolthoff . . . vs. H. Mincler [sic], the Sherman Mining Company, and the No Name Mining Company* (795); *Walter Smith and Leon Smith . . . vs. the No Name Company and the Sherman Company* (875); and *William Scott and George Scott . . . vs. Martin A. Smith et al.* (991). See also minutes of Board Directors First National Bank, Dec. 14, 1878.

13. R. G. Dun to J. Dun, Jan. 26, 1877.

14. R. G. Dun to J. Dun, Jan. 26 and June 5, 1877.

15. R. G. Dun to J. Dun, Oct. 31, 1877, and Jan. 28, 1878.

16. R. G. Dun to J. Dun, Sept. 17, 1879. R. G. Dun to Wm. Teller, Sept. 16, 1879. See also *Boulder News and Courier*, April 11 and July 25, 1879, June 25, 1880.

17. *Native Silver Mining Company of Boulder County Colorado* (New York: n.p., 1880), pp. 4–8. Fossett, *Colorado* (1876), p. 388. *Boulder County News*, Nov. 27, 1874, Feb. 26, Mar. 12, and June 18, 1875.

18. *Rocky Mountain News* (Denver), Aug. 12, 1871. *Caribou Post*, Aug. 19, Sept. 16, Oct. 7, Nov. 18, 1871, and Jan. 13, 1872. Rossiter Raymond, *Silver and Gold* (New York: J. B. Ford & Co., 1873), p. 360.

19. *Colorado Banner*, March 1, 1877; *Boulder County News*, June 23, 1876, Jan. 26, 1877; and *Central City Register*, July 5, 1876. See also *Engineering and Mining Journal* (New York), Aug. 11, 1877.

20. *Rocky Mountain News*, Oct. 2, 1878; *Colorado Banner*, July 4 and Nov. 7, 1878; see also *Boulder County News*, Oct. 26, 1877; *Central City Register*, July 5, 1876, May 5 and Sept. 29, 1877. *Colorado Banner*, May 10 and June 7, 1877. *Engineering and Mining Journal*, July 13 and Oct. 12, 1878. David Brunton interview in T. A. Richard, *Interviews with Mining Engineers* (San Francisco: Mining and Scientific Press, 1922), pp. 71–72.

21. *Colorado Banner*, Feb. 22 and June 14, 1877, and April 25, 1878; *Weekly Central City Register-Call*, Aug. 30, 1878; *Boulder News and Courier*, June 25, 1880. See also *Charles F. Hendrie and Henry Bolthoff . . . vs. Mining Company New Jersey*, Boulder District Court, Feb. 8, 1878. *Engineering and Mining Journal*, Oct. 12, 1878, Dec. 6, 1879, and Jan. 24, 1880.

22. *Boulder County News*, April 8, 1871, Jan. 26, April 5, July 12, 1872, Jan. 16, 1874; *Caribou Post*, Jan. 20 and April 27, 1872; *Engineering and Mining Journal*, Oct. 12, 1878; *Rocky Mountain News*, Oct. 2, 1878; *Boulder News and Courier*, April 4, 1879. *Rocky Mountain Sun*, Aug. 5, 1883.

23. See the *Boulder County News*, July 13 and 27, 1870, April 8, 1872, Aug. 22, 1873, Aug. 14 and Nov. 20, 1874; *Central City Register*, June 22, 1870, and Jan. 8, 1873. Thomas B. Corbett, *Colorado Directory of Mines* (Denver: *Rocky Mountain News* Printing Co., 1879), p. 110.

24. *Central City Register*, April 12, 1876, and *Rocky Mountain News*, June 2, 1876.

"It Takes a Mine to Work a Mine"

1. *Rocky Mountain News*, July 19, 1876.

2. *Central City Register*, Sept. 6, 1876. *Denver Mirror*, June 23, 1877, and *Rocky Mountain News* (weekly), Jan. 1, 1879.

3. E. Smith to D. Moffat, Dec. 9, 1876, Caribou Papers, First National Bank of Denver.

4. *Jerome B. Chaffee vs. the Mining Company Nederland, Arvin H. Henry, the First National Bank of Denver et al.* (787). The case of *James Pippin vs. the Mining Company Nederland and George Corning* (623), Boulder District Court, describes the distribution of the sale proceeds and surplus money. Chaffee was still being sued over the Caribou transaction as late as 1885. *Rocky Mountain News*, June 12, 1885.

5. W. Fullerton to D. Moffat, March 8, 1877, and Fullerton to J. A. Dun, March 8, 1877, Dun Papers. *Rocky Mountain News*, Feb. 27, 1877.

6. R. G. Dun to J. Dun, March 29, 1878. See also the *Engineering and Mining Journal*, Oct. 12, 1878.

7. The above description of the mine was taken from the *Boulder News and Courier*, April 4, 1879; *Central City Register-Call*, May 30, 1879; Frank Fossett, *Colorado* (New York: C. G. Crawford, 1879), pp. 263–265, and Corbett, *Colorado Directory of Mines*, p. 77.

8. Warranty deed, filed Boulder County, May 16, 1879; the original was dated April 25.

9. *Boulder News and Courier*, Sept. 19 and Nov. 28, 1879; *Central City Register-Call*, Sept. 19, 1879. *Engineering and Mining Journal*, June 21 and Aug. 16, 1879.

10. R. G. Dun to Reed and Teller, June 9, 1879; R. G. Dun to J. Dun, July 8, 1879. *Caribou Consolidated Mining Company vs. R. G. Dun, J. A. Dun, and Herman Minkler [sic]* (1127). *Rocky Mountain News*, April 20, 1880. See also *R. Dun vs. Eben Smith et al.*, United States Circuit Court, Denver, Colorado (338), and *James Dun vs. Caribou Consolidated Mining Company*, United States Circuit Court, Denver, Colorado (418). *James Dun vs. Caribou Consolidated Mining Company*, United States Circuit Court, Denver, Colorado (400).

11. *Denver Republican*, quoted in *Rocky Mountain News*, May 15, 1880. *Rocky Mountain News*, Jan. 25 and 27, 1880.

12. *The Caribou Consolidated Mining Company and Joseph Irwin vs. Gilbert Lehmer and Samuel Richards* (1148). *Boulder News and Courier*, Feb. 27 and March 19, 1880; *Rocky Mountain News*, March 2, 1880, and Dec. 7, 1883.

13. R. G. Dun, April 11, 1878. *Boulder News and Courier*, May 21, 1880.

14. *New York Times*, March 30, 1880. *Engineering and Mining Journal* (New York), Jan.–April 1880. *Mining Record*, April 17, 1880.

15. R. G. Dun to J. Dun, Nov. 15, Dec. 11 and 27, 1879, and Jan. 9, 1880. R. G. Dun to H. Minckler, Jan. 9, 1880.

16. R. G. Dun to J. Dun, Jan. 27 and 29, 1880; R. G. Dun to Minckler, Feb. 20, 1880.

17. R. G. Dun to J. Dun, Feb. 24, 1880.

18. *Rocky Mountain News*, April 20, 1880. *James A. Dun vs. Eben Smith* (1157). *Jerome B. Chaffee vs. James A. Dun* (1156). *Engineering and Mining Journal*, Jan. 17 and 24, 1880.

19. R. G. Dun to J. Dun, April 8 and 24 and May 13, 1880. The *Central City Register-Weekly*, July 9, 1880, stated Dun was issued $500,000 in stocks.

20. *Boulder News and Courier*, April 9, 1880. R. G. Dun to J. Dun, June 25, 1880. *Mining Record*, May 15, 1880. *Engineering and Mining Journal*, June 5 and 26, 1880.

21. R. G. Dun to J. Dun, Aug. 5, 1880; R. G. Dun to Eben Smith, Sept. 8, Oct. 11, and Oct. 20, 1880.

Mines and Miners

1. *Colorado Banner* (Boulder), March 6, 1879.

2. Statistics on the Caribou found in the Caribou Papers, First National Bank of Denver.

3. Caribou and Idaho Mine records. Caribou Papers, First National Bank of Denver. See also *James A. Dun vs. Caribou Consolidated Mining Company*, United States Circuit Court, Denver, Colorado (400).

4. Caribou Papers, First National Bank of Denver. The Harvey letters include a notice of a bid on the Caribou shaft. See also letter from D. B. Miller to H. and W. Teller, Sept. 20, 1875, Teller Papers; Caribou and Idaho Mine records, Martin Collection; *Mining Review* (Georgetown), Nov. 1874; Fossett, Colorado (1876), p. 262; *Central City Register-Call*, May 30, 1879. *Boulder County News*, Aug. 10, 1877.

5. *Mining Review*, Aug. 1875.

6. *Colorado Banner*, July 31, 1879. See also Harvey to John B. Moyle, Sept. 15, 1874, Harvey Col. Interviews with Harold Martin, July 19, 1960, and Elizabeth Amelia (Todd) Lee, Aug. 2, 1960. (Mrs. Lee was born in Caribou, June 14, 1876.)

7. *Rocky Mountain News* (Denver), May 12, 1874. Original census returns, Caribou, Boulder County, Colorado, 1880.

8. Material for the paragraph was found in Miners Lien Book, Boulder County; Caribou Mine records; Martin Col. Harvey to John B. Moyle, Sept. 15, 1874, and Harvey to De Bruyn Prince, Aug. 26 and 28, 1874, Harvey Col.; *Boulder County News*, June 13, 1872, and June 5, 1874; *Central City Register-Call*, Aug. 8, 1879; *Boulder Camera*, Aug. 28, 1919; Census, 1880.

9. Material for the foregoing section on the Caribou Mine from Caribou Papers, First National Bank of Denver.

10. *Boulder County News*, Dec. 13, 1872, and Feb. 27, 1874.

11. R. G. Dun to J. Dun, Nov. 10, 1876. See also Nov. 11 and 28 letters to Jim.

12. *Colorado Banner*, May 10, 1877; *Boulder News and Courier*, July 25, 1879, and April 16 and 23, 1880; *Central City Register-Call*, Aug. 8, 1879.

13. *Boulder County News*, March 20, April 8 and 17, and May 1, 1874; *Rocky Mountain News*, April 2, 1874.

14. Van Diest, *Grand Island Mining District*, p. 11, and *Engineering and Mining Journal* (New York), Aug. 11, 1877.

Businessman's Bonanza

1. Tice, *Over the Plains*, pp. 110–111. The *Caribou Post*, May 11, 1872, had this to say about Tice: "we believe the author is a good, true and honest man."

2. *New York Times*, Sept. 23, 1871.

3. Tice, *Over the Plains*, p. 118. *Caribou Post* (undated), quoted in the *Daily Central City Register* (Central City), June 2, 1871.

4. *Caribou Post*, July 8, 1871; *Caribou Post* (undated), quoted in *Central City Register*, May 19, 1871; *Boulder County News* (Boulder), May 20, 27, and Aug. 26, 1871; *Rocky Mountain News* (Denver), July 15, 1871.

5. *Colorado Business Directory and Annual Register for 1875* (Denver: J. A. Blake, 1875), p. 81. *Colorado State Business Directory* (Denver: J. A. Blake, 1879), p. 59. *Rocky Mountain News*, July 15, 1879. Murphy's name also appeared Murphey.

6. *Boulder County News*, Feb. 2, 1877.

7. Business records of Caribou Mine, Caribou Papers, First National Bank of Denver.

8. *Rocky Mountain News*, July 15, 1871, and *Boulder County News*, July 15, 1871.

9. Raymond, *Statistics of Mines* (1874), p. 369. *Boulder County News*, Sept. 25 and Nov. 27, 1874.

10. *Colorado Banner* (Boulder), Aug. 16, 1877, and April 25, 1878.

11. Quote from *Daily Central City Register*, July 15, 1874. See also Tice, *Over the Plains*, p. 111; *Rocky Mountain News*, July 15, 1871; *Caribou Post*, July 8, 1871; *Boulder County News*, July 19, 1872.

12. *Boulder County News*, July 23, 1875. See also issues of Sept. 4, 1874, July 9, 1875, April 28, 1876, and November 30, 1877; *Colorado Banner*, Jan. 23, 1879.

13. R. G. Dun to J. Dun, Feb. 14, 1880. Donald Dictation, Bancroft Library, 1880.

14. Boulder and Caribou Wagon Road Company Secretary Book, pp. 5–13. Bixby et al., *History of Clear Creek and Boulder Valleys, Colorado*, p. 393. *Caribou Post*, July 22, 1871.

15. *Boulder County News*, Dec. 7 and 21, 1877; *Colorado Banner*, Dec. 27, 1877, and March 7, 1878; *Boulder News and Courier* (Boulder), Sept. 5, 1879. *Caribou Post*, Oct. 17, 1871. Engineering and *Mining Record*, April 5, 1885.

16. *New York Times*, Sept. 28, 1876; *Boulder County News*, April 14 and 28 and Sept. 22, 1876; *Mining Review* (Denver), April 17, 1876.

17. *Rocky Mountain News*, April 29 and May 3, 1873; *Boulder County News*, May 9 and June 13, 1873; *Central City Register*, April 30, 1873. Apparently there were ten bricks paving the entrance before the Teller House.

18. Tice, *Over the Plains*, p. 109.

"A Town Well Worth Having"

1. *Boulder County News*, Oct. 9, 1874; *Colorado Banner* (Boulder), April 6, 1876; *Rocky Mountain News* (Denver), June 28 and July 9, 1878; *Camera* (Boulder), March 17, 1899; *Denver Tribune*, April 5, 1882. The *Daily* petition to incorporate the town of Caribou is in the files of the *Camera*.

2. *Colorado Banner*, April 25 and July 4, 1878, and Jan. 23, 1879; *Boulder News and Courier*, April 4, 1879, and April 9, 1880. *Native Silver Mining Company*, p. 5.

3. *Colorado Banner*, April 25, 1878.
4. *Central City Register*, May 5, 1875.
5. *Boulder County News*, Nov. 29, 1872.
6. Tice, *Across the Plains*, p. 122.
7. *Boulder County News*, Feb. 15, 1871, June 7, 1872, July 18, 1873, and July 2 and 9, 1875; *Central City Register*, April 15, 1874; *Colorado Banner*, March 22, 1877; *Denver Tribune*, March 7, 1878.
8. *Colorado Banner*, April 17, 1876; *Boulder County News*, Jan. 9, 1874, and Aug. 4, 1876.
9. *Caribou Post*, August 12, 1871. See also Bixby et al., *History of Clear Creek and Boulder Valleys*, p. 427. The *Post*'s first issue appeared May 27; the early editions have been lost, but the Denver Public Library has a run from July 1871–Aug. 1872.
10. *Caribou Post*, August 17, 1872. See also the March 30, 1872, issue.
11. *Caribou Post*, Oct. 7, 1871; *Boulder County News*, June 20, 1873; Census, 1880; *Boulder News and Courier*, July 1, 1881, and May 4, 1883.
12. *Boulder County News*, Sept. 6, 1878.
13. *Boulder County News*, Sept. 22, 1871, Sept. 27, 1872, Sept. 12, 1873, Sept. 25, 1874, Sept. 17, 1875, July 7 and Oct. 20, 1876, Oct. 4, 1878, and Oct. 17, 1879.
14. Examples are *Rocky Mountain News*, July 15, 1871, about 700; *Boulder County News*, March 7, 1873, 500, Feb. 19, 1875, 800; and *Colorado State Business Directory* (1879), 400. Even at the time, however, there was a divergence of estimates. For example, the *Business Directory* (1877) states a population of 400 and the *Boulder County News* estimated 700.
15. The ratio came out to 4 inhabitants to 1 qualified voter by dividing 137 into 549. The 137 figure represents the 105 votes cast, plus 30 percent, or 32, to allow for those men who did not vote. This, however, is just an estimated percentage. The 1873 figure is probably high as there were still a proportionately greater number of men than women in the camp.
16. Bixby et al., *History of Clear Creek and Boulder Valleys*, p. 427. *Boulder County News*, Nov. 6, 1874. See also Fossett, *Colorado* (1876), p. 389; *Boulder County News*, June 17, 1871. *Central City Register*, April 7, 1875.
17. *Boulder County News*, May 17, 1872.

"Preaching Every Sunday, Shoo Fly Every Night"

1. Both quotes from the *Boulder County News*, Nov. 27 and Sept. 25, 1874, respectively.
2. *Daily Central City Register*, July 15, 1874. See also *Caribou Post*, Aug. 5 and Sept. 30, 1871; *Rocky Mountain Presbyterian*, April and Sept. 1872; *Rocky Mountain News* (Denver), Sept. 23, 1873; *Boulder County News*, Aug. 7, 1874. *Colorado Business Directory and Annual Register for 1876* (Denver: J. A. Blake, 1876), p. 79.
3. Mary Collins, *Pioneering in the Rockies* (Boulder: privately printed, n.d.), pp. 93–97. For information on Stocks, see Isaac Beardsley, *Echoes from Peak and Plain* (Cincinnati: Curts and Jennings, 1898), pp. 416–418; *Rocky Mountain News*, June 28, 1878; *Boulder News and Courier*, Jan. 3, April 4, and Aug. 1, 1879 and April 9, 1880.
4. *Boulder County News*, Sept. 6, 1878, and *Boulder News and Courier*, April 4, 1879. The school was in district no. 19, Boulder County.

5. *Colorado Banner*, May 17, 1877; *Boulder County News*, April 6, 1877. Her name was also spelled Bumbeau.

6. Elizabeth Stanton, Susan Anthony, and Matilda Gage (eds.), *History of Woman Suffrage*, v. 3, p. 719. *Caribou Post*, Sept. 2 and 30, 1871; *Daily Central City Register*, Aug. 25, 1871; *New York Tribune*, Sept. 23, 1871; *Boulder County News*, May 2, 1872; *Colorado Banner*, April 12 and 26, 1877. A Mrs. Shields spoke for woman suffrage at Caribou in Sept. 1877, *Rocky Mountain News*, Sept. 28, 1877.

7. *Colorado Banner*, May 10, 1877; *Boulder County News*, May 4 and 18, 1877. See also *Central City Register*, July 5, 1876; *Rocky Mountain News*, March 29, 1874; *Boulder County News*, Nov. 30, 1877; *Colorado Banner*, Aug. 16, 1877.

8. *Colorado Banner*, May 17, 1877.

9. Interview with Heimer Murphy, daughter of Joseph J. Murphy, *Camera* files, no date. *Boulder News and Courier*, Jan. 3, 1879.

10. *Boulder County News*, July 15, 1871, and July 23, 1875; *Colorado Banner*, June 14, 1877. *Rocky Mountain News*, July 6, 1872.

11. *Boulder County News*, June 15, 1877.

12. *Boulder County News*, Jan. 10, 1873.

13. *Daily Central City Register*, June 12, 1870. Also see July 22 and Aug. 8 issue of the daily and June 15 of the weekly. For the Caribou Shoo Fly, *Boulder County News*, Sept. 20, 1872, and March 14, 1873; *Central City Register*, April 7, 1875.

14. Entries taken from Harvey's Copying Book, July 26–Sept. 1874.

15. Material for the preceding paragraphs was found in Caroline Bancroft, "Folklore of the Central City District," *California Folklore Quarterly* IV (Oct. 1945), pp. 315–342; David H. Stratton, "The Cousin Jacks of Caribou," *Colorado Quarterly* I (Spring 1953), pp. 371–384; Lynn I. Perrigo, "The Cornish Miners of Early Gilpin County," *Colorado Magazine* XIV (May 1937), pp. 92–101; Francis C. Young, *Echoes from Arcadia* (Denver: Lanning Bros., 1903), pp. 91–92; A. K. Hamilton Jenkin, *The Cornish Miner* (London: George Allen & Unwin Ltd., 1927), especially chapters six and seven.

16. *Caribou Post*, January 13, 1872.

17. *Boulder County News*, July 9, 1875.

18. Smith to Moffat, Dec. 9, 1876, Caribou Papers, First National Bank of Denver.

19. *Colorado Banner*, March 6, 1879.

20. *Boulder County News*, April 5 and May 3, 1872; *Colorado Banner*, May 10, 1877.

21. This composite picture was drawn from the following sources: *Boulder News and Courier*, Sept. 19, 1879; *Colorado Banner*, Sept. 18, 1879; Collins, *Pioneering in the Rockies*, p. 88.

22. *Boulder News and Courier*, Oct. 17, 1879. See also *Rocky Mountain News*, Sept. 17 and 19, 1879. *Boulder News and Courier*, Sept. 19, 1879.

23. *Central City Register*, quoted in the *Boulder County News*, Feb. 6, 1874. *Caribou Post*, July 22 and Dec. 16, 1871.

Hope Springs Eternal

1. *Boulder News and Courier*, April 8 and Nov. 12, 1880, July 8 and Dec. 30, 1881; *Denver Republican*, Nov. 30, 1881; *Rocky Mountain News* (Denver), July 1 and

Dec. 18, 1881, Feb. 25, 1882; *Engineering and Mining Journal* (New York), May 22, 1880 and June 25, 1881.

2. R. G. Dun to E. Smith, Jan. 5, 1881, and R. G. Dun to J. T. Graham, June 14, 1881. See also R. G. Dun to E. Smith, Feb. 25 and April 20, 1881; R. G. Dun to M. A. Gilkerson, May 1, 1881, and R. G. Dun to J. T. Graham, July 27, 1881.

3. R. G. Dun to W. G. Scarlett, Jan. 19, 1881. R. G. Dun to J. Dun, Nov. 16, 1881.

4. R. G. Dun to J. T. Graham, March 24, 1882.

5. R. G. Dun to J. Dun, Dec. 13, 1882. *Boulder News and Courier*, July 21, 1882. *Mining Record*, Feb. 25, p. 181, June 3, p. 513, and July 29, 1882, p. 109. *Denver Tribune*, Sept. 30, 1882. *Rocky Mountain News*, Aug. 23, 1882, in a moment of exhilaration claimed the mine would be producing when "the present generation has passed away."

6. *Boulder County Herald*, Aug. 16, 1882. *Denver Republican*, Aug. 10, 1882.

7. *Rocky Mountain News*, Jan. 20 and Feb. 20, 1883. *Boulder News and Courier*, Feb. 2 and March 2, 1883. *Daniel Campbell and George McCord vs. People of the State of Colorado*, District Court, Boulder County, Colorado, 1606 (1883). R. G. Dun to C. G. Buckingham, Jan. 24, 1883. It is not known if Giffin was acting on behalf of Dun when paying the seventy-five cents on the dollar. *Mining Record*, Jan. 6, 1883, has several comments.

8. R. G. Dun to E. Smith, Jan. 9, 1883. Smith apparently was trying to interest Dun in another mining property, but Dun turned him down because of the Caribou troubles.

9. R. G. Dun to J. R. Frith, Jan. 22–27, 1884.

10. R. G. Dun to J. R. Frith, Feb. 6, 1883, and R. G. Dun to S. A. Giffin, Feb. 7, 1883. See also R. G. Dun to S. A. Giffin, Feb. 21, 1883.

11. *Boulder County Herald*, Feb. 21, 1883. See also *Rocky Mountain News*, Mar. 13 and 27, 1883. *Joseph R. Frith vs. Caribou Consolidated Mining Company, a corporation*, District Court, Boulder County, Colorado, 1657 and 1678 (1883).

12. R. G. Dun to J. R. Frith, March 2, 1883. Also see R. G. Dun to J. R. Frith, Feb. 26 and Mar. 17, 1883; R. G. Dun to J. B. Metcalf, March 7, 1883.

13. *Boulder County Herald*, July 4, 1883. R. G. Dun to J. R. Frith, June 26 and Oct. 18, 1883. For further information see the *Boulder County Herald*, April 18 and Aug. 29, 1883.

14. R. G. Dun to R. George Dun, March 1, 1884. See also R. G. Dun to J. R. Frith, Jan. 22–27, 1884.

15. *Rocky Mountain News*, Dec. 25, 1883. *Report of the Director of the Mint . . . in the United States, 1884* (Washington: Government Printing Office, 1885), p. 183.

16. R. G. Dun to W. James, Aug. 30, 1888. See also R. G. Dun to J. Frith, Nov. 16, 1885; R. G. Dun to M. A. Smith, Jan. 26, 1886, and April 30, 1888; R. G. Dun to S. A. Giffin, Nov. 10, 1886; R. G. Dun to W. Donald, Nov. 13, 1886. *Boulder County Herald*, Dec. 15, 1886, Jan. 12, March 16, and Sept. 28, 1887, and July 18 and Sept. 5, 1886. *Boulder News*, Aug. 28, 1888. Chauvenet, *Caribou Silver Mines*, pp. 7 and 23.

17. Quote from R. G. Dun to W. James, Feb. 13, 1889; also letters of Jan. 28 and Nov. 14, 1889, to James. R. G. Dun to M. A. Smith, Dec. 11, 1889. *Boulder County Herald*, Feb. 20, March 13, and May 1, 1889.

18. R. G. Dun to H. Minckler, June 26, 1883; R. G. Dun to J. R. Frith, March 17, May 29, and June 26, 1883. For additional information see *Boulder News and Courier*, June 25, 1880, and July 15, 1881; *Boulder County Herald*, Feb. 20 and July 3, 1889; R. G. Dun to E. Smith, June 16, 1881; R. G. Dun to G. Teal, March 27, 1882. R. G. Dun to H. Minckler, Feb. 13 and March 2, 1883.

19. *Caribou Post*, Oct. 7, 1871. Corbett, *Colorado Directory of Mines*, p. 108. *Boulder Herald*, Feb.–Aug. 1885.

20. *Rocky Mountain News*, Aug. 19, 1884; *Boulder County Herald*, March 18, 1885, Sept. 29 and Nov. 24, 1886; *Boulder News and Banner*, Dec. 6, 1887, *Engineering and Mining Journal*, July 2 and July 16, 1887.

21. Quote from *Boulder County Herald*, Dec. 22, 1886; *Boulder News and Courier*, March 24, 1882; *Rocky Mountain News*, Mar. 30, 1882, Aug. 19, 1884; *Boulder County Herald*, Jan. 31, 1883, Mar. 18, 1885, Sept. 29, 1886.

22. "Agreement between H. A. W. Tabor and the Poorman Silver Mines" indicates the arrangements of the 1888 sale, The Poorman Silver Mines (of Colorado), microfilm, Bancroft Library. *Boulder County Herald*, April 25, 1888, Feb. 20 and Nov. 13, 1889. *Poorman* (Denver: Poorman Mining Company, 1888?), pp. 4–12.

23. Moore et al., *Geology and Uranium*, p. 521.

24. *Boulder County Herald*, May 1, 1889.

25. R. G. Dun to J. W. Fox, Dec. 27, 1889.

26. *Boulder News and Courier*, July 15, 1881. *Boulder County, Colorado* (Boulder: Banner Office Print, 1882), p. 5. *Boulder County Herald*, July 1, 1885, and Mar. 13, 1889.

27. S. F. Emmons, "Geological Sketch of the Rocky Mountain Division," *Tenth Census of the United States*, vol. 13 (Washington: Government Printing Office, 1885), pp. 123–124. Several people interviewed gave more mining deaths than this for the decade, but they could have been confused as to when the accident actually happened. Probably more than one man was killed, however.

"Times Ain't Quite as Lively"

1. *Boulder News and Courier*, March 24, 1882.

2. *Boulder News and Courier*, July 1, 1881, and Sept. 8, 1882. *Colorado State Business Directory*, 1883 and 1889 (Denver: James R. Ives & Co., 1883 and 1889), pp. 90 and 161.

3. *Boulder County Herald*, July 1, 1885. See also May 13 issue and *Boulder News and Courier*, April 9 and Nov. 12, 1880, and July 1, 1881; *Rocky Mountain News* (Denver), March 12, 1881.

4. See *Boulder County Herald*, Aug. 26–Sept. 16, 1885. For the band, see *Boulder News and Courier*, July 1, 1881, and *Boulder County Herald*, Nov. 3 and 24, 1886.

5. *Boulder County Herald*, May 11, 1887.

6. Election returns were found in *Boulder News and Courier*, Nov. 5 and 12, 1880, and Nov. 10, 1882; *Boulder County Herald*, April 11, 1883, Nov. 12 and 19, 1884, Nov. 10, 1886, Nov. 14, 1888, and Nov. 12, 1890. *Denver Tribune*, April 5, 1882. In a purely local contest in 1882 the Republicans barely won, capturing four out of seven offices.

7. *Boulder County Herald*, Aug. 19, 1885.

8. United States Census, 1880 and 1890. Colorado State Census, 1885.

9. Material for this section was found in the original returns of the Colorado State Census, 1885 (National Archives Film, 158). Comparisons are drawn with the original returns of the United States Census, 1880. The semi-decennial census was provided for in the March 3, 1879, act of Congress that made provision for the Tenth Census. If the state complied with the federal census forms, the United States treasury would pay 50 percent of the expenses. Only three states and two territories took advantage of the opportunity.

10. This paragraph and those that follow are drawn from varied sources, all interviews of Caribou residents. Personal interviews with Mrs. Elizabeth Lee, August 2, 1960, and Mrs. Lee and Mrs. Rose Barnett, Aug. 18, 1960, and Mrs. Barnett to author, Feb. 28, 1961, are the main sources. Less helpful but still important were personal interviews with Martin Parsons, July 28, 1960, and Harold Martin, July 19, 1960. A whole series of interviews can be found in the *Boulder Camera*, including the following used here: Dec. 29, 1934, Jan. 1 and 26 and March 22, 1944, Sept. 13 and 15, 1952, and two undated articles, one an interview with the daughter of Joseph Murphy, found in the files of the *Camera*, and an interview with Ed Salsman (from the *Camera*) in the author's collection.

11. Interview with Mrs. Lee and Mrs. Barnett, Aug. 18, 1960.

12. Undated printed interview in files of *Camera*.

13. Beardsley, Echoes, p. 418.

Waning Hopes

1. "The Poorman Silver Mines (of Colorado) Limited," Articles of Association and Tabor Investment Co.—Poorman Silver Mines Limited, Agreement. Microfilm, Bancroft Library. Hereafter Poorman S.M. *Daily Camera* (Boulder), Sept. 5, 1891.

2. Poorman S.M. Articles of Association, List of Stockholders, Nov. 9, 1891, Jan. 6, 1893, and Jan. 12, 1906. Summary of Capital and Shares, Jan. 6, 1893. Gow was particularly active in mining speculation, being financially interested and on the Board of Directors of the Mining Development Syndicate (of Colorado) Limited and the Gold and Silver Extraction Company of America Limited.

3. *Report of the Director of the Mint*, 1892, p. 120. See also *Boulder Herald*, Sept. 9 and Dec. 23, 1891, and Aug. 24, 1892; *Daily Camera*, Sept. 5, 1891; *Boulder News*, July 20, 1893.

4. Poorman S.M. Letter Secretary (name illegible) to the Registry of Joint Stock Companies, Feb. 5, 1908. *Edinburgh Gazette*, Dec. 22, 1908.

5. R. G. Dun to T. A. Richardson, Feb. 12, 1891. R. G. Dun to W. James, Feb. 11, 1891 and R. G. Dun to S. A. Giffin, Jan. 12, 1891. R. G. Dun to James W. Fox, Dec. 23, 1889.

6. *Boulder Herald*, Sept. 16 and Dec. 23, 1891, Feb. 3, March 16, and Sept. 21, 1892.

7. *Daily Camera*, Sept. 30, 1892. See also *Boulder Herald*, Sept. 28 and Oct. 5, 1892. R. G. Dun to S. A. Giffin, April 4, 1892. *Silver Standard*, June 25, 1892.

8. R. G. Dun to S. A. Giffin, Feb. 2, 1897.

9. *Boulder Herald*, Aug. 27, 1890. See also Feb. 25, 1891, and Oct. 12, 1892. *Boulder News*, Dec. 7, 1893.

10. *Boulder Herald*, May 27, 1891, and *Daily Camera*, Sept. 30, 1892.

11. W. H. Harvey, *Coin's Financial School* (Chicago: Coin Publishing Co., 1894), p. 112.

12. *Boulder County News*, May 18 and Aug. 10, 1877.

13. *Speeches on the Coinage of Silver, First Session 49th Congress 1886* (privately printed for H. M. Teller), vol. II, pp. 527, 541–543. To appreciate the hold silver was gaining on other sections of the country, read the speeches by J. Weaver (Iowa) and J. Taylor (Tenn.) in the same volume. For local reaction, see *Boulder News and Courier*, Dec. 17, 1880, and Mar. 23, 1883, and the *Boulder County Herald*, Jan. 7, 1885, and Nov. 3, 1886.

14. *Boulder County Herald*, July 27 and Nov. 16, 1892. See also Leon W. Fuller, "Colorado's Revolt Against Capitalism," *Mississippi Valley Historical Review*, Dec. 1934, pp. 343–360.

15. *Daily Camera*, Nov. 3, 1892, and Sept. 30, 1892. *Boulder County Herald*, Nov. 2, 1892.

16. Interviews with Mrs. Lee, Aug. 2, 1960, and Mrs. Lee and Mrs. Barnett, Aug. 18, 1960.

17. W. H. Harvey, *Coin's Financial School and Coin's Financial School Up to Date* (Chicago: Coin Publishing Co., 1895).

18. Vachel Lindsay, "Bryan, Bryan, Bryan, Bryan." See also *Literary Digest*, July 11, Oct. 31, 1896, *Rocky Mountain News* (Daily), July 1, Nov. 2, 1896, and *The New York Times*, July 8 and Nov. 2, 1896.

19. *Daily Camera*, Oct. 9, 1899. See also issues of April 14, 1896, and March 17 and June 30, 1899. *Boulder County Herald*, June 29, Aug. 31, Sept. 28, 1898, and April 5 and May 14, 1899. *Mining Reporter* (Denver), July 7, 1898.

20. *Daily Camera*, Aug. 19, 1898. *Boulder County Herald*, June 29, 1898, and April 5, May 17, and Aug. 5, 1899. *Boulder Daily Camera*, March 3, 1944.

21. Interview with Mrs. Lee and Mrs. Barnett, Aug. 18, 1960. *Boulder County Herald*, Dec. 27, 1899. *Daily Camera*, Dec. 27, 1899.

No Tomorrow

1. *Boulder Daily Camera*, Jan. 17, 1944.

2. *Boulder City and County Directory* (Boulder: W. G. Brown, 1904), p. 175. See also the *Colorado State Business Directory*, 1900–1905.

3. Interviews with Charles Smith, Aug. 9, 1960, and Eugene R. Trollope, Aug. 29, 1960.

4. Excerpts taken from the *Boulder Daily Camera*, Nov. 15, 1905, and the *Boulder County Herald*, Nov. 15, 1905.

5. *Boulder County Miner*, Aug. 21 and Sept. 4, 1919. *Boulder Daily Camera*, Aug. 30 and Sept. 2, 1919. *Boulder-News Herald*, Aug. 30, 1919.

Requiem

1. See W. Turrentine Jackson, *Treasure Hill* (Tucson: University of Arizona Press, 1963), p. 224. Ray Allen Billington, *America's Frontier Heritage* (Chicago: Holt, Rinehart and Winston, 1966), pp. 136–137.

2. See Billington, p. 179.

3. See Billington, pp. 221–222.

4. Jackson, pp. 227–228. The reader is strongly urged to examine Jackson's conclusions carefully, pp. 222–228. See also my own article, "Colorado's Urban-Mining Safety Valve," *Colorado Magazine*, fall 1971.

Bibliographical Introduction

Caribou, like the majority of Western mining camps, has been subjected to little sound historical examination, but has been the source of some popular speculation. Unfortunately, this situation has tended to perpetuate the myth at the expense of reality.

No full length study has ever been written exclusively on this camp. Inadequate sketches are found in some of the older standard histories of Colorado. Two works dealing with Caribou and the *Grand Island Mining District* have been published, Donald Kemp's *Silver, Gold and Black Iron* (1960) and John and Doris Buchanan's *The Story of the Ghost Town Caribou* (1957). John Buchanan, the pioneer twentieth-century historian of Caribou, was the principal writer and interviewer in the excellent 1944 series published in the *Boulder Camera*. This series was largely incorporated later into his interesting and popularly written short pamphlet. Kemp's book is noteworthy for its selection of pictures, not for the story. Using only well-known secondary and very few primary sources, the author patched together a history that does not have the merit it could or should have had.

More articles have been written about Caribou. John Buchanan (*Colorado Magazine*, Nov. 1944) and David Stratton (*Colorado Magazine*, April 1953) have short general accounts, and Stratton has one on the Cousin Jacks of Caribou in the *Colorado Quarterly* (spring 1953). Waldo Wedel's article (*Colorado Magazine*, summer 1964) is of purely antiquarian interest.

The intriguing search to recover the history of Caribou produced all the excitement of piecing together a historical puzzle. The resource material available is varied; the best for an overall presentation is the local newspapers. For the early 1870s Central City papers provide the most thorough news reservoir; for the remaining years the various Boulder papers offer the best coverage. During the boom years the Denver papers periodically had camp and mine items, many taken verbatim from Boulder and Central papers. The *Caribou Post* for 1871 is unsurpassed, unfortunately declining rapidly in 1872 until it carried little, if any, local news. For strictly the mining coverage *The Mining Review*, published in Georgetown and later Denver, merits the careful attention of the researcher. *The Engineering and Mining Journal* (New York) furnished excellent national coverage and occasional Caribou items.

The best-documented mine was the Caribou. Here the author was fortunate to have access to three valuable collections: for the early years the records in the collection of the late Harold Martin, son of one of the original discoverers; for the mid-1870s the Caribou papers located in the archives of the First National Bank of Denver; and finally the significant R. G. Dun letters, covering the 1870s to 1900. Supplemented by other sources, this mine's history can be fairly well sketched. Even here, though, the researcher finds himself against blank walls. As early as May 1883, Dun, writing to J. R. Frith, complained, "You will see that there are no records of importance dating back of Oct. '80. Please make a close search for the antecedent books and/or endeavor to find out if they were destroyed."

On the technical aspects of mining, Peter Van Diest's publications, the August 11, 1877, issue of the *Engineering and Mining Journal*, and Richardson and Cook's *Report of the Caribou and Native Silver Mines* provide first-hand accounts. Corbett's *Colorado Directory of Mines* and Fossett's *Colorado* (1876 and 1879) are both valuable. Raymond Rossiter's multivolume *Statistics of Mines and Mining* (1871–1876) gives the overall view, and the best recent study is Moore, Cavender, and Kaiser, *Geology and Uranium Deposits of the Caribou Area*.

The Caribouites can be examined (with a watchful and critical historical eye) in the varied collection of interviews found in the *Boulder Camera* from the 1930s into the 1960s. Forest Crossen has reprinted some in his multivolumed *Western Yesterdays*. A gentle warning needs to be issued concerning the reliability of memories with the passage of time. Regrettably, not much nineteenth-century Caribou correspondence has survived: however that of Richard Harvey provides a fascinating glimpse. The accounts of John Tice and Grace Greenwood have been quoted frequently in this book and give the best Eastern and Midwestern views of the camp and the people. Excellent sources for a multitude of statistics are the original census records of 1880 and 1885. Unfortunately, those of 1890 have been lost; 1900 is finally available for complete research. Thelma Roberts's *Red Hell, the Life Story of John Goode, Criminal* purports to describe the early years of Caribou. There is little doubt that Goode once lived in Caribou, although this account may be challenged as exaggerated and unfactual, or at best suffering from a lapse of time between the event and its telling.

Caribou was not an isolated phenomenon. It was part of a statewide mining era and a segment of the entire Western mining frontier. Rodman Paul's *Mining Frontiers of the Far West, 1848–1880*, and William Greever's *Bonanza Frontier* excellently describe the total picture. *Stampede to Timberline* by Muriel Wolle is enjoyable reading and well worth the reader's time; particularly outstanding are her sketches of places now gone. However, this writer was never able to substantiate her story of the prostitutes being driven out of Caribou down to Cardinal.

The bibliography that follows lists the sources directly utilized in this study.

Unpublished Material

Bates, L. M. Letters, found in the Teller Papers, Western History Collections, University of Colorado.

Book B Grand Island District.

Boulder & Caribou Wagon Road Company, Secretary Book, Dec. 25, 1870–Jan. 5, 1891. Western History Collections, University of Colorado.

Boulder County Miscellaneous Record Book H.

Boulder County School Districts, Record Book, Colorado State Archives.

Boulder County RePlat of Plat Book 2, Vol. 1.

Caribou Mine Miscellaneous Papers. First National Bank of Denver Archives.
Caribou Mine Reports, Colorado Bureau of Mines.
Caribou Mine and Mining Company Records, Western History Collections, University of Colorado.
Caribou Tunnel vs. James Parsons, et al. District Court, 1st Judicial District, Golden, Jefferson County, Colorado. Records in Western History Collections, University of Colorado.
Census, 1880, Population Schedules (Original Returns), Boulder County.
Colorado State Census, 1885 (Original Returns), Enumeration District No. 2.
Deed of Warranty J. Chaffee to Caribou Consolidated, filed May 16, 1879.
Dun, R. G. Records, relating to activities at Caribou, Colorado, 1872–1900. Compiled and sent to the author by Owen A. Sheffield.
Harvey, Richard. Copying Book. State Historical Society of Colorado.
Idaho Mines records. Mrs. William Martin Collection. Western History Collections, University of Colorado.
Miner's Lien Book, Boulder County.
Moffat, David. Records. First National Bank of Denver Archives.
Myncompagnie Nederland Records.
Orahood, Harper B. Papers, Western History Collections, University of Colorado.
The Poorman Silver Mines (of Colorado) Limited. Bancroft Library, Berkeley, California.
Potosi Mine Reports, Colorado Bureau of Mines.
Teller, Henry M. Papers, Western History Collections, University of Colorado.

District Court, Boulder County, Boulder, Colorado

James Pippin vs. Mining Company Nederland and George C. Corning (623).
Augustine Langford vs. the Mining Company Nederland, a corporation, James Pippin, and George C. Corning (626).
Jerome B. Chaffee vs. the Mining Company Nederland (628).
Moses Anker and M. A. Shaffenburg, late co-partners in business . . . vs. the Mining Company Nederland (629).
Moses Anker vs. the Mining Co. Nederland (633).
George Scott and William Scott . . . vs. the Sherman Mining Company (705).
John J. Ellingham vs. Sherman Mining Company and No Name Mining Company, a corporation (782).
Charles F. Hendrie and Henry Bolthoff, Partners doing business as Hendrie Bros. and Bolthoff (Plaintiffs) vs. Mining Company New Jersey (Defendant), action on attachment (no number).
Jerome B. Chaffee vs. the Mining Company Nederland, Arvin H. Henry, First National Bank of Denver, Walter and Charles Buckingham et al. (787).
William M. Roworth and Richard C. Lake . . . vs. H. Mincler [sic], the Sherman Company, and the No Name Mining Company, a foreign corporation (793).
John Best vs. H. Mincler [sic], the Sherman Mining Company, and the No Name Company, a foreign corporation (794).
Charles F. Hendrie and Wm. Hendrie and Henry Bolthoff . . . vs. H. Mincler [sic], the Sherman Mining Company, and the No Name Mining Company, a foreign corporation (795).

First National Bank of Denver vs. the Sherman Mining Company and the No Name Mining Co. (802).

Walter Smith and Leon Smith . . . vs. the No Name and the Sherman Company (875).

William Scott and George Scott . . . vs. Martin A. Smith, Levi M. Bates et al. (991).

Caribou Consolidated Mining Company vs. R. G. Dun, J. A. Dun, and Harman Minkler [*sic*] (1127).

The Caribou Consolidated Mining Company and Joseph Irwin vs. Gilbert Lehmer and Samuel Richards (1148).

Jerome B. Chaffee vs. James A. Dun (1156).

Caribou Consolidated Mining Company vs. Neil D. McKenzie (1598).

People of the State of Colorado vs. Daniel C. Campbell, alias D. C. Campbell, and George McCord, alias George McCoy, alias George McCoyd (1606).

Joseph R. Frith vs. the Caribou Consolidated Mining Company . . . (1657, 1678).

United States Circuit Court

Robert G. Dun vs. Jerome B. Chaffee, Eben Smith, and the Caribou Consolidated Mining Company (266).

Robert G. Dun vs. Jerome B. Chaffee, Eben Smith, and the Caribou Consolidated Mining Company (338).

Caribou Consolidated Mining Company vs. Robert G. Dun, James A. Dun, and Harman Minkler [*sic*] (396).

James A. Dun vs. Caribou Consolidated Mining Company (400).

James A. Dun vs. Caribou Consolidated Mining Company (418).

Interviews

Sam Conger. Mss. IX–XV, State Historical Society of Colorado.

Mrs. Rose T. Barnett, Aug. 18, 1960.

Mrs. Elizabeth A. Lee, Aug. 2 and 18, 1960.

Harold Martin, July 19 and 26, 1960, and Feb. 9, 1961.

William Martin, Bancroft Manuscripts, Western History Collections, University of Colorado.

Hugh McCammon, Bancroft Manuscripts, Western History Collections, University of Colorado.

Matthew Ollsen, April 19, 1961.

Martin Parsons, July 28, 1960.

Charles Smith, Aug. 9, 1960.

Mr. & Mrs. Harold Straughn, Aug. 2, 1960.

Eugene R. Trollope, Aug. 29, 1960.

Newspapers and Journals

The Boulder County Herald (weekly), Feb. 18, 1880–Feb. 22, 1893; Nov. 14, 1894; Sept. 30 and Nov. 19, 1896; June 6, 1898–Jan. 17, 1900; Feb. 11–Sept. 23, 1903; Oct. 11–Nov. 29, 1905.

Boulder County Miner (weekly), scattered issues 1918–1919.

The Boulder County News (weekly), Oct. 12, 1869–Nov. 8, 1878.

Boulder County Tribune, Sept. 30, 1892.

Boulder Daily Camera, Aug. 14, Sept. 5–6, 1891; Nov. 3, 1892; July 2, 1894–Dec. 31, 1895; April 14 and Nov. 18, 1896; Nov. 17, 1897; March 16, 1899–Jan. 8, 1900; Sept. 9, 1903; Nov. 15, 1905; scattered issues Aug.–Sept. 1919, 1944–1948, 1950–1953, and 1960–1961.

The Boulder News and Banner (weekly), Nov. 1, 1887–June 5, 1888.

Boulder News and Courier (weekly), Jan. 3, 1879–Oct. 26, 1883.

Boulder-News Herald (daily), Aug. 30 and Sept. 2, 1919.

The Caribou Post (weekly), July 8, 1871–Aug. 17, 1872.

The Colorado Banner (Boulder weekly), Sept. 30, 1875–Sept. 18, 1879.

The Daily Register-Call (Central City), March–July 1870; March 1, June 28, 1871; Aug. 17–Sept. 27, 1872; April 23–April 30, 1873; July 15, 1874; Dec. 9–Dec. 31, 1875; Sept. 15, 23, 1879.

Denver Daily Tribune, June 30, 1874; April 5 and Sept. 30, 1882.

Denver Mining Record, Nov. 29, 1924; May 18, 1929.

Denver Mirror, June 23, 1877.

Denver Post, May 11, 1919.

The Denver Republican (daily), Feb. 18, May 4, and Nov. 30, 1881; Jan. 1, Aug. 10, and Feb. 18, 1882; Jan. 6, 1887; Sept. 10, 1903.

Engineering and Mining Journal (New York), July 1870–Dec. 1884; scattered issues 1885–1905.

Georgetown Miner, Sept 11, 1875.

Greeley Tribune, Dec. 24, 1873.

Inter-Ocean (Denver), March 14, 1880.

The Literary Digest (New York), July 11–Oct. 31, 1896.

The Local Miner (Boulder), Sept. 10, 1889.

The Mining Record (New York), Jan. 1880–Dec. 1883.

Mining Reporter (Denver), July 7, 1898; July 13 and Aug. 17, 1899.

The Mining Review (Georgetown and Denver), Sept. 1872–May 15, 1876; Aug. 29, 1876.

New York Times, Sept. 12, 1870; Sept. 23, 1871; Sept. 28, 1876; July 28, 1877; July 8–Nov. 2, 1896.

Rocky Mountain News (daily), Aug. 9, 1869–Dec. 31, 1885; July 1–Nov. 2, 1896.

Rocky Mountain News (weekly), Jan. 1, 1879.

Rocky Mountain Sun (Aspen), Aug. 5, 1883.

Rocky Mountain Presbyterian (Denver), April 1872–April 1873.

Silver Standard (Silver Plume), June 25, 1892.

Solid Muldoon (Ouray), Oct. 3, 1879.

Weekly Central City Register-Call, Aug. 19, 1869–Dec. 31, 1881.

Weekly Colorado Tribune (Denver), Sept. 14 and Dec. 7, 1870.

Published Material

Bancroft, Caroline. "Folklore of the Central City District." *California Folklore Quarterly* IV (Oct. 1945), pp. 315–342.

Bancroft, Hubert H. *California Inter Pocula*. San Francisco: The History Co., 1888.

Beardsley, Isaac. *Echoes from Peak and Plain*. Cincinnati: Curts & Jennings, 1898.

Billington, Ray Allen. *America's Frontier Heritage*. Chicago: Holt, Rinehart & Winston, 1966.

Bixby, A., et al. *History of Clear Creek and Boulder Valleys*, Colorado. Chicago: O. L. Baskin & Co., 1880.

Boulder County Colorado. Boulder: Banner Office Print, 1882.

Boulder County Directory. 1892, 1896, 1898. Published in Trinidad, 1892; Boulder 1896, 1898.

Boulder City and County Directory. Boulder: W. G. Brown, 1904.

"The Caribou Silver Mines, Colorado." *Engineering and Mining Journal* 24 (Aug. 11, 1877), pp. 105–107.

Chauvenet, Regis. *The Caribou Silver Mines*. Golden: n.p., 1887.

Collins, Mary. *Pioneering in the Rockies*. Boulder: privately printed, n.d.

Colorado Business Directory and Annual Register (changed to *Colorado State Business Directory* in 1879). Denver: J. A. Blake, 1875, 1877, 1879, 1880, 1881, 1882.

Colorado State Business Directory. Denver: James R. Ives, 1883–1885, 1887–1893.

Colorado State Business Directory. Denver: Gazetteer Publishing Co., 1896–1909.

Colorado State Mining Directory. Denver: Western Mining Directory, 1898.

Corbett, Thomas B. *Colorado Directory of Mines*. Denver: Rocky Mt. News Printing Co., 1879.

Corregan, R. A., and D. F. Lingange (eds.). *Colorado Mining Directory*. Denver: Colorado Mining Directory Co., 1883.

Egleston, Thomas. *The Metallurgy of Silver, Gold and Mercury*. New York: John Wiley & Sons, 1887, v. 1.

Emmons, S. F., and others. "Geological Sketch of the Rocky Mountain Division." *Tenth Census of the United States*. Vol. 13. Washington: Government Printing Office, 1885.

Fossett, Frank. *Colorado*. Denver: Daily Tribune Steam Printing House, 1876.

———. *Colorado*. New York: C. G. Crawford, 1879.

Fuller, Leon W. "Colorado's Revolt Against Capitalism." *Mississippi Valley Historical Review* 21 (Dec. 1934), pp. 343–360.

Greenwood, Grace (S. Lippincott). *New Life in New Lands*. New York: J. B. Ford & Co., 1873.

Hand-Book of Colorado. Denver: J. A. Blake, 1871. Also published in 1872.

Harvey, W. H. *Coin's Financial School*. Chicago: Coin Publishing Co, 1894.

———. *Coin's Financial School Up to Date*. Chicago: Coin Publishing Co., 1895.

Hayden, F. V. *Seventh Annual Report of the United States Geographical Survey*. Washington: Government Printing Office, 1874.

Henderson, Charles W. *Mining in Colorado*. Washington: Government Printing Ofice, 1926.

Jackson, W. Turrentine. *Treasure Hill: Portrait of a Silver Mining Camp*. Tucson: University of Arizona Press, 1963.

Jenkin, A. K. Hamilton. *The Cornish Miner*. London: George Allen & Univin Ltd., 1927.

Mining in Boulder County, Colorado, Silver Jubilee Edition. Boulder: Boulder Metal Mining Asociation, 1919.

Moore, F. B., W. S. Cavender, and E. P. Kaiser. *Geology and Uranium Deposits of the Caribou Area, Boulder County Colorado*. Geological Survey Bulletin 1030-N. Washington: Government Printing Office, 1957.

Native Silver Mining Company of Boulder County, Colorado. New York: n.p., 1880.

Paul, Rodman W. *Mining Frontiers of the Far West 1848–1880*. New York: Holt, Rinehart & Winston, 1963.

Perrigo, Lynn I. "The Cornish Miners of Early Gilpin County." *Colorado Magazine* XIV (May 1937), pp. 92–101.

Pickel, Hugh E., Jr. *John H. Pickel, Hugh C. McCammon, and the Silver Strike at Caribou Hill*. Seattle: Argus Press, 1964.

Poorman. Denver: Poorman Mining Company, c. 1888.

Prospectus of the Idaho Tunnel Company. Central City: Register Printing House, 1874.

Raymond, Rossiter W. *Statistics of Mines and Mining in the States and Territories West of the Rocky Mountains*. Washington: Government Printing Office, 1871–1876.

Report of the Director of the Mint upon the Statistics of the Production of the Precious Metals in the United States. Washington: Government Printing Office, 1881–1899. After 1900 included in the Annual Report of the Treasury.

Rickard, T. A. *Interviews with Mining Engineers*. San Francisco: Mining & Scientific Press, 1922.

Richardson, C. S., and G. H. Cook. *Report of the Caribou and Native Silver Mines*. Philadelphia: Allen, Lane & Scott's Printing House, 1877.

Roberts, Thelma. *Red Hell, the Life Story of John Goode, Criminal*. New York: Henkle Publisher, 1934.

Singewald, Joseph T. *The Titaniferous Iron Ores in the United States*. Department of Interior, Bureau of Mines Bulletin 64. Washington: Government Printing Office, 1913.

Speeches on the Coinage of Silver, First Session 49th Congress, 1886. Vol. II. Privately printed for Henry M. Teller.

Stanton, Elizabeth, Susan Anthony, and Matilda Gage (eds.). *History of Woman Suffrage*. Vol. 3. Rochester: Charles Mann, 1887.

Stratton, David H. "The Cousin Jacks of Caribou." *Colorado Quarterly* 1 (Spring 1953), pp. 371–384.

Tice, John H. *Over the Plains and on the Mountains*. St. Louis: Industrial Age Printing Co., 1872.

Twain, Mark. *Roughing It*. Hartford: American Publishing Co., 1872.

Van Diest, P. H. "Concentration of Caribou Ores." *Mining Review* 5 (Jan. 1875), p. 57.

———. "The Crossing of the No-Name and Caribou Lodes." *Mining Review* 6 (March 1875), p. 5.

———. *The Grand Island Mining District of Boulder County, Colorado*. Denver: *Mining Review* Publishing Co., 1875.

Wallihan, S. S., and T. O. Bigney (eds). *The Rocky Mountain Directory and Colorado Gazetteer for 1871*. Denver: S. S. Wallihan & Co., 1870.

Young, Francis C. *Echoes from Arcadia*. Denver: Lanning Bros., 1903.

Index